HISTORY

OF THE

MEDIAEVAL SCHOOL OF INDIAN LOGIC

HISTORY
OF THE
MEDIAEVAL SCHOOL OF INDIAN LOGIC

BY

MAHAMAHOPADHYAYA SATIS CHANDRA VIDYABHUSANA

M.A., Ph.D.

Professor of Sanskrit and Pali, Presidency College, Calcutta; Joint Philological Secretary, Asiatic Society of Bengal; and Fellow of the Calcutta University

Thesis approved for the Degree of Doctor of Philosophy in the University of Calcutta, 1907

GYAN

Published by

Gyan Publishing House
5, Ansari Road
Daryaganj, New Delhi-110002
Phone: 011-47034999, 9811692060
E-mail: books@gyanbooks.com

Distribution Network
gyanbooks.com
India, USA, Canada, UK, Australia, France

ISBN : 978-81-212-1176-5 (PB)
First Published, 1909

2nd Impression 2021

Printed at: Gyan Press, Delhi.

History of the Mediaeval School of Indian Logic
Author: Mahamahopadhyaya Satis Chandra
Vidyabhusana

University Studies—No. 1.

HISTORY

OF THE

MEDIÆVAL SCHOOL OF INDIAN LOGIC

BY

MAHĀMAHOPĀDHYĀYA SATIS CHANDRA VIDYABHUSANA,
M.A., PH.D.

Professor of Sanskrit and Pali, Presidency College, Calcutta; Joint Philological Secretary, Asiatic Society of Bengal; and Fellow of the Calcutta University.

(Thesis approved for the Degree of Doctor of Philosophy in the University of Calcutta,
1907.

Calcutta:

PUBLISHED BY THE CALCUTTA UNIVERSITY AND PRINTED AT THE BAPTIST MISSION PRESS.

1909.

TO

THE HON'BLE MR. JUSTICE ASUTOSH MUKHOPADHYAYA,

SARASVATI, M.A., D.L., D.Sc., F.R.A.S., F.R.S.E.,

Vice-Chancellor of the Calcutta University,

President of the Asiatic Society of Bengal, and Chairman of the Board of Indigenous Sanskrit Education, Bengal,

WHOSE LIFE IS AN UNBROKEN RECORD

OF LOFTY IDEALS

TRANSLATED INTO PRACTICE,

THIS BOOK IS DEDICATED

IN TOKEN OF PROFOUND ESTEEM

BY

HIS HUMBLE ADMIRER,

THE AUTHOR.

TABLE OF CONTENTS.

BOOK I.

THE JAINA LOGIC.

CHAPTER I.—THE ERA OF TRADITION.

CHAPTER II.—THE HISTORICAL PERIOD.

BOOK II.

THE BUDDHIST LOGIC.

Chapter 1.—The Old Buddhist References to Logic.

CHAPTER II.—SYSTEMATIC BUDDHIST WRITERS ON LOGIC.

APPENDIX A.

APPENDIX B.

APPENDIX C.

PREFACE.

WITH the object of drawing the attention of scholars to the vast literature of the Mediæval school of Indian Logic, I have in the present thesis embodied the results of some of my researches into it.[1] The Mediæval Logic of India is divided into two principal systems, *viz.*, the Jaina and the Buddhist. The materials of the Jaina portion of my thesis were derived from several rare Jaina manuscripts procured from Western India and the Deccan. I have also used the Jaina manuscripts of the Asiatic Society of Bengal and the numerous Jaina works printed in Bombay, Benares and Calcutta. From the footnotes of my thesis it will be evident that I have frequently used Professor Peterson's Reports of Operations in Search of Sanskrit manuscripts in the Bombay Circle. Though the Professor has said nothing in particular about Logic and Logicians, he has given a general index of Jaina authors which has been of the greatest use to me. I have not heard of any scholar who has yet written any special account of the Jaina Logic. Dr. Herman Jacobi's "Eine Jaina-Dogmatik" printed in Leipzig is an annotated translation of Umāsvāti's Tattvārthādhigama Sūtra, an ancient Jaina work on general philosophy and not a special treatise on Logic. A short time ago I sent a proof of my account of the Jaina Logic to Dr. Jacobi who very graciously returned it with a few marginal glosses which have been most thankfully accepted and embodied in the foot-notes of this thesis.

To show how generously that most eminent authority on Jainism condescended to help me, I quote here the

---

1 Some of these researches were published in the "Journal" of the Asiatic Society of Bengal during the last two years.

letter which he wrote in communicating to me his suggestions:

Bonn, 21st October, 1907.
Niebuhrstrasse 59.

DEAR SIR,

I have received your kind letter and the proofs of the Jaina Logic, and I heartily congratulate you on the work you have done. It will prove very useful, for you have brought together a mass of information which is not of easy access to many. In looking over the proofs I have made some marginal glosses to show you where I think you might alter your statement. Of course, everything is left to your decision.

I shall be glad to see your whole book, as I take great interest in Indian Logic and I have myself written an article on it principally for the information of our Logicians who as a rule know nothing about what has been done in this branch of Philosophy by Indian thinkers. I shall therefore feel obliged if you can spare me a copy of your work.

With kind regards,
I am,
Yours sincerely,
H. JACOBI.

A proof of the Jaina Logic was also sent to two oriental authorities on Jainism—Muni Dharmavijaya and his pupil Śrī Indravijaya at Benares. I owe them a great debt of gratitude for the kind assistance which they cheerfully rendered to me by going through the proof and offering certain suggestions and observations which have been incorporated in the foot-notes of this thesis.

As to the Buddhist Logic, no systematic information is available from Pāli texts as there is not a single regular treatise on Logic in the Pāli language; but references to ancient Brahmanic Logic can be gleaned from the publications of the Pali Text Society of London and also from other Pali works printed elsewhere. The Buddhist Sanskrit works on Logic of the Middle Age are now almost extinct in India. A few of them, which are available in Chinese versions, have been noticed by Dr. Sugiura in his "Hindu Logic as preserved in China and Japan." But almost all the Buddhist Sanskrit works on Logic are carefully preserved in faithful translations in Tibet. The materials of that portion of my thesis, which deals with Buddhist Logic, were chiefly derived from the Hodgson Collection of Tibetan xylographs deposited in the India Office, London, and the large number of Tibetan block-prints brought down to Calcutta from Gyantse during the British Mission to Tibet in 1904. I also consulted almost all the Tibetan manuscripts and block-prints bearing on Logic that lie hidden in the Tibetan monasteries of Labrang and Phodang in Sikkim which I visited during May and June 1907.[1] For the historical account of the Buddhist authors I have chiefly depended on Lama Tārānātha's Tibetan history of Indian Buddhism translated into German by A. Schiefner under the designation of "Geschichte des Buddhismus," and the Tibetan historical work called Pag-sam-jon-zang edited in the original Tibetan by Rai Sarat Chandra Das, Bahadur, C.I.E., in Calcutta. Some most important historical facts regarding the Buddhist Logicians and their works have been discovered from the colophons at the end of each of the Tibetan works which I have examined.

It was mainly through the influence of Mr. F. W. Thomas that I was enabled to borrow the Tibetan xylographs of the India Office, London, and I avail myself of this opportunity of acknowledging my humble appreciation of the generosity of that distinguished scholar. My respectful thanks are also due to the Government of India, who kindly lent me several block-prints out of the vast Tibetan collection brought down to Calcutta by the Tibet Mission of 1904. I should be guilty of great ingratitude if I were not to mention my obligations to Mr. A. Earle, I.C.S., Director of Public Instruction, Bengal, Mr. C. H. Bompas, I.C.S., Deputy Commissioner,

---

[1] Subsequently in October 1908 I visited Pamiangchi, which is another very old monastery in Sikkim, where all facilities were kindly afforded to me by their Highnesses the Maharaja and Maharani of Sikkim as well as by Mr. Crawford, I.C.S., the then Deputy Commissioner of Darjeeling.—S. C. V.

Darjeeling, and Mr. Claude White, C.I.E., Political Resident, Sikkim, for the kind help they gave me in getting access to the Tibetan Monasteries of Labrang and Phodang in Sikkim.

For a time I was quite bewildered by the enormous store of material on Indian Logic which I had collected, and it took me many a month to select and classify a portion of it for the purpose of this thesis. When the compilation of the paper was finished, and the work was passing through the press, Mr. W. W. Hornell, B.A., of the Indian Educational Service, kindly undertook to revise it, but he was able to revise only the first chapter of the Jaina Logic before leaving India. Accordingly, the rest of the work was, at my request, revised by Mr. W. C. Wordsworth, M.A., of the Presidency College, Calcutta. I am deeply indebted to both these gentlemen for their kind courtesy and assistance.

Whatever the merits or the utility of the present contribution may be, it has had the rare good fortune and privilege of having been looked through by a savant with whom it would be an impertinence to name in the same breath any other living authorities, oriental or occidental, on Indian philosophy. This savant, whose learning is equalled by his modesty and willingness to assist beginners in their uphill work, is no other than our revered Dr. G. Thibaut, M.A., Ph.D., D.Sc., C.I.E., now Registrar of the Calcutta University, which post may he fill long so that our countrymen may continue to derive benefit from his vast erudition.

SATIS CHANDRA VIDYABHUSANA.

INTRODUCTION.

Logic is generally designated in India as Nyāya-śāstra. It is also called Tarka-śāstra, Hetu-vidyā, Pramāṇa-śāstra, Ānvīkṣikī and Phakkikā-śāstra.

Three Schools of Indian Logic.

Indian Logic may be divided into three principal schools, *viz.*, the Ancient (600 B.C.—400 A.D.), the Mediæval (400 A.D.—1200 A.D.), and the Modern 1200 A.D.—1850 A.D.). The **Nyāya-sūtra** by Akṣapāda Gautama is the foremost, though by no means the first, work on Logic of the Ancient School; the **Pramāṇa-samuccaya** by Dignāga is a representative work of the Mediæval School, while the **Tattva cintāmaṇi** by Gaṅgeśa Upādhyāya is the main text-book of the Modern School. These three works have, since their composition, enjoyed a very wide popularity, as is evident from the numerous commentaries that have from time to time centred round them. A few of the commentaries are mentioned below:—

The Ancient School of Logic.

Text.

1. **Nyāya-sūtra** by Akṣapāda Gautama.

Commentaries.

2. Nyāya bhāṣya by Vātsyāyana.
3. Nyāya-vārtika by Udyotakara.
4. Nyāya-vārtika-tātparya-ṭīkā by Vācaspati Miśra.
5. Nyāya-vārtika-tātparya-ṭīkā-pariśuddhi by Udayanācārya.
6. Nyāyālaṅkāra by S'rī Kaṇṭha.
7. Nyāya-vṛtti by Abhayatilakopādhyāya.
8. Nyāya-vṛtti by Viśvanātha.

The Mediæval School of Logic.

Text.

1. **Pramāṇa-samuccaya** by Dignāga.

Commentaries.

2. Pramāṇa-samuccaya-vṛtti by Dignāga.
3. Pramāṇa-vārtika-kārikā by Dharmakīrti
4. Pramāṇa-vārtika-vṛtti by Dharmakīrti.
5. Pramāṇa-vārtika-pañjikā by Devendrabodhi.
6. Pramāṇa-vārtika-pañjikā-ṭīkā by S'ākyabodhi
7. Pramāṇa-vārtika-vṛtti by Ravi Gupta.
8. Pramāna-samuccaya-tīkā (Viśālāmalavatī-nāma) by Jinendrabodhi.

9. Pramāṇa-vārtikālaṅkāra by Prajñākara Gupta.
10. Pramāṇa-vārtikā ankāra-ṭikā by Jina.
11. Pramāṇa-vārtikālaṅkāra by Yamāri.
12. Pramāṇa-vārtika-ṭikā by S'aṅkarānanda.

The Modern School of Logic.

Text.

1. Tattva-cintāmaṇi by Gaṅgeśa Upādhyāya.

Commentaries.

2. Tattva-cintāmaṇi Prakāśa by Rucidatta.
3. Tattva Āloka by Jayadeva Miśra.
4. Tattva Dīdhiti by Raghunātha S'iromaṇi.
5. Tattva Rahasya by Mathurānātha.
6. Tattva Dīpanī by Kṛṣṇakānta.
7. Tattva Ṭīkā by Kaṇāda Tarkavāgīśa.
8. Tattva Āloka-sāra-mañjarī by Bhavānanda.
9. Tattva Āloka-darpaṇa by Maheśa Ṭhakkura.
10. Tattva Āloka-kaṇṭakoddhāra by Madhu Sūdana Ṭhakkura.
11. Tattva Āloka-rahasya by Mathurānātha.
12. Tattva Dīdhiti-vyākhyā-vivecana by Rudra Nyāyavācaspati.
13. Tattva Dīdhiti-ṭippanī by Jagadīśa.
14. Tattva Dīdhiti-ṭīkā by Gadādhara.
15. Tattva Dīdhiti-sāramañjarī by Bhavānanda.
16. Tattva Bhavānandī vyākhyā by Mahādeva Paṇḍita.
17. Tattva Kālīśaṅkarī-patrikā by Kālīśaṅkara.
18. Tattva Cāndrī-patrikā by Candra Nārāyaṇa.
19. Tattva Raudrī-patrikā by Rudra Nārāyaṇa.

etc. etc. etc.

Besides these there are numerous other texts and commentaries on Logic which belong to one or another of the three schools mentioned above.

The Jaina system of Mediæval Logic.

I shall say here nothing about the ancient and modern schools of Logic, my whole attention will be devoted to the mediæval school alone. It is perhaps known to very few scholars that the Mediæval Logic was almost entirely in the hands of the Jainas and Buddhists. For one thousand years, from 600 B.C. to 400 A.D., the Jainas and Buddhists were fully occupied in questions of metaphysics and religion though there are occasional references to Logic in their works of that period. At about 400 A.D. began an epoch when they seriously took up the problems of Logic, and all the text-books on the Jaina and Buddhist systems of Logic date at or after that time. Ujjainī in Malwa and Valabhi in Guzerat were the scenes of activity of the Jaina Logicians of the S'vetāmbara sect. The Digambaras flourished principally in Pāṭaliputra and Drāviḍa (including Karṇāṭa) about the 8th century A.D. The Nyāyāvatāra by Siddhasena Divākara, dated about 533 A.D., was the first systematic work on the Jaina Logic.

The Buddhist system of Mediæval Logic.

The real founders of the Mediæval Logic were the Buddhists. The first batch of the Buddhist Logicians came principally from Gāndhāra (modern Peshwar) on the Punjab frontier. Ayodhyā (Oudh) was the scene of their activity. Unfortunately we have not before us any of the original Sanskrit works on Logic produced by them. We may, however, form an approximate estimate of their Logic from the works on the Yogācāra philosophy by Maitreya, Asaṅga and Vasubandhu recovered from the Chinese sources. About 500 A.D.[1] the Huns conquered Gāndhāra, and their leaders Mihirakula and others perpetrated terrible atrocities on the Buddhists to the great detriment of Buddhistic studies there. Asaṅga and Vasubandhu (and perhaps Maitreya too) passed the best days of their lives in Ayodhyā and wrote most of their works there. King Vikramāditya who reigned in Ayodhyā about 480 A.D.[2] was at first a patron of the Sāṁkhya philosophy but afterwards greatly supported Buddhism through the influence of Vasubandhu. Bālāditya, who succeeded Vikramāditya to the throne of Ayodhyā, was a pupil of Vasubandhu and a supporter of Buddhism. The Buddhist Logic of the Yogācāra school appears thus to have originated in Ayodhyā and flourished there during 400-500 A.D. under Kings Vikramāditya and Bālāditya.

The second batch of the Buddhist Logicians flourished in Drāviḍa (the Deccan) during 500-700 A.D. when the Buddhist kings of the Pallava dynasty were supreme there. Ācārya Dignāga, about 500 A.D., was the oldest logician of Drāviḍa whose works are still extant, in faithful translations. Another logician of eminence of the Drāviḍa school was Dharmakīrti who lived about 650 A.D. His Nyāyabindu, and a commentary on it by Dharmottara called Nyāya-bindu-ṭīkā, are the only systematic works on Buddhist Logic which have come down to us in their Sanskrit originals. They would have certainly disappeared from India like a hundred other works of their kind, had it not been that a Jaina logician named Mallavādin had written a gloss on them. Seeing that the gloss would be useless without the text and commentary, the Jainas preserved all three. The Nyāyabindu, together with the commentary, preserved

---

1 Vide Beal's Buddhist Records of the Western World, vol. I., pp. xv, 168.

2 Vide Takakusu's *Paramārtha's Life of Vasubandhu* published in the Journal of the Royal Asiatic Society of Great Britain and Ireland, January 1905, p. 36.

among the palm-leaf manuscripts in the Jaina temple of S'ānti-nātha, Cambay, has been published by Professor Peterson in the Bibliotheca Indica series of Calcutta. With the downfall of the Pallavas, Logic disappeared from Drāviḍa. Vinayāditya of the Western Chaḷukya dynasty about 696 A.D. put a check to the power of the Pallavas, while Vikramāditya II, of the same dynasty, about 733 A.D., seized Kāñcī, their capital.[1] The Chalukyas were Vaiṣṇavas, and their conquest of Kāñcī was really a triumph of the Brahmanic religion over Buddhism. At about 788 A.D. the great Brāhmaṇa preacher S'aṅkarācārya appeared, and Buddhism became gradually extinct in Drāviḍa.

The third and fourth batches of Buddhist Logicians flourished simultaneously in Kāśmīra and Bengal (including Behar). Ravi Gupta, 725 A.D., was the earliest logician of the Kāśmīra school. At this time Kāśmīra was governed by the illustrious King Lalitāditya or Muktāpīḍa (about 695—732 A.D.), who built a large vihāra with a stūpa at Huṣkapur.[2] At the same time there was a great demand for Sanskrit Buddhist books in Tibet with the thorough opening of her intercourse with India in the 8th century A.D. King Khri-ral (otherwise known as Ral-pa-can) in the 9th century A.D. employed numerous Indian Pandits and Tibetan Lamas to translate Sanskrit books into Tibetan. The propaganda of translations went on in full force up to about 1101 A.D., when the glorious reign of S'rī Harṣa Deva (1089—1101 A.D.), who was a patron of learning, both Brāhmanic and Buddhistic,[3] came to a close. The Buddhist monasteries and Tibetan Lamas did not altogether disappear from Kāśmīra until the establishment of Mahomedan rule in that country in 1341 A.D., when her intercourse with Tibet ceased. Henceforth we hear no more of logicians flourishing in Kāśmīra.

In Bengal and Behar Logic flourished extensively during 700-1200 A.D., when the Buddhist kings of the Pāla dynasty reigned there. Candra Gomin, about 700 A.D., was the first logician of the Bengal school. With the downfall of the Pāla kings in 1139 A.D., Buddhist Logic disappeared from Bengal. The splendid monastery of Vikramaśilā is said to have been destroyed in 1203 A.D. (*vide* Appendix C).

In the Middle Age there were several important universities or centres of Buddhistic learning in India, such as Kāñcīpura, Nālandā, Odantapurī, S'rī Dhānyakaṭaka, Kāśmīra and

---

[1] *Vide* Sewell's "Antiquities of Madras," vol. II, pp. 150-151.

[2] *Vide* Stein's translation of Rājataraṅgiṇī IV—183.

[3] Dharmottarācārya's Pāralokasiddhi was translated into Tibetan in Kāśmīra at the monastery of Ratnaraśmi during the reign of S'rī Harṣa (*vide* Tangyur, Mdo, Ze, folio 270).

Vikramaśilā. The Buddhist logicians belonged to one or another of these universities or centres of learning. On the extinction of these Buddhistic universities, the Brahmanic universities of Mithilā and Nadia grew up. These last, in their turn, are now declining, being unable to make headway against the more scientific methods of study which are developing under the influence of the Calcutta University, established by the Imperial British Government in 1857, with the object of encouraging Eastern and Western learning side by side. In spite of strenuous efforts made by the British Government to foster study and research in Indigenous Logic, it is still at its lowest ebb, as the degrees of a modern University are held in greater regard than those of the archaic Universities of Mithilā and Nadia; and as it is often alleged that in comparison with the Logic of Europe, Indian Logic though subtle is cumbrous in its method, forbidding in its language, and less profitable in its material results.

SATIS CHANDRA VIDYABHUSANA.

CALCUTTA,
December, 1907.

BOOK I.

The Jaina Logic.

CHAPTER I.

THE ERA OF TRADITION (*circa* 607 B.C.—453 A.D.).

The Jinas and Mahāvīra.

1. The Jainas maintain that their religion is coeval with time. According to their traditions there appeared at various periods in the world's history sages whom they call *Jinas*, conquerors of their passions, or *Tīrthaṅkaras*, that is, builders of a landing place in the sea of existence. These sages preached the religion of the Jainas. The Jainas hold that in every cycle of time (*utsarpinī-* or *avasarpiṇī-kāla*) 24 sages are born. The first sage of the last series was Ṛṣabhadeva, the 24th was Mahāvīra or Vardhamāna, who attained *nirvāṇa* at Pāvā in 527 B.C.[1] The scriptures which the Jainas obey are founded on the teachings of Mahāvīra. No one disputes this, and scholars generally regard Mahāvīra as the founder of Jainism, and hold that the theory of the existence of *Jinas* previous to him, except Pārśvanātha the 23rd Tīrthaṅkara, was a subsequent invention.

---

[1] पणछस्सय वस पणमास जुदं गमिय वीरणिवुइदो सगराजो। (Trilokasāra of the Digambara sect). "Mahāvīra attained nirvāṇa 605 years 5 months before the Śaka King (78 A.D.) came to the throne," that is, in 527 B.C. As he lived 72 years he must have been born in 599 B.C.

According to Vicāraśreṇī of Merutuṅga, Tīrthakalpa of Jinaprabha Sūri, Vicāra-sāra-prakaraṇa, Tapāgaccha-paṭṭāvalī, etc., of the Śvetāmbara sect Mahāvīra attained *nirvāṇa* 470 years before Vikrama Saṁvat or in B.C. 527.

Dr. Jacobi of Bonn, in his letter dated the 21st October 1907, kindly writes to me as follows:—

"There is however another tradition which makes this event [*viz.* the *nirvāṇa* of Mahāvīra] come off 60 years later, in 467 B.C. (see Pariśiṣṭa Parvan, Introduction, p. 4 f.; also Kalpasūtra, Introduction, p. 8). The latter date cannot be far wrong because Mahāvīra died some years before the Buddha whose death is now placed between 470-480 B.C."

The Svetāmbaras and the Digambaras.

2. The Jainas are divided into two sects, the *Svetāmbaras*, those who are clothed in white, and the *Digambaras*, those who are sky-clad or naked. The *Svetāmbaras* claim to be more ancient than the *Digambaras*, whose existence as a separate sect is said to date from A.D. 82,[1] *i.e.*, 609 years after the attainment of *nirvāṇa* by Mahāvira.

Indrabhūti Gautama (607 B.C.—515 B.C.).

3. The teachings of Mahāvira as represented in the scriptures are said to have been collected[2] by a disciple of his called Indrabhūti. This disciple is often known as Gautama or Gotama. He was a *Kevalin*[3] and the first of the Gaṇa-dharas[4] or leaders of the assembly. His father's name was Brāhmaṇa Vasubhūti, and his mother's name was Brāhmaṇī Pṛthvī. He was born in

---

[1] The Svetāmbaras say :—छव्वास सयाइं नवुत्तराइं तइया सिद्धिंगयस्स वीरस्स तो बोडियाण दिट्ठी रहवीरपुरे समुप्पन्ना। "The Digambara doctrine was preached in Rathavīrapura 609 years after the attainment of nirvāṇa of Mahāvira" (Āvaśyaka niryukti—52). But the Digambaras deny this and say that the Svetāmbaras rose in Vikrama 136 or 79 A.D. Cf. Bhadrabāhucarita IV. 55 :

मृते विक्रमभूपाले षट्त्रिंशदधिके शते।
गतेऽब्दानामभूल्लोके मतं श्वेताम्बराभिधम्॥

[2] अथ सप्तर्धिसम्पन्नं श्रुतार्थं जिनभाषितम्।
द्वादशाङ्गश्रुतं सम्यक् सोपाङ्गं गौतमो व्यधात्॥

(Jaina Harivaṃśa Purāṇa.)

Indrabhūti Gautama and Sudharma Svāmi were the joint compilers of the Jaina scriptures. But Indrabhūti became a *Kevalin* or attained *kevalajñāna* (absolute knowledge) on the day on which Mahāvira attained nirvāṇa. He did not therefore occupy the chair of his teacher Mahāvīra, but relinquished it to his spiritual brother Sudharma Svāmi. Cf. इन्द्रभूति प्रभृतीनां त्रिपदीं व्याहरत् प्रभुः॥ (Hemacandra's Mahāvīracarita, chap. v, MSS. lent by Muni Dharmavijaya and Indravijaya).

[3] Possessor of absolute knowledge. For a further reference to this title see R. G. Bhandarkar's Report, 1883-84, p. 122.

[4] यत्प्रज्ञाप्रसरेऽतिशायिनि तथा प्राचीयमैत्र्योज्ज्वले
जैनी गौरचरत्रिपद्यपि यथा सद्यः पदैः कोटिशः।
यस्योपाङ्गमहोदया समभवत्त्रैलोक्यसंचारिणी
वन्द्योऽसौ गणभृद्व्रजाग्रिमधुरामिन्द्रभूतिः सताम्॥ ४॥

(Siddhajayantī-caritra-ṭīkā, noticed in Peterson's 3rd Report, App. 1, p. 38.)

the village of Gorbara[1] in Magadha and died at Guṇava in Rājagṛha (Rajgir) at the age of ninety-two, 12 years after the attainment of *nirvāṇa* by Mahāvīra.[2] Assuming that Mahāvīra attained *nirvāṇa* in 527 B.C., Indrabhūti's birth must be assigned to 607 B.C. and his death to 515 B.C.

The Canonical Scriptures of the Jainas.

4. Those scriptures of the Jainas which are generally regarded as canonical are divided into 45 *siddhāntas* or *āgamas* classified as 11 Aṅgas, 12 Upāṅgas, etc. "For the benefit of children, women, the old, and the illiterate,"[3] these were composed in the Ardha-Māgadhi or Prākṛta language. On the same principle the scriptures of the Buddhistic canon were originally written in Māgadhī or Pāli. It is maintained that originally the Aṅgas were 12 in number. The 12th Aṅga, which was called the Dṛṣṭivāda or the presentation of views, was written in Sanskrit.[4]

The Dṛṣṭivāda.

5. The **Dṛṣṭivāda** is not extant. It consisted apparently of five parts, in the first of which logic is said to have been dealt with. The Dṛṣṭivāda is reputed to have existed in its entirety at the time of Sthūlabhadra[5] who, according to the Tapāgacha-paṭṭāvali, died in the year in which the 9th Nanda was killed by Candra Gupta (*i.e.*, about 327 B.C.). By 474 A.D. the Dṛṣṭivāda

---

1 श्रीमन्तं मगधेषु गोर्वर इति ग्रामोऽभिरामः श्रिया
तस्योत्पन्नमसन्नचित्तमनिशं श्रीवीरसेवाविधौ ।
ज्योतिःसंश्रयगौतमान्वयवियत्प्रद्योतनद्योमणिं
तापोत्तीर्णसुवर्णवर्णवपुषं भक्त्येन्द्रभूतिं स्तुवे ॥

(Gotamastotra by Jinaprabha Sūri, extracted in Kāvyamālā, 7th Gucchaka, p. 110).

2 For particulars about Indrabhūti Gautama, *vide* Dr. J. Klatt's Paṭṭāvali of the Kharataragaccha in the Indian Antiquary, Vol. XI, Sept. 1882, p. 246; and Weber's Die Handschriften-verzeichnisse der Königlichen Bibliothek zu Berlin, pp. 983 and 1030, in which are noticed Sarvarājagaṇi's Vṛtti on Gaṇadhara-sārdha-śatakam of Jinadattasūri, and Srī-paṭṭāvali-vācanā of the Kharataragaccha.

3 Haribhadra-sūri, in his Daśa-vaikālika-vṛtti (Chap. III), observes:—

बालस्त्रीवृद्धमूर्खाणां नृणां चारित्रकाङ्क्षिणाम् ।
अनुग्रहार्थं तत्त्वज्ञैः सिद्धान्तः प्राकृतः कृतः ॥

4 Vardhamāna-sūri, in his Ācāra-dinakara, quotes the following passage from Āgama:—

मुत्तूण दिट्ठिवायं कालिय उक्कालियंग सिद्धंतं ।
थीबालवायणत्थं पाइय मुइयं जिणवरेहिं ॥

5 *Vide* Cūrṇika of Nandī Sūtra, page 478, published by Dhanapat Sing, Calcutta, and Peterson's 4th Report on Sanskrit MSS., p. cxxxvi.

had disappeared altogether. Nothing is known as to the way in which logic was treated in the Dṛṣṭivāda.[1]

6. The subject-matter of logic is touched upon in several of the 45 Prākṛta scriptures of the Jainas. In the **Anuyoga-dvāra-sūtra**,[2] **Sthānāṅga-sūtra**, **Nandī-sūtra**, etc., there is a description of *Naya*, or the method of comprehending things from particular standpoints. In the **Nandī-sūtra**, **Sthānāṅga-sūtra**, **Bhagavatī-sūtra**, etc.,[3] there is a complete classification of valid knowledge (*Pramāṇa*).

7. The word "Hetu" is found in these Prākṛta scriptures, but its use in these works makes it clear that it had not at this period acquired a very definite significance. In the Sthānāṅga-sūtra[4] it is used not only in the sense of reason, but also as a synonym for valid knowledge (*Pramāṇa*) and inference (*Anumāna*). *Hetu* as identical with valid knowledge (*Pramāṇa*) is stated to be of four kinds, *viz*:—

Hetu.

(1) knowledge derived from perception (*Pratyakṣa*);
(2) knowledge derived from inference (*Anumāna*);
(3) knowledge derived through comparison (*Upamāna*); and
(4) knowledge derived from verbal testimony or reliable authority (*Āgama*).

---

[1] For a full history of the Dṛṣṭivāda (called in Prākṛta Diṭṭhivāo) see Weber's Sacred Literature of the Jains, translated by Weir Smyth in the Indian Antiquary, Vol. XX, May 1891, pp. 170-182.

[2] In the Anuyoga-dvāra-sūtra *Naya* is divided into seven kinds, viz., *naigama*, *saṁgraha*, *vyavahāra*, *ṛju-sūtra*, *śabda*, *samabhirūḍha* and *evaṁbhūta*. For an explanation of these terms see Umāsvāti (in articles 21-26), who instead of dividing *Naya* into seven kinds, first divides it into five kinds, and then subdivides one of the five, *viz.*, *śabda*, into three kinds.

[3] In the Sthānāṅga-sūtra knowledge (*jñāna*) is divided into (1) *Pratyakṣa* (direct knowledge) and (2) *Parokṣa* (indirect knowledge). *Pratyakṣa* again is subdivided as *Kevala jñāna* (entire knowledge) and *Akevala jñāna* (defective knowledge). The *Akevala jñāna* is subdivided as *avadhi* and *manaḥ-paryāya*. The *Parokṣa jñāna* is subdivided as *abhini-bodha* (*mati*) and *śruta*. *Vide* the Sthānāṅga-sūtra, pp. 45-48, and the Nandī-sūtra, pp. 120-134; both published by Dhanapat Sing and printed in Calcutta. See also what is said in the account of Umāsvāti *seq.*

[4] अथवा हेउ चउव्विहे पन्नत्ते तं जहा
पच्चक्खे अनुमाणे उवमे आगमे।
अथवा हेउ चउव्विहे पन्नत्ते तं जहा
अत्थि तं अत्थि सो हेउ अत्थि तं।
णत्थि सो हेउ णत्थि तं अत्थि सो
हेउ णत्थि तं णत्थि सो हेउ॥

(Sthānāṅga-sūtra, pp. 309-310, published by Dhanapat Sing and printed in Calcutta.)

8. When *Hetu* is used in the sense of inference (*Anumāna*), it is classified according to the following types :—

(1) This *is*, because that *is :* There is a fire, because there is smoke.

(2) This *is not*, because that *is :* It is not cold, because there is a fire.

(3) This *is*, because that *is not :* It is cold here, because there is no fire.

(4) This *is not*, because that *is not :* There is no *śiṁśapā* tree here, because there are no trees at all.[1]

Bhadrabāhu (433—357 B.C.).

9. An elaborate discussion of certain principles of logic is found in a Prākṛta commentary on the Daśa-vaikālika-sūtra called Daśavaikālika-niryukti. This commentary was the work of one Bhadrabāhu[2] of the Prācina Gotra. For 45 years this sage lived the ordinary life of the world; 17 years he passed in the performance of religious vows (*Vratas*) and for 14 years he was acknowledged by the Jainas to be the foremost man of his age (*Yuga-pradhāna*).[3] He was a *Srutakevalin*,[4] that is, one versed in the 14 *Pūrvas* of the Dṛṣṭivāda.

10. The abovementioned incidents are generally accepted as facts in the life of the author of the commentary. There is some doubt, however, as to the time in which he lived.[5] According to the records[6] of the *Śvetāmbaras* he was born in 433 B.C. and died in 357 B.C. The *Digambaras*, however, maintain there were two Bhadrabāhus; that the first lived to 162 years from the *nirvāṇa*

---

1 *Vide* footnote 4 on page 4.

2 For particulars *vide* Dr. J. Klatt's Kharataragaccha-paṭṭāvali in the Indian Antiquary, Vol. XI. Sept. 1882, p. 247; Weber II, p. 999; Peterson's 4th Report on Sanskrit MSS., p. lxxxiv; and Dr. H. Jacobi's edition of the Kalpasūtra, Introduction, pp. 11-15.

3 In the Vicāra-ratna-saṁgraha by Jayasoma-sūri noticed by Peterson in his 3rd Report on Sanskrit MSS., pp. 307-308, Bhadrabāhu is included among the Yuga-pravaras or Yuga-pradhānas.

4 For further particulars about this title see R. G. Bhandarkar's Report, 1883-84, p. 122.

5 In Weber II, p. 999, in which the Gurvāvalī-sūtra of Mahopādhyāya Dharmasāgaragaṇi is noticed, we read of Sambhūtivijaya and Bhadrabāhu "Ubhau-pi ṣaṣṭhapaṭṭadharau."

6 अपश्चिमः पूर्वभृतां द्वितीयः
श्रीभद्रबाहुश्च (?) गुरुः शिवाय ।
ज्ञानोपयोगाद्विररचय यो
ररक्ष सङ्घं धरणार्चितांह्रिः ॥ १९ ॥
निर्युक्ति विद्यान्तपयोधिराप
स्वर्गं च वीरात् खनगेन्दुवर्षे १७० ।

of Mahāvīra, that is, up to 365 B.C., and that the second[1] to 515 years from the *nirvāṇa* of Mahāvīra, that is, up to 12 B.C. They do not state definitely which of these Bhadrabāhus was the author of the Daśavaikālika-niryukti, but they hold the view that the second was the author of several of the existing Jaina works. The *Svetāmabara* records do not contain any mention of the second Bhadrabāhu, but in the Ṛṣimaṇḍala-prakaraṇa-vṛtti,[2] a commentary of the *Svetāmbaras,* and in the Caturviṁśati prabandha it is stated that Bhadrabāhu lived in the south in Pratiṣṭhāna and was a brother of Varāhamihira. Now Varāhamihira is popularly believed to have lived in the first century B.C. It is possible therefore, even according to the S'vetāmbaras, that the Daśavaikālika-niryukti was the work of a commentator who, to rely on popular belief, lived about the time of the opening of the Christian era.

11. Whenever he lived, the author of the Daśavaikālikaniryukti also wrote commentaries (niryuktis) on the following Jaina scriptures :—Āvaśyaka-sūtra, Uttarādhyayana-sūtra, Ācārāṅga-sūtra, Sūtra-kṛtāṅga-sūtra, Daśāśruta-skandha-sūtra, Kalpa-sūtra, Vyavahāra-sūtra, Sūrya-prajñapti-sūtra, and Ṛṣibhāṣita-sūtra.

12. Bhadrabāhu did not set himself to analyse knowledge with the object of evolving a system of logic. His object was to illustrate the truth of certain principles of the Jaina religion. To do this, he, in his Daśavaikālika-niryukti,[3] elaborated a syllogism consisting of ten parts (*daśāvayava-vākya*) and then demonstrated how the religious principles of Jainism satisfied the conditions of this formula.

तयोर्द्वितीयः श्रुतविच्च भद्रः
श्रीस्थूलभद्रश्च ददातु शर्म ॥ १४ ॥

Gurvāvalī by Munisundara-sūri published in the Jaina Yaśovijaya-granthamālā of Benares, p. 4.

1 *Vide* the Sarasvatī-gaccha-paṭṭāvalī in the Indian Antiquary, October 1891, and March 1892.

2 *Vide* Dr. R. G. Bhandarkar's Reports on Sanskrit MSS. during 1883-84, p. 138. Bhadrabāhu must have lived as late as the 6th century A.D., if he was really a brother of that Varāhamihira who was one of the nine Gems at the court of Vikramāditya. Munis Dharmavijaya and Indravijaya maintain that Bhadrabāhu's brother was not the same Varāhamihira that adorned the court of Vikramāditya.

3 ते उ पइन्न विभत्ती हेउ-विभत्ती विवक्खपडिसेहो ।
दिट्ठंतो आसंका तप्पडिसेहो निगमणं च ॥ १३७ ॥

Daśavaikālika-niryukti, p. 74, published under the patronage of Dhanapat Sing by the Nirṇaya Sāgara Press, Bombay; and Dr. E. Leumann's edition of Daśavaikālika-niryukti, p. 649.

13. The following is an example:—

(1) The proposition (*Pratijñā*),—" to refrain from taking life is the greatest of virtues."

The Syllogism.

(2) The limitation of the proposition (*Pratijñā-vibhakti*)—" to refrain from taking life is the greatest of virtues according to the Jaina scriptures."

(3) The reason (*Hetu*),—" to refrain from taking life is the greatest of virtues, because those who so refrain are loved by the gods and to do them honour is an act of merit for men."

(4) The limitation of the reason (*Hetu-vibhakti*),—" none but those who refrain from taking life are allowed to reside in the highest place of virtue."

(5) The counter-proposition (*Vipakṣa*),—" but those who despise the Jaina scriptures and take life are said to be loved by the gods and men regard doing them honour as an act of merit. Again, those who take life in sacrifices are said to be residing in the highest place of virtue. Men, for instance, salute their fathers-in-law as an act of virtue, even though the latter despise the Jaina scriptures and habitually take life. Moreover, those who perform animal sacrifices are said to be beloved of the gods."

(6) The opposition to the counter-proposition (*Vipakṣa-pratiṣedha*),—" those who take life as forbidden by the Jaina scriptures do not deserve honour, and they are certainly not loved by the gods. It is as likely that fire will be cold as that they are loved by the gods or that it is regarded by men as an act of merit to do them honour. Buddha, Kapila and others, really not fit to be worshipped, were honoured for their miraculous sayings, but the Jaina *Tīrthaṅkaras* are honoured because they speak absolute truth."

(7) An instance or example (*Dṛṣṭānta*),—" the *Arhats* and *Sādhus* do not even cook food, lest in so doing they should take life. They depend on householders for their meals."

(8) Questioning the validity of the instance or example (*Āśaṅkā*),—" the food which the householders cook is as much for the *Arhats* and *Sādhus* as for themselves. If, therefore, any insects are destroyed in the fire, the *Arhats* and *Sādhus* must share in the householders' sin. Thus the instance cited is not convincing."

(9) The meeting of the question (*Āśaṅkā-pratiṣedha*),—" the *Arhats* and *Sādhus* go to householders for their food without giving notice and not at fixed hours. How, therefore, can it be said that the householders cooked food for the *Arhats* and *Sādhus*? Thus the sin, if any, is not shared by the *Arhats* and *Sādhus*."

(10) Conclusion (*Nigamana*),—" to refrain from taking life is therefore the best of virtues, for those who so refrain are loved by the gods, and to do them honour is an act of merit for men."

Syādvāda.

14. Bhadrabāhu in his Sūtra-kṛtāṅga-niryukti[1] mentions another principle of the Jaina logic called *Śyādvāda* (*Syat* " may be " and *Vāda* " assertion," or the assertion of possibilities) or *Saptabhaṅgī-naya* (the sevenfold paralogism).

15. The *Syādvāda*[2] is set forth as follows :—(1) May be, it is, (2) may be, it is not, (3) may be, it is and it is not, (4) may be, it is indescribable, (5) may be, it is and yet is indescribable, (6) may be, it is not and it is also indescribable, (7) may be, it is and it is not and it is also indescribable.

Umāsvāti (1—85 A.D.).

The categories. Pramāṇa and Naya.

16. Jaina philosophy recognises seven categories, *viz.*, (1) the soul (*Jīva*), (2) the soul-less (*Ajīva*), (3) action (*Āśrava*), (4) bondage (*Bandha*), (5) restraint (*Saṁvara*), (6) destruction of the consequences of action (*Nirjarā*), and (7) release or salvation (*Mokṣa*). According to the Tattvārthādhigama-sūtra which with a *Bhāṣya* or commentry was composed by one Umāsvāti, these categories can only be comprehended by *Pramāṇa*, which in this *sūtra* fluctuates between the two meanings of valid knowledge and the sources of valid knowledge, and of *Naya*, the method of comprehending things from particular standpoints.

17. This Umāsvāti is better known as Vācaka-śramaṇa : he was also called Nāgaravācaka, this title being probably a reference to his Śākhā (spiritual genealogy). The Hindu philosopher Mādhavācārya calls him Umāsvāti-vācakācārya.[3] He lived for 48 years, 8 months, and 6 days and attained *nirvāṇa* in Saṁvat

---

[1] असियसयं किरियाणं
अकिरियाणं च होइ चुलसीति ।
अभाणिय सत्तट्ठी
वेणइयाणं च बत्तीसा ॥ ११ ॥

(Sūtra-kṛtāṅga-niryukti, skandha 1, adhyāya 12, p. 448, edited by Bhim Sing Manak and printed in the Nirṇaya Sāgara Press, Bombay.)

Cf. Sthānāṅga Sūtra, p. 316, published by Dhanapat Sing, Benares edition.

[2] Cf. Sarvadarśana-saṁgraha translated by Cowell and Gough, p. 55. For full particulars about Syādvāda or Saptabhaṅgī-naya *vide* Saptabhaṅgī-taraṅginī by Vimala Dāsa printed in Bombay.

[3] *Vide* Sarvadarśana-saṁgraha, chapter on Jaina darśana.

142, *i.e.*, in 85 A.D. In the Tattvārthādhigama-sūtra Umāsvāti gives the following account [1] of himself :—He was born in a village called Nyagrodhikā, but he wrote the Tattvārthādhigama-sūtra in Pāṭaliputra or Kusumapura (modern Patna). He belonged to the Kaubhīṣaṇin-gotra. His father was Svāti and he was consequently sometimes called Svāti-tanaya. He was also known as Vatsī-sūta, because his mother was Umā of the Vatsa-gotra. In the Tīrthakalpa of Jinaprabha-sūri it is stated that Umāsvāti was the author of 500 Sanskrit prakaraṇas (treatises). He is said to have belonged to the *Svetāmbara* sect though, as stated in article 2 above, it is probable that the distinction between that sect and the *Digambaras* had not yet come into existence.

Parokṣa, indirect knowledge, and *Pratyakṣa*, direct knowledge.

18. It has been observed in article 16 above that in the Tattvārthādhigama-sūtra *Pramāṇa* fluctuates between the meanings of valid knowledge and the sources of valid knowledge. In its former sense

---

[1] न्यग्रोधिकाप्रसूतेन विहरता पुरवरे कुसुमनाम्नि ।
कौभीषणिना स्वातितनयेन वात्सीसुतेनार्घ्यम् ॥ ३ ॥
अर्हद्वचनं सम्यग्गुरुक्रमेणागतं समुपधार्य ।
दुःखार्तं च दुरागमविहतमतिं लोकमवलोक्य ॥ ४ ॥
इदमुच्चैर्नागरवाचकेन सत्त्वानुकम्पया दृब्धम् ।
तत्त्वार्थाधिगमाख्यं स्पष्टमुमास्वातिना शास्त्रम् ॥ ५ ॥

(Tattvārthādhigama-sūtra, Chap. X, p. 233, edited by Mody Keshavlal Premchand in the Bibliotheca Indica Series, Calcutta.)

A similar account is found in the commentary on the Tattvārthādhigama-sūtra by Siddhasenagaṇi. This account is mentioned by Peterson in his 4th Report on Sanskrit Manuscripts, p xvi.

For Further particulars about Umāsvāti see Peterson's 4th Report on Sanskrit Manuscripts, p. xvi, where he observes that in the Digambara Paṭṭāvalī published by Dr. Hoernle in the Indian Antiquary, XX, p. 341, Umāsvāmin (probably the same as Umāsvāti) is included as the sixth Digambara Sūri of the Sarasvatī-gaccha, between Kundakunda and Lohācārya II. According to Dr. Hoernle (*vide* "Two Paṭṭāvalīs of the Sarasvatīgaccha" by Dr. Hoernle in the Indian Antiquary, Vol. XX, October 1891, p. 351) the date of Umāsvāmin's accession is 44 A.D., and he lived for 84 years, 8 months and 6 days. Dr. Hoernle adds, the Kāṣṭhāsaṃgha arose in the time of Umāsvāmin.

Umāsvāti's Tattvārthādhigama-sūtra with his *bhāṣya*, together with Pūjā-prakaraṇa, Jambudvīpa-samāsa and Praśamarati, has been published by the Asiatic Society of Bengal, Calcutta, in one volume which ends thus :—

कृतिः सिताम्बराचार्यस्य महाकवेरुमास्वातिवाचकस्य इति ॥

(Jambudvīpa-samāsa, p. 38, published as Appendix C to the Tattvārthādhigama-sūtra in the Bibliotheca Indica Series.)

Pramāṇa, according to this Sūtra, is of two kinds: (1) *Parokṣa*, indirect knowledge, which is acquired by the soul through external agencies such as the organs of sense, and (2) *Pratyakṣa*, direct knowledge which is acquired by the soul without the intervention of external agencies... *Parokṣa*, indirect knowledge, includes *mati*[1] and *śruta*, for these are acquired by the soul through the medium of the senses and the mind. Knowledge which is attained by *Yoga* (concentration) in its three stages of *avadhi*, *manaḥparyāya* and *kevala* is a species of *Pratyakṣa*, direct knowledge, because it is acquired by the soul not through the medium of the senses.

19. Umāsvāti contends[2] that inference (*Anumāna*), comparison (*Upamāna*), verbal testimony or reliable authority (*Āgama*), presumption (*Arthāpatti*), probability (*Sambhava*), and non-existence (*Abhāva*) are not distinct sources of valid knowledge: he includes them under *Parokṣa* (indirect knowledge). According to his theory the majority of them are the result of the contact of the senses with the objects which they apprehend; and some of them are not sources of valid knowledge at all.

20. It is interesting to note that according to Umāsvāti and the earlier Jaina philosophers all sense-perceptions (visual perception, auditory perception, etc.) are indirect apprehensions in as much as the soul acquires them not of itself but through the medium of the senses. The words *Parokṣa* and *Pratyakṣa* are thus used by these authors in senses quite opposite to those which they bear both in Brāhmaṇic logic and in the later Jaina logic.

---

1 *Mati* is knowledge of existing things acquired through the senses and the mind.

Śruta is knowledge of things (past, present and future) acquired through reasoning and study.

Avadhi is knowledge of things beyond the range of our perception.

Manaḥparyāya is knowledge derived from reading the thoughts of others.

Kevala is unobstructed, unconditional and absolute knowledge.

2 In the *bhāṣya* on aphorism 12, of chapter 1 of the Tattvārthādhigama-sūtra, Umāsvāti observes:—

अनुमानोपमानागमार्थापत्तिसम्भवाभावानपि च प्रमाणानीति केचिन्मन्यन्ते तत्कथमेतदिति अत्रोच्यते । सर्वाण्येतानि मतिश्रुतयोरन्तर्भूतानि इन्द्रियार्थसन्निकर्षनिमित्तत्वात् ॥

(Tattvārthādhigama-sūtra, p. 15).

In his *bhāṣya* on 1—6 of the Tattvārthādhigama-sūtra Umāsvāti observes:—

चतुर्विधमित्येके ।

(Tattvārthādhigama-sūtra, p. 9.)

In his *bhāṣya* on 1—35 he mentions the four Pramāṇas thus:—

यथा वा प्रत्यक्षानुमानोपमानाप्तवचनैः प्रमाणैरेकोऽर्थः प्रमीयते स्वविषयनियमात् न च ता विप्रतिपत्तयो भवन्ति तद्वन्नयवादा इति ॥

(Tattvārthādhigama-sūtra, p. 35).

Naya, the method of comprehending things from particular standpoints.

21. *Naya* [1] is the method by which things are comprehended from particular standpoints. It is of five kinds:—(1) *Naigama*, the non-distinguished (2) *Saṁgraha*, the general, (3) *Vyavahāra*, the practical, (4) *Ṛju-sūtra*, the straight expression, (5) *Sabda*, the verbal.

Naigama.

22. *Naigama*, the non-distinguished, is the method by which an object is regarded as possessing both general and specific properties, no distinction being made between them. For instance, when you use the word "bamboo," you are indicating a number of properties, some of which are peculiar to the bamboo, while others are possessed by it in common with other trees. You do not distinguish between these two classes of properties.

Saṁgraha.

23. *Saṁgraha*, the collective, is the method which takes into consideration generic properties only, ignoring particular properties.

Vyavahāra.

24. *Vyavahāra*, the practical, is the method which takes into consideration the particular only. The general without the particular is a nonentity. If you ask a person to bring you a plant, he must bring you a particular plant, he can not bring plant in general.

Ṛju-sūtra.

25. *Ṛju-sūtra*, the straight expression, is the method which considers a thing as it exists at the moment, without any reference to its past or its future. It is vain to ponder over a thing as it was in the past or as it will be in the future. All practical purposes are served by considering the thing itself as it exists at the present moment. For instance, a man who in a previous birth was my son is now born as a prince, but he is of no practical use to me now. The method of *Ṛju-sūtra* recognises nothing but the entity itself (*bhāva*) and does not consider the name (*nāma*), the image (*sthāpanā*), or the causes which constituted it (*dravya*). The fact that a cowherd is called *Indra* does not make him lord of the heavens. An image of a king can not perform the functions of a king. The causes which exist in me now and will necessitate my being born hereafter with a different body can not enable me to enjoy that body now.

These four kinds of *Pramāṇa* seem to refer to those in the Nyāya Sūtra of the Hindu logician Akṣapāda Gautama. But the same four kinds are also referred to as sub-divisions of *Hetu* in the Sthānāṅga Sūtra of the Jainas, p. 309. published by Dhanapat Sing and printed in Calcutta.

1 नैगमसंग्रहव्यवहारर्जुसूत्रशब्दा नयाः ॥ १-३४ ॥

(Tattvārthādhigama-sūtra, p. 32.)

Sabda.

26. *Sabda*,[1] the verbal, is the method of correct nomenclature. It is of three kinds, *viz.*, *Sāmprata*, the suitable, *Samabhirūḍha*, the subtle, and *Evaṁbhūta*, the such-like. In Sanskrit a jar is called *ghaṭa*, *kumbha* or *kalasa*, and these are synonymous terms. *Sāmprata* consists in using a word in its conventional sense, even if that sense is not justified by its derivation. For example the word "*Satru*" according to its derivation means "destroyer," but its conventional meaning is "enemy." *Samabhirūḍha* consists in making nice distinctions between synonyms, selecting in each case the word which on etymological grounds is the most appropriate. *Evaṁbhūta* consists in applying to things such names only as their actual condition justifies. Thus a man should not be called *Sakra* (strong), unless he actually possesses the *Sakti* (strength) which the name implies.

---

[1] Umāsvāti in his *bhāṣya* on 1-35 observes :—

यथार्थाभिधानं शब्दः। नामादिषु प्रसिद्धपूर्व्वाच्छब्दादर्थे प्रत्ययः साम्प्रतः सत्सु अर्थेषु असंक्रमः समभिरूढः। व्यञ्जनार्थयोरेवम्भूत इति॥

(Tattvârthâdigama-sūtra, p. 32.)

CHAPTER II.

THE HISTORICAL PERIOD (COMMENCING FROM 453 A.D.).

THE WRITTEN RECORDS OF THE JAINAS.

27. The teachings of Mahāvira as contained in the Jaina *Āgamas* are said to have been handed down by memory for several centuries until in Vira Saṁvat 980 or A.D. 453, they were codified in writing by Devardhi Gaṇi,[1] otherwise known as Kṣamāśramaṇa, at a council held at Valabhi. According to this theory the authentic history of the Jaina literature commences from 453 A.D., and all that preceded that period is to be regarded as merely traditional.

SIDDHASENA DIVĀKARA (ABOUT 533 A.D.).

28. The first Jaina writer on systematic logic, during the historical period, appears to be Siddhasena Divākara. Before his time there had not perhaps existed any distinct treatise on Jaina logic, its principles having been included in the works on metaphysics and religion. It was he who for the first time laid the foundation of a science called Logic (*Nyāya*) among the Jainas by compiling a treatise called **Nyāyāvatāra**[2] in 32 short stanzas.

---

1 *Vide* Dr. Klatt's Paṭṭāvali of the Kharataragaccha in the Indian Anitquary, Sept. 1882, Vol. XI, p. 247; and Dr. Jacobi's Kalpasūtra, Introduction, p. 15. See also Vinaya Vijaya Gaṇi's commentary on the Kalpasūtra which quotes the following text :—

वलहिपुरंमि नयरे ।
देवड्ढि पमुह सयलसंघेहिं ।
पुव्वे आगम लिहिउ ।
नवसय असी आउ वीराउ ॥ १ ॥

(Sukhabodhikā Ṭīkā to Kalpasūtra, p. 433, printed in Kathiwar by Hira Lal Haṁsarāja.)

In Devardhi Gaṇi's redaction of the Kalpasūtra (*vide* Dr. Jacobi's edition of the Kalpasūtra, p. 67) we read :—

Samaṇassa bhagavao Mahāvīrassa jāva savva-dukkha-ppahīṇassa navavāsasayāiṁ vikkaṁtaiṁ dasamassa ya vāsa-sayassa, ayaṁ asī ime saṁvacchare kāle gacchai iti (148).

2 *Vide* No. 741 in the list of MSS. purchased for the Bombay Government as noticed by Peterson in his 5th Report, p. 289. A manuscript of the Nyāyāvatāra with Vivṛti was procured for me from Bhavanagara, Bombay, by Muni Dharmavijaya and his pupil Sri Indravijaya.

29. Siddhasena Divākara is also the famous author of the **Sammatitarka-sūtra** which is a work in Prākṛta on general philosophy containing an elaborate discussion on the principles of logic. This author, who belonged to the S'vetāmbara sect, has been mentioned by Pradyumna Sūri (*q.v.*) in his Vicāra-sāra-prakaraṇa [1] and by Jina Sena Sūri in the Ādipurāṇa dated 783 A.D.

30. Siddhasena Divākara, who was a pupil of Vṛddha-vādi-sūri, received the name of Kumuda-candra [2] at the time of ordination. He is said to have split, by the efficacy of his prayers, the Linga, the Brāhmaṇical symbol of Rudra, in the temple of Mahākāla at Ujjayinī, and to have called forth an image of Pārśvanātha by reciting his Kalyāṇa-mandira-stava. He is believed by Jainas to have converted Vikramāditya to Jainism 470 years after the *nirvāṇa* of Mahāvīra, that is, in 57 B.C.[3]

31. But Vikramāditya of Ujjainī does not seem to be so old as he has been identified by scholars with Yaśodharma Deva, king of Malwa, who, on the authority of Alberuni, defeated the Huns at Korur in 533 A.D. This view of scholars agrees well with the statement of the Chinese pilgrim Hwen-thsang, who, coming to India in 629 A.D., says that a very powerful king, presumably Vikramāditya, reigned at Ujjainī 60 years before his arrival there.[4] Moreover, Varāhamihira, who was one of the nine Gems at the court of Vikramāditya, is known to have lived between 505 A.D. and 587 A.D.[5] It is therefore very probable that

---

[1] पंचेव य वरिससए सिद्धसेणदिवायरो य जयपयडो ।
नवसय चौसहिए सत्तसुय चक्करविसयपक्ख ॥ २९ ॥

(Vicāra-sāra-prakaraṇa, noticed by Peterson in his 3rd Report, p. 272.)

[2] Cf. Prabhāvakacaritra VIII, V. 57.

[3] For other particulars about Siddhasena Divākara see Dr. Klatt's Paṭṭāvalī of the Kharataragaccha in the Indian Antiquary, Vol. XI. Sept. 1882, p. 247. *Vide* also Dr. R. G. Bhandarkar's report on Sanskrit MSS., during 1883-84, pp. 118, 140. Also the Prabandha-cintāmaṇi translated by Mr. Tawney in the Bibliotheca Indica series of Calcutta, pp. 10-14.

[4] *Vide* Beal's Buddhist Records, Vol. II, p. 261.

[5] Varāhamihira chose S'aka 427 or A.D. 505 as the initial year of his astronomical calculation, showing thereby that he lived about that time:

सप्ताश्विवेदसंख्यं शककालमपास्य चैत्रशुक्लादौ ।
अर्धास्तमिते भानौ यवनपुरे सौम्यदिवसाद्ये ॥ ८ ॥

Pañcasiddhāntikā, chap. 1, edited by Dr. G. Thibaut and Sudhākara Dvivedi.

Vide also Dr. Thibaut's Introduction to the Pañcasiddhāntikā, p. xxx.

Vikramāditya and his contemporary Siddhasena Divākara lived at Ujjainī about 533 A.D. I am inclined to believe that Siddhasena was no other than *Kṣapaṇaka* [1] (a Jaina sage) who is traditionally known to the Hindus to have been one of the nine Gems that adorned the court of Vikramāditya.

32. The Nyāyāvatāra written in Sanskrit verse gives an exposition of the doctrine of *Pramāṇa* (sources of valid knowledge) and *Naya* (the method of comprehending things from particular standpoints).

Pramāṇa or valid knowledge. Perception.

33. *Pramāṇa* is valid knowledge which illumines itself as well as other things without any obstruction. It is of two kinds: (1) direct valid knowledge or perception (*Pratyakṣa*) and (2) indirect valid knowledge (*Parokṣa*). Direct valid knowledge (*Pratyakṣa*) is two-fold: (1) practical (*Vyāvahārika*) which is the knowledge acquired by the soul through the five senses (the eye, ear, nose, tongue and touch) and the mind (*Manas*), and (2) transcendental (*Pāramārthika*) which is the infinite knowledge that comes from the perfect enlightenment of the soul: it is called *Kevala* or absolute knowledge.

Verbal Testimony.

34. Indirect valid knowledge (*Parokṣa*) is also of two kinds: (1) inference (*Anumāna*) and (2) verbal testimony (*Śābda*). Verbal testimony is the knowledge derived from the words of reliable persons including knowledge from scripture. Suppose a young man coming to the side of a river cannot ascertain whether the river is fordable or not, and immediately an old experienced man of the locality, who has no enmity against him, comes and tells him the river is easily fordable: the word of the old man

---

[1] The nine Gems are:—

धन्वन्तरिः क्षपणकोऽमरसिंहः शङ्कु
वेतालभट्ट घटखर्पर कालिदासाः ।
ख्यातो वराहमिहिरो नृपतेः सभायां
रत्नानि वै वररुचि र्नव विक्रमस्य ॥

(Jyotirvidābharaṇa).

In the Pañcatantra and other Brahmanic Sanskrit works as well as in the Avadānakalpalatā and other Buddhist Sanskrit works the Jaina ascetics are nicknamed as Kṣapaṇaka:

भगवद्भाषितं तत्तु सुभद्रेण निवेदितम् ।
श्रुत्वा क्षपणकः क्षिप्रमभूद् द्वेषविषाकुलः ॥ ९ ॥
तस्य सर्व्वज्ञतां वेत्ति सुभद्रो यदि मद्गिरा ।
तदेष क्षपणमयां त्यक्ष्यति श्रमणादरात् ॥ १२ ॥

(Avadānakalpalatā, Jyotiṣkāvadāna).

is to be accepted as a source of valid knowledge called personal testimony or *Laukika Sābda*. Scripture is also a source of valid knowledge for it lays down injunctions on matters which baffle perception and inference: for instance, it teaches that misery is the consequence of vice. Knowledge derived from this source is called scriptural testimony or *Sāstraja Sābda*. *Scripture* is defined as that which was first cognised by a competent person, which is not such as to be passed over by others, which is not incompatible with the truths derived from perception, which imparts true instruction and which is profitable to all men and is preventive of the evil path.[1]

Inference.

35. Inference (*Anumāna*) is the correct knowledge of the major term (*Sādhya*) derived through the middle term (*Hetu*, reason, or *Linga*, sign) which is inseparably connected with it. It is of two kinds: (1) inference for one's own self (*Svārthānumāna*) and (2) inference for the sake of others (*Parārthānumāna*).

36. The first kind is the inference deduced in one's own mind after having made repeated observations. A man by repeated observations in the kitchen and elsewhere forms the conclusion in his mind that fire must always be an antecedent of smoke. Afterwards, he is not certain whether a hill which he sees has fire on it or not. But, noticing smoke, he at once brings to mind the inseparable connection between fire and smoke, and concludes that there must be fire on the hill. This is the inference for one's own self.

37. If the inference is communicated to others through words, it is called an inference for the sake of others. A type of this kind of inference is as follows:—

(1) The *hill* (minor term or *Pakṣa*) is full of *fire* (major term or *Sādhya*);
(2) because it is full of *smoke* (middle term or *Hetu*);
(3) whatever is full of smoke is full of fire, as, *e.g.*, a *kitchen* (example or *Dṛṣṭānta*);
(4) so is this hill full of smoke (application or *Upanaya*):
(5) therefore this hill is full of fire (conclusion or *Nigamana*).

Terms of a syllogism.

38. In a proposition the subject is the minor term (*Pakṣa*) and the predicate the major term (*Sādhya*). The minor term is that with which the connection of the major term is to be shown: In the proposition

---

[1] आप्तोपज्ञमनुल्लङ्घ्यमदृष्टेष्टविरोधकम् ।
तत्त्वोपदेशकृत् सार्वं शास्त्रं कापथघट्टनम् ॥
(Verse 9, Nyāyāvatāra).

"the hill is full of fire," the *hill* is the minor term and *fire* major term. The middle term (*Hetu*) is defined as that which cannot occur otherwise than in connection with the major term. Thus in the proposition: "the hill is full of fire because it is full of smoke," *smoke* is the middle term which cannot arise from any other thing than fire which is the major term. The example (*Dṛṣṭānta*) is a familiar case which assures the connection between the major term and the middle term: It is of two kinds: (1) homogeneous *Sādharmya*), such as "the hill is full of fire because it is full of smoke, as a *kitchen*," and (2) heterogeneous (*Vaidharmya*) which assures the connection between the middle term and major term by contrariety. that is, by showing that the absence of the major term is attended by the absence of the middle term, such as "where there is no fire there is no smoke as in a *lake*."

39. In an inference for the sake of others the minor term (*Pakṣa*) must be explicitly set forth, otherwise the reasoning might be misunderstood by the opponent, *e.g.* This hill has fire because it has smoke.

This instance, if the minor term is omitted, will assume the following form :—

Having fire, | Because having smoke.

Here the opponent might not at once recollect any instance in which fire and smoke exist in union, and might mistake a lake for such an instance. In such a case the whole reasoning will be misunderstood.

40. If that of which the major term or predicate is affirmed is opposed by evidence, the public opinion, one's own statement, etc., we have that which is known as the fallacy of the minor term (*Pakṣābhāsa*) of which there are many varieties.

Fallacy of the minor term.

The semblance or fallacy of the minor term (*Pakṣābhāsa*) arises when one attributes to it as a proved fact that which is yet to be proved, or which is incapable of being proved, or when it is opposed to perception and inference, or inconsistent with the public opinion or incongruous with one's own statement, thus :—

(1) "The jar is animate (*paudgalika*)"—this is a conclusion which is yet to be proved to the opponent.

(2) "Every thing is momentary"—this is a Saugata conclusion which, according to the Jainas, is incapable of being proved.

(3) "The general (*sāmānya*) and particular (*viśeṣa*) things are without parts, are distinct from each other and are like themselves alone"—this is opposed to perception.

(4) "There is no omniscient being"—this is, according to the Jainas, opposed to inference.

(5) "The sister is to be taken as wife"—this is inconsistent with the public opinion.

(6) "All things are non-existent."—this is incongruous with one's own statement.

Inseparable connection.

41. Inseparable connection (*Vyāpti*) is the invariable accompaniment of the middle term by the major term. In the inference: "this hill is full of fire, because it is full of smoke," the connection between fire and smoke, that is, the invariable presence of fire with smoke, is called *Vyāpti* or Inseparable Connection. It is of two kinds: (1) Intrinsic and (2) Extrinsic.

42. Intrinsic inseparable connection (*Antar-vyāpti*) occurs when the minor term (*pakṣa*) itself as the common abode of the middle term (*hetu*) and major term (*sādhya*) shows the inseparable connection between them, thus:—

(1) This hill (minor term) is full of *fire* (major term):

(2) because it is full of *smoke* (middle term).

Here the inseparable connection between fire and smoke is shown by the hill (minor term) in which both of them abide.

43. Extrinsic inseparable connection (*Bahir-vyāpti*) occurs when an example (*dṛṣṭānta*) from the outside is introduced as the common abode of the middle term (*hetu*) and major term (*sādhya*) to assure the inseparable connection between them, thus:—

(1) This hill is full of *fire* (major term);

(2) because it is full of *smoke* (middle term);

(3) as a *kitchen* (example).

Here the reference to the kitchen is no essential part of the inference: but is introduced from without as a common instance of a place in which fire and smoke exist together, and so it reaffirms the inseparable connection between them.

44. Some logicians hold that, that which is to be proved, that is, the major term (*sādhya*), can be established by intrinsic inseparable connection (*Antarvyāpti*) only: hence the extrinsic inseparable connection (*Bahir-vyāpti*) is superfluous.

Fallacies of the middle term.

45. The semblance of reason or fallacy of the middle term (*Hetvābhāsa*) arises from doubt, misconception or non-conception about it (the middle term). It is of three kinds:—

(1) The unproved (*Asiddha*): This is fragrant because it is a sky-lotus.

Here the reason (middle term), *viz.*, the sky-lotus, is unreal.

(2) The contradictory (*Viruddha*): "This is fiery because it is a body of water."

Here the reason alleged is opposed to what is to be established.

(3) The uncertain (*Anaikāntika*): "Sound is eternal because it is always audible."

Here the reason or middle term is uncertain because audibleness may or may not be a proof of eternity.

Fallacy of example.

46. The fallacy of example (*Dṛṣṭāntābhāsa*) may arise in the homogeneous or heterogeneous form from a defect in the middle term (*hetu*) or major term (*sādhya*) or both; or from doubt about them.

47. Fallacies of the homogeneous example (*Sādharmya-dṛṣṭāntābhāsa*) are as follows :—

(1) Inference is ***invalid*** (major term), because it is a ***source of knowledge*** (middle term), like *perception* (homogeneous example).

Here the example involves a defect in the major term (*sādhya*), for perception is not invalid.

(2) Perception is ***invalid*** (major term), because it is a ***source of valid knowledge*** (middle term), like a ***dream*** (homogeneous example).

Here the example involves a defect in the middle term (*hetu*), for the dream is not a source of valid knowledge.

(3) The omniscient being is not ***existent*** (major term), because he is not ***apprehended by the senses*** (middle term), like a ***jar*** (homogeneous example).

Here the example involves a defect in both the major and middle terms (*sādhya* and *hetu*), for the jar is both existent and apprehended by the senses.

(4) This person is ***devoid of passions*** (major term), because he is ***mortal*** (middle term), like the ***man in the street*** (homogeneous example).

Here the example involves doubt as to the validity of the major term, for it is doubtful whether the man in the street is devoid of passions.

(5) This person is ***mortal*** (major term), because he is ***full of passions*** (middle term), like the ***man in the street*** (homogeneous example).

Here the example involves doubt as to the validity of the middle term, for it is doubtful, whether the man in the street is devoid of passions.

(6) This person is ***non-omniscient*** (major term), because he is ***full of passions*** (middle term), like the ***man in the street*** (homogeneous example).

Here the example involves doubt as to the validity of both the major and middle terms, for it is doubtful whether the man in the street is full of passions and non-omniscient.

It is stated in the Nyāyāvatāra-vivṛti that some unnecessarily lay down three other kinds of fallacy of the homogeneous example (*Sādharmya-dṛṣṭāntābhāsa*), viz. :—

(1) Unconnected (***Ananvyaya***), such as : This person is ***full of passions***

(major term), because he is a *speaker* (middle term), like a *certain man in Magadha* (example).

Here though a certain man in Magadha is both a speaker and full of passions, yet there is no inseparable connection between "being a speaker" and "being full of passions."

(2) Of connection unshown (*Apradarśitānvaya*), such as :—

Sound is *non-eternal* (major term), because it is *produced* (middle term), as a jar (example).

Here though there is an inseparable connection between "produced" and "non-eternal," yet it has not been shown in the proper form as :—

"Whatever is produced is non-eternal as a jar."

(3) Of inverted connection (*Viparītānvaya*), such as :—

Sound is non-eternal (major term), because it is *produced* (middle term).

Here if the inseparable connection (*vyāpti*) is shown thus—

"Whatever is non-eternal is produced as a jar," instead of—

"Whatever is produced is non-eternal as a jar," the example would involve the fallacy of inverted connection.

48. Fallacies of the heterogeneous example (*Vaidharmya-dṛṣṭāntābhāsa*) are of six kinds, thus :—

(1) Inference is *invalid* (major term), because it is a *source of knowledge* (middle term): whatever is not invalid is not a source of knowledge, as a *dream* (heterogeneous example).

Here the example involves in the heterogeneous form a defect in the major term (*sādhya*) for the dream is really invalid though it has been cited as not invalid.

(2) Perception is *non-reflective* or *nirvikalpaka* (major term), because it is a *source of knowledge* (middle term): whatever is reflective or *savikalpaka*, is not a source of knowledge, as *inference* (heterogeneous example).

Here the example involves in the heterogeneous form a defect in the middle term (*sādhana*), for inference is really a source of knowledge though it has been cited as not such.

(3) Sound is eternal and *non-eternal* (major term), because it is an *existence* (middle term): whatever is not eternal and non-eternal is not an existence, as a jar (heterogeneous example).

Here the example involves in the heterogeneous form a defect in both the major and middle terms (*sādhya* and *sādhana*), for the jar is both "eternal and non-eternal" and "an existence."

(4) Kapila is not *omniscient* (major term), because he is not a *propounder of the four noble truths* (middle term): whoever is omniscient is the propounder of the four noble truths, as *Buddha* (the heterogeneous example).

Here the example involves in the heterogeneous form a doubt as to the validity of the major term (*sādhya*), for it is doubtful whether Buddha was omniscient.

(5) This person is *untrustworthy* (major term), because he is *full of passions* (middle term): whoever is trustworthy is not full of passions, as *Buddha* (heterogeneous example).

Here the example involves doubt as to the validity of the

middle term (*hetu*), for it is doubtful whether Buddha is not full of passions.

(6) Kapila is not devoid of *passions* (major term), because he did *not give his own flesh to the hungry* (middle term): whoever is devoid of passions did give his own flesh to the hungry, as *Buddha* (heterogeneous example).

Here the example involves doubt as to the validity of both the major and middle terms (*sādhya* and *sādhana*), for it is doubtful whether Buddha was devoid of passions and gave his own flesh to the hungry.

It is stated in the Nyāyāvatāra-vivṛti that some unnecessarily lay down three other kinds of fallacy of the heterogeneous example (*Vaidharmya-dṛṣṭāntābhāsa*), *viz.*—

(1) Unseparated (*Avyatireki*): This person is not *devoid of passions* (major term), because he is a *speaker* (middle term): whoever is devoid of passions is not a speaker, as a *piece of stone* (heterogeneous example).

Here though a piece of stone is both "devoid of passions" and "not a speaker," yet there is no invariable separation (*vyatireka vyāpti*) between "devoid of passions" and "a speaker."

(2) Of separation unshown (*Apradarśitavyatireka*):

Sound is *non-eternal* (major term), because it is *produced* (middle term); as ether (example).

Here though there is an invariable separation between "*produced*" and "eternal," yet it has not been shown in the proper form, such as: "Whatever is non-non-eternal is not produced, *e.g.*, ether."

(3) Of contrary separation (*Viparīta-vyatireka*):

Sound is *non-eternal* (major term), because it is produced (middle term): whatever is not produced is non-non-eternal, *e.g.*, ether (example).

Here the example has been put in a contrary way, for the proper form should have been: Whatever is non-non-eternal is not produced, *e.g.*, ether."

49. Refutation (*Dūṣaṇa*) is the pointing out of defects or fallacies in the statements of the opponent in any of the forms enumerated above. The semblance of a refutation (*Dūṣaṇābhāsa*) is the contrivance to allege defects where there are no defects at all.

50. The immediate effect of *Pramāṇa* (valid knowledge) is the removal of ignorance. The consequence of the transcendental perception (*Pāramārthika Pratyakṣa Pramāṇa*) is bliss and equanimity consisting in salvation (*Mokṣa* or final emancipation), while that of the other kinds of *Pramāṇa* (direct and indirect knowledge) is the facility which they afford us to choose the desirable and reject the undesirable things.

Naya or the method of comprehending things from particular standpoints.

51. *Naya* is the method of comprehending things from particular standpoints. Thus we may conceive rose either as a flower possessing the attributes common to all flowers or as a thing possessing attributes which are peculiar to the rose as distinguished from other flowers. The *Naya* is of seven kinds: *naigama*, *saṁgraha*, *vyavahāra*, *ṛjusūtra*, *śabda*, *samabhirūḍha*, and *evaṁbhūta*.

52. Knowledge which determines the full meaning of an object through the employment, in the scriptural method, of one-sided *nayas*, is called *Syādvāda-śruta.* It is the perfect knowledge of things taken from all possible standpoints. Thus a thing may be, may not be, both may or may not be, etc., according as we take it from one or other standpoint.

The soul (*Jīva*) is the knower, the illuminator of self and non-self, doer, enjoyer, undergoes changes of condition and is self-conscious, being different from the earth, water, etc.

This system of *Pramāṇa* and *Naya*, with which all of us are familiar, and which serves to perform all practical functions, has no beginning and no end.

SIDDHASENA GAṆI (600 A.D.).

53. Siddhasena Gaṇi, who belonged to the S'vetāmbara sect, was the author of a commentary on Umāsvāti's Tattvārthādhigama-sūtra called Tattvārthaṭīkā,[1] in which the logical principles of *Pramāṇa* (the sources of knowledge), and *Naya* (the method of comprehending things from particular standpoints) have been fully discussed. He was a pupil of Bhāsvāmin[2] who was a spiritual successor of Siṁhasūri, himself a disciple of Dinna Gaṇi. Siddhasena Gaṇi[3] is generally believed to have been a contemporary of Devardhigaṇi Kṣamāśramaṇa, who flourished 980 years after Mahāvīra, or about 453 A.D. But as he has in his Tattvārthaṭīkā quoted Siddhasena Divākara and was posterior to Siṁhagiri or Siṁhasūri, a contemporary of Vikramāditya, I am inclined to suppose that he lived after 533 A.D., or about 600 A.D.

SAMANTABHADRA (600 A.D.).

54. Samantabhadra, who belonged to the Digambara sect of Southern India, was the famous author of a well-known com-

---

1 A palm-leaf manuscript of the Tattvārthaṭīkā in the temple of S'āntinātha, Cambay, has been noticed by Peterson in his 3rd Report, pp. 83-86.

2 तस्मादभूच्छिष्यवरः सत्त्वानामसमेसुखीकरकलापः ।
तत्त्वार्थटीकामिमां व्यधात् सिद्धसेनगणिः ॥ ७

(Tattvārthaṭīkā, noticed in Peterson's 3rd Report, p. 85.)

3 Siṁhasūri is identified by Peterson with Siṁhagiri who was a contemporary of Vikramāditya.

(Peterson's 4th Report, pp. cxxxi and cxxviii.)

Muni Dharmavijaya and his pupil Indra-vijaya tell me that Siddhasena Gaṇi was a contemporary of Devardhigaṇi Kṣamāśramaṇa,

mentary on Umāsvāti's Tattvārthādhigama-sūtra called **Gandhahasti-mahābhāṣya.** The introductory part of this commentary is called **Devāgamastotra**[1] or Āptamīmāṁsā, and is replete with discussions of logical principles besides a review of the contemporary schools of philosophy including the Advaita Vāda.[2] The Āptamīmāṁsā has been cited by the Hindu philosopher Vācaspati Miśra[3] in explaining Saṅkarācārya's criticism of the Syādvāda doctrine in the Vedānta-sūtra.

55. Samantabhadra, who was styled a Kavi and whose works were commented on by Vidyānanda[4] and Prabhācandra, was also the author of the Yuktyanuśāsana, the Ratnakaraṇḍaka (also called Upāsakādhyayana), the Svayambhū-stotra, and the Caturviṁ-

---

who flourished 980 years after the *nirvāṇa* of Mahāvīra. *Vide* also Uvāsagadasāo edited by A. F. R. Hoernle, Appendix III, page 50.

1 In the Pāṇḍavapurāṇa he is extolled as the author of the Devāgamastotra :—

समन्तभद्रो भद्रार्थो भातु भारतभूषणः

देवागमेन येनात्र व्यक्तो देवागमः कृतः ॥

(Pāṇḍavapurāṇa, noticed in Peterson's 4th Report, p. 157.)

2 अद्वैतैकान्तपक्षेऽपि दृष्टो भेदो विरुध्यते ।

कारकाणां क्रियायाश्च नैकं स्वस्मात् प्रजायते ॥ २४ ॥

(Āptamīmāṁsā, verse 24.)

3 Vācaspati Miśra in his Bhāmati-ṭikā on Saṅkara's exposition of the Vedānta Sūtra 2-2-33 quotes the following verse :—

स्याद्वादः सर्वथैकान्तत्यागात् किंवृत्तचिद्विधेः ।

सप्तभङ्गनयापेक्षो हेयादेयविशेषकृत् ॥

(Bhāmatī, Bibliotheca Indica, p. 458.)

The same verse occurs in the Āptamīmāṁsā as follows :—

स्याद्वादः सर्वथैकान्तत्यागात् किं वृत्तचिद्विधः ।

सप्तभङ्गनयापेक्ष हेयादेय विशेषकः ॥ १०४ ॥

(MSS. of the Āptamīmāṁsā, verse 104, borrowed from Mr. Jain Vaidya of Jaipur.)

Vidyānanda at the closing part of his commentary on the Āptamīmāṁsā (called Āpta-mīmāṁsālaṅkṛti-ṭikā aṣṭasāhasrī) refers to Samantabhadra thus :—

येनाशेषकुनीतिवृत्तिसरितः प्रेक्षावतां शोषिताः

यद्वाचोऽप्यकलङ्कनीतिरुचिरास्तत्त्वार्थसार्थद्युतः ।

स श्रीस्वामि समन्तभद्र यतिभृत् भूयाद् विभुर्भानुमान्

विद्यानन्दघनप्रदोऽनघधियां स्याद्वादमार्गाग्रणीः ॥

(Folio 218, Āptamīmāṁsālaṅkṛti-ṭikā, Govt. Collection, in the Asiatic Society of Bengal, No. 1525.)

śati-jina-stuti. He is mentioned by Jina Sena in the Ādipurāṇa composed about 838 A.D., and is referred to by the Hindu philosopher Kumārila.[1] Kumārila, a contemporary of the Buddhist logician Dharmakīrti, is generally held to have lived in the 7th century A.D. Samantabhadra is supposed to have flourished about 600 A.D.

56. The Āpta-mīmāṁsā consists of 115 stanzas in Sanskrit, divided into ten chapters called *Paricchedas*, in the course of which a full exposition of the seven parts of the *Syād-vāda* or *Sapta-bhaṅgī-naya* has been given. The first and second parts of the doctrine, *viz.*, *Syād-asti* ("may be, it is"), and *Syād-nāsti* ("may be, it is not"), have led to most interesting discussion of the relation between *asti*, that is, *bhāva* or existence, and *nāsti*, that is, *abhāva* or non-existence.

57. Non-existence (*Abhāva*) is divided into four kinds: (1) antecedent non-existence (*prāgabhāva*), *e.g.*, a lump of clay becomes non-existent as soon as a jar is made out of it, so the jar is an antecedent non-existence with reference to the lump of clay; (2) subsequent non-existence (*pradhvaṁsābhāva*), *e.g.*, the lump of clay is a subsequent non-existence with reference to the jar; (3) mutual non-existence (*anyonyābhāva* or *anyāpoha*), *e.g.*, a jar and a post are mutually non-existent with reference to each other; and (4) absolute non-existence (*samavāyābhāva* or *atyantābhāva*), *e.g.*, the inanimate is not a living object. It is observed[2] that on the supposition of mere existence to the entire exclusion of non-existence, things become all-pervading, beginningless, endless, indistinguishable and inconceivable. For

---

Prabhācandra in his commentary on the Ratnakaraṇḍaka (or Upāsakādhyayana) observes:—

येनाज्ञानतमो विनाश्य निखिलं भव्यात्मचेतोगतं
सम्यग्ज्ञानमहांशुभिः प्रकटितः सागारमार्गोऽखिलः ।
स श्रीरत्नकरण्डकामलरविः संसृत्सरिच्छोषको
जीयादेष समन्तभद्रमुनिपः श्रीमत्प्रभेन्दुर्जिनः ॥

(Upāsakādhyayana with the commentary of Prabhācandra noticed in Peterson's 4th Report, pp. 137-38.)

1 *Vide* Dr. R. G. Bhandarkar's Report on Sanskrit MSS. during 1883-84, p. 118, and J.B.B.R.A.S., for 1892, p. 227.

2 भावैकान्ते पदार्थानामभावानामपह्नवात् ।
सर्वात्मकमनाद्यन्तमस्वरूपमभावकम् ॥ ९ ॥
कार्यद्रव्यमनादि स्यात् प्रागभावस्य निह्नवे ।
प्रध्वंसस्य च धर्मस्य प्रच्यवेऽनन्ततां व्रजेत् ॥ १० ॥
सर्वात्मकं तदेकं स्यादन्यापोहव्यतिक्रमे ।
अन्यत्र समवायेन व्यपदिश्येत सर्वथा ॥ ११ ॥

instance, if the antecedent non-existence is denied, action and substance are to be supposed as beginningless, while on the denial of the subsequent non-existence, they become endless, and in the absence of mutual non-existence they become one and all-pervading, while on absolute non-existence being denied they are to be supposed as existing always and everywhere.

58. In the same way on the supposition of mere non-existence to the entire exclusion of existence, it becomes impossible to establish or reject anything (since it is non-existent). If on the other hand existence and non-existence, which are incompatible with each other, are simultaneously ascribed to a thing, it becomes indescribable. Therefore the truth is as follows :—

(1) A thing *is* existent—from a certain point of view.
(2) It *is non*-existent—from another point of view.
(3) It is *both* existent and non-existent *in turn*—from a third point of view.
(4) It is *indescribable* (that is, both existent and non-existent simultaneously)—from a fourth point of view.
(5) It *is* existent and *indescribable*—from a fifth point of view.
(6) It *is non*-existent and *indescribable*—from a sixth point of view.
(7) It *is both* existent and *non*-existent and *indescribable*—from a seventh point of view.

AKALAṄKADEVA (ABOUT 750 A.D.).

59. Akalaṅka, otherwise known as Akalaṅkadeva or Akalaṅkacandra, was a famous logician who belonged to the Digambara sect. He was designated as a *Kavi*[1] (poet)—a title of special honour given to writers of repute. He wrote a commentary on Samantabhadra's Āptamīmāṁsā called Aṣṭa śatī[2] which is a

---

अभावैकान्तपक्षेऽपि भावापह्नववादिनाम्।
अबोधवाक्यप्रमाणं न केन साधनदूषणम् ॥ ११ ॥
विरोधान्नोभयैकात्म्यं स्याद्वादन्यायविद्विषाम्।
अवाच्यतैकान्तेऽप्युक्तिर्नावाच्यमिति युज्यते ॥ १२ ॥
कथंचित्ते सदेवेष्टं कथंचिदसदेव तत्।
तथोभयमवाच्यं च नययोगान्न सर्वथा ॥ १४ ॥

(Āptamīmāṁsā, MSS., verses 9-14, lent to me by Mr. Jain Vaidya of Jaipur.)

[1] For an explanation of the term "Kavi" *vide* R. G. Bhandarkar's Report on Sanskrit MSS. during 1883-84, page 122.

[2] A manuscript of the Aṣṭa-śatī was kindly supplied to me by Mr. Jain Vaidya of Jaipur early in 1907.

most precious work on the Jaina philosophy dealing mainly with logic. Māṇikyanandi's Parīkṣāmukha-sūtra (q.v.) was based on another work on logic, called **Nyāya-viniścaya**, written by Akalaṅka, to whom the following works are also attributed: Laghīyastraya, Akalaṅka-stotra, Svarūpa-sambodhana and Prāyaścitta. Laghusamantabhadra [1] in his Aṣṭa-sāhasri-viṣama-pada-tātparya-ṭīkā calls Akalaṅka as *Sakala-tārkika-cakra-cūḍā-maṇi* or "the crest-gem of all logicians."

60. In the Pāṇḍava-purāṇa [2] reference is made to a legend according to which Akalaṅka was embarrassed in a controversy with a Buddhist antagonist. Finding that the antagonist was effectively prompted by Māyādevī concealed in a jar, Akalaṅka is said to have put an end to that prompting or inspiration by kicking the jar over with his foot.

61. Akalaṅka, though mentioned along with Dharmakīrti [3] as a logician, flourished at a considerably later time. He is held to have been a contemporary of Rāṣtrakūṭa king Subhatuṅga [4] or Kṛṣṇarāja I. As Kṛṣṇa-rāja's son, Govind II, lived in Saka 705 [5] or 783 A.D., Kṛṣṇa-rāja I, and consequently his contemporary Akalaṅka, must have flourished about 750 A.D.

VIDYĀNANDA (ABOUT 800 A.D.).

62. Vidyānanda, mentioned by the Hindu philosopher Mādhavācārya,[6] was a Digambara logician of Pāṭaliputra. He was the author of the **Āpta-mīmāṁsālaṅkṛti**, otherwise called **Aṣṭasāhasrī**, an exhaustive sub-commentary on the Āpta-

---

1 *Vide* Aṣṭasāhasri-viṣamapada-tātparyaṭīkā by Laghusamanta-bhadra, noticed by Peterson in his 5th Report, p. 217.

2 अकलङ्कोऽकलङ्कः स कलौ कलयतु श्रुतम् ।
पादेन ताडिता येन मायादेवी घटस्थिता ॥

(Pāṇḍavapurāṇa, noticed by Peterson in his 4th Report, p. 157.)

3 वाचकमुख्यविरचितानि सकलशास्त्रचूडामणिभूतानि तत्त्वार्थसूत्राणीति यद्येवमकलङ्कधर्मकीर्त्यादिवत् प्रकरणमेव किं नारभ्यते किमनया सूत्रकारत्वाहोपुरुषिकया ।

(Pramāṇa-mīmāṁsā, by Hemacandra, noticed by Peterson in his 5th Report, p. 148.)

4 *Vide* K. B. Pathak's article on "Bhartṛhari and Kumārila" in the Journal of the Bombay Branch of the Royal Asiatic Society, Vol. XVIII, 1892.

5 *Vide* R. G. Bhandarkar's "Early History of the Deccan," 2nd edition, p. 78.

6 *Vide* the chapter on the Jaina system in the Sarvadarśana-saṃgraha translated by Cowell and Gough, p. 56.

mīmāṁsā, containing an elaborate exposition of various logical principles. Vidyānanda, in the opening and the closing lines of his Aṣṭasāhasrī,[1] makes an indirect reference to Samantabhadra and Akalaṅka respectively, while in chapter X of the work he distinctly says that he followed the Aṣṭaśati of Akalaṅka in explaining the Āptamīmāṁsā. Another logical treatise called **Pramāṇa-parīkṣā** is also attributed to him. He was also the author of the S'loka-vārtika and Āpta-parīkṣā.

63. He has, in his Aṣṭasāhasrī, criticised the doctrines of the Sāṁkhya, Yoga, Vaiśeṣika, Advaita, Mīmāṁsaka and Saugata, Tāthāgata or Bauddha philosophy; and has also mentioned Dignāga, Udyotakara, Dharmakīrti,[2] Prajñākara,[3] Bhartṛhari,[4] S'abarasvāmi, Prabhākara and Kumārila. Vidyānanda was

---

1 The opening lines of the Aṣṭa-sāhasrī are :—

श्रीवर्द्धमानमभिवन्द्य समन्तभद्रमुद्भूतबोधमहिमानमनिन्द्यवाचम् ।
शास्त्रावताररचितस्तुतिगोचराप्तमीमांसितं कृतिरलंक्रियते मयास्य ॥ १ ॥

The closing lines of the Aṣṭasāhasrī are :—

श्रीमदकलङ्कशशधरकुलविद्यानन्दसम्भवा भूयात् ।
गमीमांसालंकृतिरष्टसाहस्री सतामृद्ध्यै ॥

The lines in Chapter X referred to run thus :—

श्रीमदकलङ्कविवृतां समन्तभद्रोक्तिमत्र संक्षेपात् ।
परमागमार्थविषयामष्टसाहस्रीं प्रकाशयति ॥

(Aṣṭasāhasrī, MSS., Asiatic Society of Bengal.)

2 यदुक्तं धर्मकीर्तिना :—

अतद्रूप परावृत्त वस्तुमात्र प्रवेदनात् ।
सामान्यविषयम्प्रोक्तं लिङ्गभेदाप्रतिष्ठितेः ।

(Quoted in Aṣṭasāhasrī, chap. I.)

अर्थोपयोगेऽपि पुनः स्मार्त्तं शब्दानुयोजनम् ।
अक्षधीर्यद्यपेक्षेत सोऽर्थो व्यवहितो भवेत् ।

(Quoted in Aṣṭasāhasrī, chap. I.)

प्रज्ञाकरस्येदं वचः :—

क्रमप्रतीतेरेवं स्यात् प्रथमस्यावना मतिः ।
तत्सामर्थ्यात् पुनः पश्चाद् यतः कर्त्ता प्रतीयते ॥

(Quoted in Aṣṭasāhasrī, chap. I.)

न सोऽस्ति प्रत्ययो लोके यः शब्दानुगमादृते ।
अनुविद्धमिवाभाति सर्वं शब्दे प्रतिष्ठितम् ॥

(This verse of Vākyapadīya by Bhartṛhari is quoted in the Aṣṭasāhasrī, *vide* J.B.B.R.A.S. for 1892, p. 221.)

otherwise named Pātra Kesari or Pātra Kesari Svāmi who has been praised by Jina Sena in the Ādi Purāṇa [1] composed about Śaka 760 [2] or A.D. 838. He is believed to have lived early in the 9th century A.D. [3] at Pātaliputra.[4]

Māṇikya Nandi (about 800 A.D.).

64. Māṇikya Nandi was a Digambara author, whose **Parīkṣā-mukha-śāstra** [5] or **Parīkṣā-mukha-sūtra** is a standard work on the Jaina logic. As his work is based on that of Akalaṅka,[6] he must have lived after 750 A.D. The earliest commentary on the Parīkṣā-mukha-śāstra is the Prameya-kamala-mārtaṇḍa of Prabhācandra. Vidyānanda, Māṇikya Nandi and Prabhā-candra have been pronounced to be contemporaries.[7] So Maṇikya Nandi seems to have lived about 800 A.D.

65. The Parīkṣā-mukha-sūtra is divided into six chapters thus: (1) the characteristic of valid knowledge (*Pramāṇa-svarūpa*); (2) direct apprehension or perception (*Pratyakṣa*); (3) indirect apprehension (*Parokṣa*); (4) the object of valid knowledge (*Viṣaya*); (5) the result of valid knowledge (*Phala*); (6) the semblances or fallacies (*Ābhāsa*).

---

[1] भट्टाकलङ्कश्रीपालपात्रकेसरिणां गुणाः ।
विदुषां हृदयारूढा हारायन्तेऽतिनिर्मलाः ॥ ५३ ॥

(Ādīpurāṇa, quoted by Mr. K. B. Pathak, J.B.B.R.A.S., for 1892, p. 222.)

Mr. Pathak has quoted Samyaktvaprakāśa to show that Vidyānanda and Pātrakesari were identical:—

तथा श्लोकवार्त्तिके विद्यानन्दापरनाम पात्रकेसरिस्वामिना यदुक्तं तच्च लिख्यते तत्त्वार्थश्रद्धानं सम्यग्दर्शनम् ।

(J.B.B.R.A.S., for 1892, pp. 222, 223.)

[2-3] *Vide* K. B. Pathak's article on Bhartṛahari and Kumārila in J.B.B.R.A.S., for 1892, pp. 227, 229.

[4] *Vide* Brahma-nemidatta's Kathākoṣa, life of Pātrakesari *alias* Vidyānanda.

[5] A manuscript of the Parīkṣāmukha-śāstra was kindly lent to me by Mr. Jain Vaidya of Jaipur (Rajputana), and subsequently another manuscript of the work was procured from the Deccan College, Poona.

[6] Peterson in his 4th Report, p. 155, notices Parīkṣāmukhaṁ saṭīkam. The Ṭikā is the Prameya-ratna-mālā or Parīkṣāmukhapañjikā of Anantavīrya, which opens thus:

अकलङ्कवचोऽम्भोधेरुद्दध्रे येन धीमता ।
न्यायविद्यामृतं तस्मै नमो माणिक्यनन्दिने ॥ १ ॥

[7] *Vide* K. B. Pathak's article on Bhartṛhari and Kumārila in J.B.B.R.A.S., for 1892, pp. 219, 220, 221. Mr. Pathak says that Māṇikya Nandi has mentioned Vidyānanda, but in the text of the Parīkṣā-mukha-śāstra itself I have not come across any such mention.

66. *Pramāṇa*, valid knowledge, is defined as the knowledge which ascertains the nature of what was uncertain to one's self. It generally arises in the form: "I know the jar by myself," which consists of a subject, an object, an act, and an instrument. Just as a lamp illumines itself as well as the surrounding objects, so the *Pramāṇa* sets forth the knower as well as the thing known.

Valid knowledge.

67. *Pramāṇa* is of two kinds: (1) direct knowledge (*Pratyakṣa*) which arises through the senses, etc., and (2) indirect knowledge (*Parokṣa*) consisting of recollection (*Smṛti*), recognition (*Pratyabhijñāna*), argumentation (*Tarka* or *Ūha*), inference (*Anumāna*), and the scripture (*Āgama*). Recollection is a knowledge of the form "that" which arises through the awaking of impressions, thus: "that Devadatta." Recognition is a knowledge which arises from perception through recollection in the forms, "this is that," "this is like that," "this is different from that," "this is the counterpart of that," etc., thus: "this is that Devadatta," "the *bos gavaeus* is like the cow," "the buffalo is different from the cow," "this is far from that," "this is a tree," etc. Argumentation is a knowledge of the connection between the middle term and the major term based on the presence or absence of the latter, in the form, "if this is, that is, if this is not, that is not," thus smoke arises only if there is fire, but it cannot arise if there is no fire. Inference[1] is the knowledge of the major term arising through the middle term: there is fire here because there is smoke.

Kinds of valid knowledge.

68. Pervasion[2] or inseparable connection (*Vyāpti or Avinābhāva*) is the universal attendance of the middle term by the major term in simultaneity or succession: thus fire and smoke may abide simultaneously or the latter may follow the former.

Terms of a Syllogism.

If the middle term and the major term exist simultaneously, the former is called *vyāpya*, pervaded or contained, and the latter *vyāpaka*, pervader or container.

But if the middle term follows the major term, the former is called effect (*kārya*), and the latter cause (*kāraṇa* or *hetu*), thus fire is the cause of smoke. Ordinarily, however, the major term is called *sādhya* or that which is to be proved, and the middle term is called *sādhana* or that by which it is to be proved. Sometimes the major term is also called *dharma* or predicate, and the middle term *liṅga*, mark or sign.

The minor term is called *Pakṣa*, the place or locus in which the major term abides, or *Dharmin*, the subject, thus: "this

---

[1] साधनात् साध्यविज्ञानमनुमानम् ॥ ९ ॥ (Parīkṣā-mukha-sūtra).

[2] सहक्रमभावनियमोऽविनाभावः ॥ ११ ॥ (Parīkṣā-mukha-sūtra).

place is fiery"; "sound is mutable": here "this place" and "sound" are the minor terms. Some philosophers, who divide the middle term (reason) into three phases, dispense with the minor term in an inference.

The middle term (*Hetu*) is defined as that which is inseparably connected with the major term, or in other words, which cannot come into existence unless the major term exists. For instance, smoke could not come into existence unless the fire existed.

Different phases of the middle term.

69. The middle term or reason (*Hetu*) is divided as (1) perceptible (*upalabdhi*), and (2) imperceptible (*anupalabdhi*). Each of these again may occur in the form of an affirmation (*Vidhi*) or negation (*pratiṣedha*).

70. The *perceptible* reason in the *affirmative* form admits of six subdivisions according as it is :—

(i) the pervaded (*vyāpya*)—sound is mutable because it is factitious ;

(ii) an effect (*kārya*)—this man has got intellect because there are (intellectual) functions in him ;

(iii) a cause (*kāraṇa*)—there is a shadow here because there is an umbrella ;

(iv) prior (*pūrva*)—the Rohiṇi stars will rise for the Kṛttikās have risen.

(v) posterior (*uttara*)—the Bharaṇī stars certainly rose for the Kṛttikās have risen ;

(vi) simultaneous (*sahacara*)—the man had a mother for he had a father ; or this mango has a particular colour because it has a particular flavour.

71. The *perceptible* reason in the *negative* form admits of six subdivisions as follows :—

(i) the pervaded (*vyāpya*)—there is no cold sensation because of heat ;

(ii) an effect (*kārya*)—there is no cold sensation because of smoke ;

(iii) a cause (*kāraṇa*)—there is no happiness in this man because of the shaft in his heart ;

(iv) prior (*pūrva*)—the Rohiṇi stars will not rise at once for the Revatī [only] has risen.

(v) posterior (*uttara*)—the Bharaṇī did not rise a moment ago for the Puṣyā has risen.

(vi) simultaneous (*sahacara*)—there is no doubt of the existence of the other side of this wall for this side of it is perceived.

72. The *imperceptible* reason in the *negative* form admits of seven subdivisions as follows :—

(i) identity (*svabhāva*)—there is no jar here because it is imperceptible;

(ii) the pervaded (*vyāpya*)—there is no S'iṁśapā here because there is no tree at all;

(iii) an effect (*kārya*)—there is no smouldering fire here because there is no smoke;

(iv) a cause (*kāraṇa*)—there is no smoke here because there is no fire;

(v) prior (*pūrva*)—the Rohiṇī stars will not rise in a moment for the Kṛttikās are not perceptible;

(vi) posterior (*uttara*)—the Bharaṇī did not rise a moment ago for the Kṛttikās are not perceptible;

(vii) simultaneous (*sahacara*)—in this even balance there is no bending upwards because it is not perceptible.

73. The *imperceptible* reason in the affirmative form admits of three subdivisions thus :—

(i) an effect (*kārya*)—in this man there is some disease because there is no healthy movement in him;

(ii) a cause (*kāraṇa*)—this man is sorrowful because he has no union with his beloved ones;

(iii) identity (*svabhāva*)—there is uncertainty here because certainty is not discernible;

Example.

73. The middle term and the major term are the parts of an inference, but the example (*udāharaṇa*) is not. Nevertheless for the sake of explaining matters to men of small intellect, the example (*udāharaṇa* or *dṛṣṭānta*), nay, even the application (*upanaya*) and the conclusion (*nigamana*) are admitted as parts of an inference. The example is of two kinds: (1) the affirmative or homogeneous (*anvayi* or *sādharmya*) which shows the middle term as covered by the major term, such as: wherever there is smoke, there is fire, as in a *kitchen*; and (2) the negative or heterogeneous (*vyatireki* or *vaidharmya*) by which the absence of the middle term is indicated by the absence of the major term, *e.g.*, wherever there is no fire, there is no smoke, as in a *lake*.

Inference.

74. Inference is of two kinds, *viz.*, (1) inference for one's own self (*svārthānumāna*), and (2) inference for the sake of others (*parārthānumāna*). An instance of the latter kind of inference is given below :—

(1) Sound (minor term) is mutable (major term)—proposition;

(2) because it is factitious (reason or middle term);

(3) whatever is factitious is mutable, as a jar (affirmative or homogeneous example) ;
(4) sound is factitious (application) ;
(5) therefore sound is mutable (conclusion).

Or

(3) whatever is not mutable is not factitious, as the milk of a barren woman's breast (negative or heterogeneous example) ;
(4) but sound is factitious (application) ;
(5) therefore sound is mutable (conclusion).

Verbal Testimony.

75. Testimony (*Āgama*) is a knowledge of objects derived from the words of reliable persons or scripture in virtue of their natural fitness or suggestiveness—*e.g.*, the north pole exists.

Objects of valid knowledge.

76. Objects of valid knowledge are either general (*sāmānya*) or particular (*viśeṣa*). The general is of two kinds : (1) homogeneous (*tiryak*), including many individuals of like nature as, the "cow" is a general notion which signifies many individual cows as Śabalā, Khamba, Mumbha, etc. ; and (2) heterogeneous (*ūrddhvatā*), including many individuals of dissimilar nature, as, "gold" is a general notion comprising a bracelet, necklace, ear-ring, etc. The particular is also of two kinds : (1) relating to things (*vyatireka*), *e.g.*, cow, buffalo, elephant, dog, are four particular things distinguished from one another ; and (2) relating to action such as pleasure, pain, etc., experienced by the soul.

Result of valid knowledge.

77. The result or consequence of valid knowledge is the cessation of ignorance enabling one to choose the desirable and reject the undesirable.

Various kinds of Fallacies.

78. Fallacy or semblance consists of the knowledge of that which is different from the real thing. It is of many kinds, such as the fallacy—

(1) of perception (*pratyakṣābhāsa*), *e.g.*—to mistake a post for a man ;
(2) of recollection (*smaraṇābhāsa*)—in trying to recollect Jinadatta to say : "O, that Devadatta" ;
(3) of recognition (*pratyabhijñānābhāsa*)—on seeing a greyhound to say : "this is a tiger" ;
(4) of argumentation (*tarkābhāsa*)—"whoever is his son must be black" ;
(5) of the minor term (*pakṣābhāsa*) —"sound is impermanent" : This is a fallacy of the minor term according to the Mimāṁsakas, for they do not attribute

impermanency to sound; or fire is not hot because it is a substance as water;

(6) of the middle term or reason (*hetvābhāsa*)—sound is eternal because it is factitious;

(7) of example (*dṛṣṭāntābhāsa*)—sound is eternal because it is corporeal, like a jar;

(8) of verbal testimony (*āgamābhāsa*)—"there is a heap of sweetmeats on the side of the river, run you boys"; "there are a hundred elephants on his finger"; "the Jainas are allowed to eat in the night" [as a fact they are not so allowed according to their scripture].

References to contemporaneous systems of philosophy.

79. Māṇikya Nandi in the Parīkṣāmukha-sūtra (chapter vi, aph. 56-57) has mentioned the Laukāyatika, Saugata, Sāṁkhya, Yoga, Prābhākara, Jaiminiya, etc. In the 3rd chapter of the work he has alluded to—"a certain philosopher who maintaining three phases of the reason or middle term (*hetu*) dispenses with the minor term (*pakṣa*)."[1]

80. He concludes his work by referring to it as a mirror through which a man can see what is to be accepted and what rejected.[2]

PRABHĀ CANDRA (ABOUT 825 A.D.).

81. Prabhā Candra styled a *Kavi*, a member of the Digambara sect, was the author of the famous logical treatise called the **Prameya-kamala-mārtaṇḍa**, the earliest commentary on the Parīkṣāmukha-sūtra of Māṇikya Nandi. He was also the author of the Nyāya-kumuda-candrodaya (or briefly Candrodaya), a commentary on the Laghīyastraya of Akalaṅka. He has in his Prameya-kamala-mārtaṇḍa mentioned Bhagavān Upavarṣa,

---

1 साध्याविनाभावित्वेन निश्चितो हेतुः ॥ १० ॥

को वा त्रिधा हेतुमुक्त्वा समर्थयमानो न पक्षयति ॥ ११ ॥

(Parīkṣāmukha-sūtra, MSS. lent to me by Mr. Jain Vaidya of Jaipur).

2 परीक्षामुखमादर्शं हेयोपादेयतत्त्वयोः ।

संविदे मादृशो बालः परीक्षादक्षवद् व्यधाम् ॥

(Parīkṣāmukha-sūtra, chap. VI, MSS. lent to me by Mr. Jain Vaidya of Jaipur).

S'abarasvāmi, Bhartṛhari, Bāṇa,[1] Kumārila,[2] Prabhākara, Dignāga, Udyotakara Dharmakīrti, Vidyānanda and others. He himself has been mentioned by Jina Sena in the Ādi Purāṇa[3] composed about S'aka 760 or A.D. 838. Prabhā Candra, as a contemporary of Maṇikya Nandī and Vidyānanda, is believed to have lived in the first half of the 9th century A.D.

Mallavādin (about 827 A.D.).

82. He belonged to the S'vetāmbara sect and was the famous author of a commentary on the Buddhist logical treatise Nyāyabinduṭikā called Dharmottara-ṭippanaka. According to a Jaina legend,[4] Malla was the son of King S'īlāditya's sister. He was called *vādin* or logician, because, having vanquished the Buddhists in a dispute, he re-established the Jaina faith and brought to its former glory the great figure of Ādinātha on Mount S'atruñjaya (in Kathiwar).

83. A palm-leaf manuscript[5] of the Dharmottara-ṭippanaka

---

[1] Prabhā Candra has quoted the following verse from Bāṇa's Kādambarī:—

रजोजुषे जन्मनि सत्त्ववृत्तये
स्थितौ प्रजानां प्रलये तमःस्पृशे ।
अजाय सर्गस्थिति-नाश-हेतवे
त्रयीमयाय त्रिगुणात्मने नमः ॥

(Prameya-kamala-mārtaṇḍa, Deccan College, MSS., p. 21*a*, quoted by Mr. K. B. Pathak in J.B.B.R.A.S., for 1892, p. 221.)

[2] Prabhā Candra refers to Kumārila otherwise called Bhaṭṭa thus :—

यथा चार्थापत्तिरपि प्रमाणान्तरं तथाप्यर्थापत्तिरपि दृष्टः श्रुतो वा अर्थोऽन्यथा नोपपद्यते इत्यदृष्टार्थकल्पना, कुमारिलोऽपि एतदेव भाष्यकारमतो व्याचष्टे ।

(Prameya-kamala-mārtaṇḍa, quoted by Mr. K. B. Pathak in the J.B.B.R.A.S., for 1892, p. 227).

[3] In the Ādi Purāṇa Prabhā Candra is thus mentioned :—

चन्द्रांशुशुभ्रयशसं प्रभाचन्द्रं कविं स्तुवे ।
कृत्वा चन्द्रोदयं येन शश्वदाह्लादितं जगत् ॥ ४७ ॥

(Quoted by Mr. K. B. Pathak in J.B.B.R.A.S., for 1892, p. 222.)

On p. 227 of the same journal the date of the Adipurāṇa is fixed at Saka 760 or 838 A.D.

[4] Peterson 4, pp. 3-4, in which is mentioned the legend from the Prabandhacintāmaṇi (Rāmacandra's edition, Bombay, p. 273).

[5] इति धर्मोत्तरटिप्पनके श्रीमल्लवाद्याचार्यकृते तृतीयः परिच्छेदः समाप्तः मङ्गलं महाश्रीः ॥

is preserved at Anhilwad Patan and is said to be dated Saṁvat 1231 or 1174 A.D. According to the Prabhāvaka-caritra [1] Mallavādin was also the author of a Padmacaritra and lived in Vira Saṁvat 884 or 357 A.D. But this is impossible as Dharmottara (q.v.), on whose Nyāyabinduṭikā Mallavādin wrote Ṭippanaka, lived about 837 A.D. On the other hand Mallavādin is mentioned [2] by Hem Candra Sūri who lived during 1088—1172 A.D. It seems therefore probable that the year 884 in which Mallavādin lived does not refer to Vīra Saṁvat, but to Vikrama Saṁvat. On that supposition Mallavādin lived in 827 A.D. and was a contemporary of Dharmottara.

Pradyumna Sūri (about 980 A.D.).

84. He [3] belonged to the Rājagaccha of the S'vetāmbara sect. In Māṇikyacandra's Pārśvanātha-caritra,[4] his prowess in logical discussions is referred to in the following terms :—

"There was born the preceptor Pradyumna Sūri—the first healer of disease of the world—who entirely removed all corruptions from the body of men (or detected all defects in disputation committed by men) and who, using sharp logical expressions, made his irrelevant opponents to sweat and thereby to be cured of the fever of pride."

संवत् १२३१ वर्षे भाद्रपद शुदि १२ रवौ अद्येह अंचावशिपाम वास्तव्य ध० दारवंड्डतव० चाचड़ेन धर्मार्थं धर्मोत्तर-टिप्पनकं लिखापितम् ॥

(Noticed in Peterson 5, App. p. 3.)

1 *Vide* Klatt, Vienna Oriental Journal, Vol. IV, p. 67.

2 अनु मल्लवादिनं तार्किकाः ।
तस्मादन्ये हीना इत्यर्थः ॥

(Siddha Hema S'abdānuśāsana Bṛhat Ṭīkā, 2-2-39).

3 For further particulars about Pradyumna Sūri see Peterson's 4th Report, p. lxxix.

4 पुंसां विपश्चितां विकारमखिलं निर्दूषयन् दूषणं-
व्याख्याः समवदन् भवामयभिषक् प्रद्युम्नसूरिर्गुरुः ।
येन स्वेदयता प्रयुज्य परुषां तर्कोल्बणां भारतीं
वादीन्द्राः प्रतिवादिनो सममरं दर्पज्वरं त्याजिताः ॥ ४ ॥
दिग्मल्लरचनामात्मवेद्यपदं समारुहे ।
यः प्रत्यक्षं नरेन्द्रस्य जयमलयमः पुनः ॥ ५ ॥
श्रीरामनामिधो राजगच्छमुकुटवारिधिः ।
सूरिः प्रद्युम्नसूर्याख्यः पूर्वं यः पूर्वजोऽभवत् ॥ १८ ॥

85. In the same work reference is made to his victory over the Digambaras of Veṅkapaṭṭa in the presence of the king of that province. He delighted the kings of various countries by no fewer than eighty-four triumphs in discussion. He was eleventh in ascent from Māṇikyacandra Sūri, who wrote his Pārśvanātha-caritra in Saṁvat 1276 or 1219 A.D. Pradyumna must have flourished about 980 A.D., for he was the preceptor of Abhayadeva Sūri (q.v.) who lived a little before 1039 A.D.

ABHAYADEVA SŪRI (ABOUT 1000 A.D.).

86. Abhayadeva Sūri belonged to the S'vetāmbara sect [1] and was the pupil and successor of Pradyumna Sūri of the Rāja-gaccha. He was an eminent logician and author of **Vādamahārṇava**, a treatise on logic called the Ocean of Discussions, and of a commentary on the Sammati-tarka-sūtra called **Tattvārtha-bodha-vidhāyinī**.[2] " He is described as a lion that roamed at ease in the wild forest of books on logic. That the rivers of various conflicting opinions might not sweep away the path of

---

सपादलक्षगोपालत्रिभुवनगिर्यादिदेशगोपालान् ।
यश्चतुरधिकाशीत्या वादजयैरंजयामास ॥ २८ ॥
श्रीअभयदेवसूरिस्तच्छिष्यस्तर्कभूरभूत् ।
अभ्यासनालितुमुलाङ्गीयंदास्यमशिश्रियत् ॥ २९ ॥

(Pārśvanātha-caritra as noticed by Peterson in his 3rd Report, pp. 57-164.)

1 तर्कग्रन्थविचारदुर्गमवनीसञ्चारपञ्चानन-
स्तस्मादभयदेवसूरिरजनि श्वेताम्बरग्रामणीः ।
सद्वाक्यश्रुतिलालसा मधुकरी कोलाहलाशङ्किनी
हित्वा विष्टरपङ्कजं श्रितवती ब्राह्मी यदीयाननम् ॥ ६ ॥
उच्चनिम्नगाः सत्पथभेदमेता
भुवं करिष्यन्ति जडैः समेताः ।
इतीव रोधाय चकार तासां
ग्रन्थं नवं वादमहार्णवं यः ॥ ७ ॥
विद्वन्मण्डलमौलिमण्डनमणिः प्रेङ्खत्तपोऽधर्मवि-
र्निर्दन्योऽपि जिनेश्वरः समजनि श्रीमांस्ततः सद्गुरुः ।
यः स्फूर्जद्गुणपुञ्जगुञ्जनमतीजिष्णोः पुरः प्रस्खलान् ।
वादे वादिवरान् विजित्य विजयश्रीसंपदं स व्यधात् ॥ ८ ॥

(Pārśvanātha-caritra by Māṇikyacandra noticed by Peterson in his 3rd Report, pp. 158-59.)

2 See R. Mitra's Catalogue, X, pp. 39-40.

the good, Abhayadeva [1] wrote his Vāda-mahārṇava." He was succeeded by Jineśvara Sūri, a contemporary of King Muñja.[2] He was the ninth predecessor of Siddhasena Sūri, who wrote Pravacana-sāroddhāra-vṛtti in Saṁvat 1242 or 1185 A.D. It was probably this Abhayadeva Sūri, who was "world-renowned" and a teacher of S'ānti Sūri [3] who died in Saṁvat 1096 or 1039 A.D.

LAGHUSAMANTABHADRA (ABOUT 1000 A.D.).

87. He [4] wrote a commentary on the Aṣṭasāhasrī of Vidyā nanda called the **Aṣṭasāhasrī-viṣamapada-tātparya-ṭīkā** [5] and seems to have belonged to the Digambara sect and lived about 1000 A.D.

ANANTA-VĪRYA (ABOUT 1039 A.D.).

88. Ananta-vīrya was the Digambara author of a commentary on the Parīkṣāmukha of Māṇikya Nandi called **Parīkṣā-mukha-pañjikā** or **Prameya-ratnamālā**, as also a commentary on Akalaṅka's Nyāya-viniścaya called the **Nyāya-viniścaya-vṛtti.** He wrote the former for S'anti-ṣena at the request of Hirapa, son of Vijaya and Nāṇambā.[6] Now S'āntiṣena, supposed to be identical with S'ānti S'ūri, died in Saṁvat 1096 or A.D. 1039. His contemporary Ananta-vīrya must, therefore, have flourished

---

1 For particulars about Abhayadeva Sūri see Peterson's 4th Report, p. iii.

2 Weber's Die Handschriften-verzeichnisse, etc., p. 851, vv. 1, 2, and pp. 121, vv. 4-5. Jineśvara Sūri was probably a spiritual brother of Dhaneśvara Sūri.

3 यस्माभूद्गुरुरागमे गुणनिधिः श्रीसर्वदेवाह्वयः
सूरौ श्रीऽभयदेव सूरिरभितख्यातप्रमाणेऽपि च ।
तस्येयं सुगुणद्वयादधिगत (?) दक्षांतमविद्यागुण (?)
प्रत्याख्याय चिरं भुवि प्रचरतु श्रीशान्तिसूरेः कृतिः ॥

(Uttarādhyayana bṛhadvṛtti by S'āntyācārya noticed by Dr. R. G. Bhandarkar in his Report on Sanskrit MSS. for 1883-84, p. 44.) See also Weber's Die Handschriften-verzeichnisse der Königlichen Bibliothek zu Berlin, p. 827.

4 *Vide* Peterson's Sixth Report, p. xxiii.

5 The Aṣṭasāhasrī-viṣama-pada-tātparya-ṭīkā has been noticed in Peterson's Fifth Report, pp. 216-219, where we read :

देवं स्वामिनममलं विद्यानन्दं प्रणम्य निजभक्त्या ।
विवृणोम्यष्टसहस्रीविषमपदं लघुसमन्तभद्रोऽहम् ॥

6 वैजेयप्रियपुत्रस्य हीरपस्योपरोधतः ।
शान्तिषेणार्थमारब्धा परीक्षामुखपञ्जिका ॥ १ ॥

(Parīkṣā-mukhaṁ saṭīkam, noticed in Peterson's Fourth Report, p. 155.)

about that time.[1] Ananta-vīrya must have lived before the 14th century, for he is mentioned by Mādhavācārya in the chapter on Jaina darśana in the Sarvadarśana-saṃgraha.

Deva Sūri (1086-1169 A.D.).

89. Deva Sūri, called Vādipravara or the foremost of disputants, belonged to the S'vetāmbara sect and was a pupil of Municandra Sūri. He was the author of the well-known treatise on logic called **Pramāṇa-naya-tattvālokālaṅkāra** on which he himself wrote an elaborate commentary named **Syādvāda-ratnākara.**[2] He totally vanquished the Digambara Kumuda-candrācārya in a dispute over the salvation of women [at the court of Jaya-siṁha-deva at Anahillapurapattana in N. Guzerat] and thereby practically stopped the entrance of the Digambaras into that town. The dispute[3] took place in Saṁvat 1181 or 1124 A.D.

90. Ratnaprabha Sūri, a pupil of Deva Sūri, in his Upadeśamālā-ṭīkā,[4] composed in Saṁvat 1238 or A.D. 1181, writes :—

"Lord S'rī Deva Sūri, who was the crest-gem of the pupils of the esteemed Municandra Sūri and succeeded him in his paṭṭa (sacred chair), conquered the Digambaras in the council-room of

---

1 *Vide* the Indian Antiquary, Vol. XI, p. 253; and Dr. R. G. Bhandarkar's Report on Sanskrit MSS. during 1883-84, p. 129.

2 स्याद्वादरत्नाकर इत्यस्ति ग्रन्थो महत्तमः ।
वादिवृन्दारकश्रीमद्देवसूरिविनिर्मितः ॥ ४ ॥

Malladhāri Rājaśekhara Sūri's Pañjikā on Syādvāda-ratnākarāvatāi k.

3 चन्द्राश्वशिववर्षेऽत्र वैशाखे पूर्णिमादिने ।
आकारितौ वादिशालायां तौ वादिप्रतिवादिनौ ॥

(Prabhāvakacar., XXI, v. 95, quoted by Dr. Klatt in his article on "Historical Records of the Jains" in the Indian Antiquary, Vol. XI, Sept. 1882, p. 254.)

4 Ratnaprabha Sūri observes :—

शिष्यः श्रीमुनिचन्द्रसूरिमहभिर्मौं सार्वचूडामणिः
पट्टे से विनिवेशितस्तदनु स श्रीदेवसूरिप्रभुः ।
आस्थाने जयसिंहदेवनृपतेर्येनाखिलदिग्वाससां
श्रीनिर्वाणसमर्थनेन विजयस्तम्भः समुत्तम्भितः ॥
तत्पट्टप्रभवो भवद्भय नृपमाभिरामोदयाः
श्रीभद्रेश्वरसूरयः प्रविधियस्तस्मानसप्रीतये ।
श्रीरत्नप्रभसूरिभिः प्रभवता श्रीदेवसूरिप्रभोः
शिष्यैः सेयमकारि सम्मदकृते वृत्तिर्विमेधार्थिनाम् ॥

(Upadeśamālāṭīkā noticed by Peterson in his 3rd Report, p. 167.)

King Jaya-simha-deva and raised a pillar of victory by maintaining the nirvāṇa or salvation of women [that is, holding that even women are capable of attaining nirvāṇa]."

91. In Samvat 1204 or 1147 A.D. Deva Sūri founded a caitya, raised a bimba at Phalavardhigrāma, and established an image of Neminātha at Arāsana.[1] He was born in Samvat 1143 or 1086 A.D., attained the rank of Sūri in 1174 Samvat or 1117 A.D., and ascended to heaven in Samvat 1226 or 1169 A.D.[2]

Subjects of the Pramāṇa-naya-tattvālokālankāra.

92. The Pramāṇa-naya-tattvālokālaṅkāra[3] consists of eight chapters (paricchedas), *viz.*—(1) Determination of the nature of valid knowledge (*pramāṇa-svarūpa-nirṇaya*); (2) determination of the

---

Munisundara Sūri in his Gurvāvalī composed in Samvat 1466 gives a similar account :—

श्रीनादिंनचतुरशीति सुवादिलीला-
लब्धोल्लसज्जयरमामदकेलिधाम्नौ ।
वादार्णवे कुमुदचन्द्रदिगम्बरेन्द्रः
श्रीसिद्धभूमिपतिसंसदि पत्तनेऽस्मिन् ॥ ७४ ॥
स्याद्वादरत्नाकरतर्कवेधा
सुरे स केषां नहि देवसूरिः ।
यत्तच्चतुर्विंशतिसूरिमाध्यं
यस्यैव नाम्ना विदितं बभूव ॥ ७५ ॥
वेदमुनीशमितेऽब्दे
देवगुरुर्जगदनुपमोऽभ्युदितः ।
श्रीमुनिचन्द्रगुरोरिति
शिष्या बहवोऽभवन् विदिताः ॥ ७६ ॥

(Gurvāvalī published in the Jaina Yaśovijaya-granthamālā of Benares, pp. 18-19.)

[1] *Vide* Peterson's 4th Report, p. lv.; also Klatt, Ind. Ant. XI. p. 254.

[2] शिखिवेदशिवे जन्म दीक्षा युग्मशरेश्वरे ।
वेदाश्वशंकरे वर्षे सूरित्वमभवत् प्रभोः ॥
रसयुग्मरवौ वर्षे श्रावणे मासि संगते ।
कृष्णपक्षस्य सप्तम्यामपराह्णे गुरोर्दिने ॥
मर्त्यलोकस्थितं लोकं प्रतिबोध्य पुरन्दर-
बोधका इव ते जग्मुर्दिवं श्रीदेवसूरयः ॥

(Prabhāvakacar., XXI, vv. 287 seq., quoted by Dr. Klatt in his article on "Historical Records of the Jains" in the Indian Antiquary, Sept. 1882, Vol. XI, p. 254.) According to some authorities Deva Sūri was born in Samvat 1134 or 1077 A.D.

[3] The Pramāṇa-nayatattvālokālankāra has been printed and published in Benares in the Jaina Yaśovijaya series.

nature of perception (*pratyakṣa-svarūpa-nirṇaya*); (3) determination of the nature of recollection, recognition, argumentation and inference (*smaraṇa-pratyabhijñāna-tarkānumāna-svarūpa-nirṇaya*); (4) determination of the nature of valid knowledge derived from verbal testimony or scripture (*āgamākhya-pramāṇa-svarūpa-nirṇaya*); (5) determination of the nature of objects of knowledge (*viṣaya-svarūpa-nirṇaya*); (6) determination of the consequences and semblances or fallacies of knowledge (*phala-pramāṇa-svarūpādyābhāsa-nirṇaya*); (7) determination of the nature of one-sided knowledge (*nayātma-svarūpa-nirṇaya*); and (8) determination of the right procedure of a disputant and his opponent (*vādi-prativādi-nyāya-nirṇaya*).

As this work is written on the same plan as Māṇikya Nandi's Parikṣāmukha-sūtra or Akalaṅka's Nyāya-viniścaya as well as Siddhasena Divākara's Nyāyāvatāra, I shall pass over the common points, mentioning only the special features.

Valid knowledge.

93. *Pramāṇa* or valid knowledge is defined here as the knowledge which ascertains the nature of itself and all other things. The intercourse between the sense-organs and the objects of sense is not *pramāṇa* (valid knowledge), for though it can ascertain the nature of objects outside itself, it cannot ascertain its own nature, since it has no consciousness. *Pramāṇa* must certainly be *knowledge*, for it is capable of choosing what is desirable and rejecting what is undesirable. It must also be definite in character, for it is opposed to superimposition (*samāropa*). Superimposition is of three kinds: (1) inversion (*viparyaya*)—such as to look upon a pearl-oyster as a piece of silver; (2) doubt (*saṃśaya*)—such as: is this a post or a man? and (3) uncertainty (*anadhyavasāya*) consisting in a mere cogitation in the mind as to what the thing might be.

Direct knowledge. Perception.

94. *Pramāṇa* (valid knowledge) is of two kinds: (1) direct (*pratyakṣa*) perception, and (2) indirect (*parokṣa*). The direct knowledge or perception is of two kinds: practical (*sāṁvyavahārika*) and transcendental (*pāramārthika*). The practical direct knowledge again is subdivided as that which arises through the sense-organs (*indriya-nibandhana*) and that which does not arise through the sense-organs (*anindriya-nibandhana*) but through the mind (*manas*). Each of these passes through four stages,[1] *viz.*: (1) *avagraha*, distinguishing the type whether it be, *e.g.*, horse or man, but not discerning the characteristics;

---

[1] The explanation of *avagraha*, etc., as given here is taken from Col. Jarrett's translation of the Ain-i-Akbari, published by the Asiatic Society of Bengal, vol. III, p. 190, as the portion related to *pramāṇa* in the Jaina

(2) *īhā*, inquiring, *e.g.*, whence came the man and from what country came the horse; (3) *avāya*, arriving at a correct identification of the above, and (4) *dhāraṇā*, recollecting the thing particularised and keeping it in mind.

The transcendental direct knowledge (*pāramārthika*) is that which comes exclusively from the illumination of the soul and is profitable to emancipation. It is two-fold: (1) *vikala* (defective) including *avadhi-jñāna* (limited knowledge), *i.e.*, knowledge of special objects which, near or remote, are not differentiated, and *manaḥ-paryāya*, *i.e.*, definite knowledge of another's thoughts and the laying bare of the secrets of the heart; and (2) *sakala*, *i.e.*, perfect, which is the unobstructed intuition of the entire aspects of a thing. One who possesses that perfect transcendental knowledge is called an *arhat*, *i.e.*, one freed from all faults or obstructions.

Indirect knowledge.

95. Indirect knowledge (*parokṣa*) is of five kinds: *viz.*, (1) recollection (*smaraṇa*); (2) recognition (*pratyabhijñāna*); (3) argumentation (*tarka*); (4) inference (*anumāna*); (5) verbal testimony or the knowledge derived from the words of a reliable person or scripture (*āgama*).

Inference.

96. Inference is of two kinds: (1) *svārtha*, for one's own self, and (2) *parārtha*, for the sake of others. *Hetu* (reason or the middle term) is defined as that which cannot happen except in connection with the major term. The definition that the *hetu* (middle term) is that which possesses three characteristics, is to be rejected as involving fallacies.[1] Some maintain the threefold characteristic or division of the *hetu* (reason or middle term), but do not admit the necessity of using the minor term (*pakṣa*) in an

---

chapter of Ain-i-Akbari very closely resembles that in the *Pramāṇa-naya-tattvālokālaṅkāra*. Dr. R. G. Bhandarkara's explanation of these terms given on p. 93, footnote, of his Report on Sanskrit MSS., for 1883-84, is, however, different.

[1] निश्चितान्यथानुपपत्त्येकलक्षणो हेतुः न तु त्रिलक्षणकादिः।
तस्य हेत्वाभासस्यापि सम्भवात् ॥ ११ ॥

(Pramāṇa-naya-tattvālokālaṅkāra, Chap. III.)

This is an attack on Dharmakīrti and other Buddhist logicians who define the three characteristics of *hetu* as follows:—

त्रैरूप्यं पुनर्लिङ्गस्य अनुमेये सत्त्वमेव।
सपक्ष एव सत्त्वम्। असपक्षे चासत्त्वमेव निश्चितम्।

(Nyāyabindu, Chapter II.)

inference.[1] Again, according to others, as the connection or absence of connection between the middle and the major terms can be shown by internal inseparable connection (*antar-vyāpti*), the example forming the external inseparable connection (*bahir-vyāpti*) is useless.[2] For instance:—

The hill (minor term) is fiery (major term), because it is smoky (middle term) as a kitchen (example).

Here the hill is an integral part of the inference, and in it may be found the necessary connection between fire and smoke. Why then should we burden our inference with an example from without? The kitchen certainly shows the same connection: fire and smoke are found together there: but the kitchen is not an essential part of the inference, and so for the purpose in hand the connection which it proves may be described as the external inseparable connection. We must look to logical neatness, and the economy of mental labour, since the mind is liable to be confused when the unessential is brought across its track.

97. The application (*upanaya*) and conclusion (*nigamana*) as parts of the syllogism are also useless, but these together with the example are to be employed to convince men of small intellect.[3]

Parts of a syllogism.

Avayava or parts of a syllogism are stated to be the following:—

1. *Pakṣa-prayoga* (use of the minor term, otherwise called proposition, *pratijñā*)—the hill is fiery.
2. *Hetu-prayoga* (use of the middle term)—because it is smoky.
3. *Dṛṣṭānta* (example)—whatever is fiery is smoky just as a kitchen.
4. *Upanaya* (application)—this hill is smoky.
5. *Nigamana* (conclusion)—therefore this hill is fiery.

98. Non-existence (*abhāva* or *anupalabdhi*) is subdivided as (1) antecedent (*prāgabhāva*); (2) subsequent (*pradhvaṁsābhāva*); (3) mutual (*itaretarābhāva*); and (4) absolute (*atyantābhāva*). Various kinds of *ābhāsa* or fallacy are also enumerated. Under the verbal

---

[1] त्रिविधं साधनमभिधायैव तत्समर्थनं विदधानः कः खलु न पक्षप्रयोगम् अङ्गीकुरुते ॥२३॥
(Pramāṇa-naya-tattvālokālaṅkāra, Chap. III.)

[2] अन्तर्व्याप्त्या हेतोः साध्यप्रत्यायने शक्तावशक्तौ च बहिर्व्याप्तेरुद्भावनं व्यर्थम् ॥ २५ ॥
(Pramāṇa-naya-tattvālokālaṅkāra, Chap. III.)

[3] मन्दमतींस्तु व्युत्पादयितुं दृष्टान्तोपनयनिगमनान्यपि प्रयोज्यानि ॥ २९ ॥
(Pramāṇa-naya-tattvālokālaṅkāra, Chap. III.)

testimony (*i.e.*, *āgama*) as also under the method of one-sided interpretation (*naya*) there is given an elaborate exposition of the *Saptabhaṅgīnaya* (sevenfold paralogism). The mediate and immediate results of valid knowledge (*pramāna*) have been clearly laid down.

99. The results of knowledge and the practical use made of them are stated to be not illusory (*saṁvṛti*), but real (*pāramārthika*).

100. Under *naya* (the method of comprehending a thing from one particular point of view), the fallacies of it (*nayābhāsa*) are also enumerated thus :—

Fallacies of Naya.

(1) *Naigamābhāsa* (the fallacy of the *naigama*)—*e.g.*, in estimating a soul we make a distinction between its "existence" (generic property) and its "consciousness" (specific property).

(2) *Saṁgrahābhāsa* (the fallacy of the collective)—occurs when we call a thing real if it possesses the generic property alone, altogether losing sight of its specific properties, as when we say a bamboo is real so far as it is a tree, but it has no specific properties.

(3) *Vyavahārābhāsa* (the fallacy of the practical)—*e.g.*, the Cārvāka philosophy which makes a wrong distinction of substance, quality, etc.

(4) *Ṛjusūtrābhāsa* (the fallacy of the straight expression)—as the Tathāgata philosophy which altogether denies the reality of things.

(5) *Śabdābhāsa* (the verbal fallacy)—occurs when we recognise the distinction of times into past, present and future, but go on attaching one and the same meaning to a word in all the three times, *e.g.*, if we now use the word "kratu" (sacrifice) in the sense of "strength" which it signified a thousand years ago.

(6) *Samabhirūḍhābhāsa* (the fallacy of the subtle)—occurs when we interpret synonymous words such as Indra, Śakra, Purandara, etc., signifying altogether different things.

(7) *Evaṁbhūtābhāsa* (the fallacy of the such-like)—occurs when a thing is discarded simply because it does not, at the moment, possess the properties implied by the name, *e.g.*, Rāma is not a man (a thinking animal) because he is not at present thinking.

101. The soul (*ātmā*) which is the doer and enjoyer, and an embodiment of consciousness, is of the same size as its body.

In every person there is a separate soul which, having got rid of the bondage of its *karma* (act-fruits), attains emancipation.

Rules of Debate.

102. The last chapter expounds the method of debate. Discussion (*Vāda*) consists in assertion and counter-assertion for the establishment of a certain proposition by rejecting its opposite. The disputant or the person who opens the discussion may be eager either to gain a victory or to ascertain a truth. The truth may be sought either for one's own self as a disciple seeks it, or for others as a teacher seeks it. The same remarks apply to the opponent or respondent. There are four constituents of a council of discussion, *viz.*, (1) the disputant (*vādī*); (2) the opponent (*prativādi*); (3) the members (*sabhya*); and (4) the president (*sabhāpati*). The duty of the disputant and his opponent consists in establishing his own side and opposing the other side by means of proof. The members must be acceptable to both the parties in respect of the skill in grasping their dogmas; they must have a good memory, be very learned, and possess genius, patience and impartiality. Their duties consist in stating the assertions and replies of the disputant and his opponent with reference to the particular subject of discussion, in estimating the merits and demerits of their arguments and counter-arguments, in occasionally interrupting them for setting forth some established conclusions, and in, as far as possible, declaring the result of the discussion. The President must be endowed with wisdom, authority, forbearance and impartiality. His duty consists in judging the speeches of the parties and the members, as also in preventing quarrels, etc., among them. In the event of the parties being desirous of victory alone, they may continue the discussion with vigour as long as the members wish; but if they are eager to ascertain the truth alone, they may continue the discussion so long as the truth is not ascertained and so long as they retain their vigour.

HEMACANDRA SŪRI (1088-1172 A.D.).

103. Hemacandra Sūri[1] (surnamed Kalikāla-sarvajña), born at Dhandhuka in Ahmedabad, was a pupil of Devacandra of the Vajraśākhā. He was a contemporary of King Jaya Siṁha and is said to have been the preceptor of Mahārāja Kumāra Pāla of Guzerat about Saṁvat 1199-1229. He was the author of a large number of works such as Kāvyānuśāsana-vṛtti, Chan-

---

1 For details about Hemacandra, see Bühler's "Ueber das Lebens des Jaina Monches Hemacandra"; Peterson's 4th Report, p. cxli, and p. 82; and also Peterson's lecture on the story of Hema Candra published in the *Bombay Gazette*, August 29, 1895.

donuśāsanavṛtti, Abhidhāna-cintāmaṇi or Nāmamālā, Anekārtha-saṁgraha, Dvāśraya-mahā-kāvya, Triṣaṣṭiśalākapuruṣa-caritra (a part of which is called Mahāvīracaritra and the appendix called Pariśiṣṭaparva), Yogaśāstra, Nighaṇṭuśeṣa, etc.

104. He was also the author of a most important work on logic called **Pramāṇa-mīmāṁsā**,[1] on which he himself wrote a commentary. This work, which is divided into five chapters, is written in the *Sūtra* or aphoristic style, and not in the form of a *prakaraṇa* (commentary).

105. He was a spiritual brother of Pradyumna Sūri,[2] was born in Saṁvat 1145 or 1088 A.D., took the vow (*vrata*) in 1150 Saṁvat or 1093 A.D., attained the rank of Sūri in 1166 Saṁvat or 1109 A.D., and ascended to heaven (died) in 1229 Saṁvat or 1172 A.D.[3]

Candraprabha Sūri (1102 A.D.).

106. Candraprabha Sūri (born in Guzerat), who founded the Pūrṇimāgaccha[4] in Saṁvat 1159 or 1102 A.D., was a pupil of

---

1 A manuscript of the Pramāṇa-mīmāṁsā with the commentary by the author himself has been noticed by Peterson in his 5th Report on Sanskrit MSS., pp. 147-148. In explaining why the Pramāṇa-mīmāṁsā was written in the form of aphorisms, Hemacandra in the first chapter of the commentary says:—

वाचकमुख्यविरचितानि सकलशास्त्रचूडामणिभूतानि तत्त्वार्थसूत्राणीति यद्येव-सकलशास्त्रधर्मकौशल्यादिवत् प्रकरणमेव किं नारभ्यते किमनया सूत्रकारत्वाहोपुरुषिकया नैवं वोचः । भिन्नरुचिर्ह्ययं जनस्ततो नास्य स्वेच्छाप्रतिबन्धो लौकिकराजकीयं वा शासनमस्तीति यत्किञ्चिदेतत् तच्च वर्णसमूहात्मकैः पञ्चभिरध्यायैः शास्त्रमेतदरचयदा-चार्यः । तस्य च प्रेक्षावत्प्रवृत्त्यंगमभिधातुमिदमादिसूत्रम् । अथ प्रमाणमीमांसा अथ इत्यस्य अधिकारार्थत्वात् ।

(Quoted in Peterson's 5th Report, p. 148.)

2 श्रीमांश्चन्द्रकुलेऽभवद्गुणनिधिः प्रद्युम्नसूरिप्रभु-
र्बन्धुर्यस्य स विश्वहेमविषये श्रीहेमसूरिर्विधिः ॥

(Candrasena's commentary on Utpādasiddhiprakaraṇa, a manuscript of which is noticed in Peterson's 3rd Report, p. 209.)

3 शरवेदेश्वरे वर्षे कार्त्तिके पूर्णिमानिशि ।
जन्माभवत् प्रभोर्व्योमबाणशंभौ व्रतं तथा ॥
रसषट्केश्वरे सूरिप्रतिष्ठा समजायत ।
नन्दद्वयरवौ वर्षेऽवसानमभवत् प्रभोः ॥

(Prabhāvakacar., XXII, v. 851 seq., quoted by Klatt in Ind. Ant., Vol. XI, Sept. 1882, p. 254.)

4 For the origin of the Pūrṇimāgaccha see Dr. R. G. Bhandarkar's Report, 1883-84, p. 147.

Jayasiṁha Sūri and preceptor of Dharmaghoṣa. He[1] was the author of Darśanaśuddhi, otherwise called Samyaktva-prakaraṇa, and possibly also of the two logical treatises called the Prameyaratnakoṣa and Nyāyāvatāra-vivṛti.[2] He was a great logician, and in debate appeared as a lion before the opponents who resembled elephants.[3]

107. The Nyāyāvatāra-vivṛti is an excellent commentary on the Nyāyāvatāra of Siddhasena Divākara. In it mention is made of the Buddhist logicians Dharmottara, Arcaṭa[4] and others, and there is also a criticism of the views of Saugata, Naiyāyika, Mīmāṁsaka, Vaiśeṣika, Sāṁkhya, Cārvāka, Bauddha, Śauddhodani, Kaṇabhakṣa, Akṣapāda, Brahama-vādi, etc.

Nemicandra Kavi (about 1150 A.D.).

108. Nemicandra, born in Guzerat, who combatted the views of the Hindu philosopher Kaṇāda, was a great teacher of

---

1 For Candraprabha Sūri see also Peterson's 4th Report, p. xxvii.

2 The manuscript of Nyāyāvatāra-vivṛti, which I consulted, was obtained from Bhavanagar, Bombay, through Munis Dharmavijaya and Indravijaya. In the Nyāyāvatāra-vivṛti itself there is no mention of Candraprabha Sūri. Elsewhere I have seen it stated that it was the work of that author. The authorship must, however, for the present, remain an open question. In the colophon of the Nyāyāvatāra-vivṛti it is stated that it was the work of Siddhasena-Divākara-vyākhyānaka or simply Siddha-vyākhyānaka which was evidently a surname. Munis Dharmavijaya and Indravijaya relying on the line व्याख्यात-चूडामणि-सिद्धव्याख्याताः (quoted from Ratnaprabha Sūri's Upadeśamālā-viśeṣa-vṛtti in Peterson's 3rd Report, p. 168) are inclined to identify Siddha-vyākhyānaka with Siddharṣi who lived in Saṁvat 962 or 905 A.D. (as is evident from Peterson's 4th Report, p. cxxix). There is another commentary on the Nyāyāvatāra by Haribhadra Sūri. For Darśana-śuddhi, *vide* Peterson 3, App. p. 91; for Prameya-ratna-kośa, *vide* the Jaināgama List, published in Bombay, p. 77; and for the Nyāyāvatāra-vivṛti *vide* Peterson 3, p. xvi.

3 तीर्थे वीरविभोः सुधर्मगणभृत्सन्तानलब्धोन्नति
चारित्रोज्ज्वलचन्द्रगच्छजलधिप्रोल्लासशीतद्युतिः ।
साहित्यागमतर्कलक्षणमहाविद्यापगासागरः
श्रीचन्द्रप्रभसूरिरद्भुतमतिर्वादीभसिंहोऽभवत् ॥ १ ॥

(Daśavaikālikaṭikā by Tilakācārya, noticed in Peterson's 5th Report, p. 65.)

4 प्रमाणेत्यादि अनेन च शास्त्राद्यवृत्तचतुर्थपादप्रयोजनसंबन्ध विकलतया अनेकधिरर्थं प्रति प्रामाण्यवीगाद् अभिधेयादित्रयमदर्शनेऽप्यप्रार्थ्यसंशयपक्षेण श्रोतारः श्रवणं प्रति प्रोत्साह्यन्ते इति धर्मोत्तरो मन्यते ... ... अयं तु चायं न शास्त्रोत्पादकमेतत् प्रामाण्याभावात् तेषां चाप्रमाणात्प्रवृत्तेः ।

(Nyāyāvatāra-vivṛti, on verse 1.)

logic.[1] He was a pupil of Vairasvāmi and preceptor of Sāgarendu (Sāgaracandra) Muni, as is mentioned by Māṇikyacandra, Sāgarendu Muni's pupil, in his Pārśvanātha-caritra written in Saṁvat 1276 or 1219 A.D. As Māṇikyacandra flourished about 1219 A.D., his preceptor's preceptor Nemicandra[2] must have lived about 1150 A.D. Nemicandra was styled a *Kavi*.[3]

ĀNANDA SŪRI AND AMARACANDRA SŪRI, NICKNAMED TIGER-CUB AND LION-CUB (1093-1150 A.D.).

109. These two, born in Guzerat, were great logicians who, even in their boyhood having overcome their elephant-like opponents in dispute, were nicknamed, respectively, *Vyāghra-śiśuka* (Tiger-cub) and *Siṁha-śiśuka* (Lion-cub.)[4] They[5] were the twin pupils and successors of Mahendra Sūri in the Nāgendra-gaccha, and were succeeded by Haribhadra Sūri. As Siddharāja from whom they received their nicknames ascended the throne in Saṁvat 1150 or 1093 A.D., they must have flourished at the beginning of the 12th century A.D. It is probably these two

---

1 षड्तर्कीकमलाविलासधवलितच्छत्रपोऽत्यर्पिपत्
कल्पद्रोदयचन्द्रमाः समजनि श्रीनेमिचन्द्रप्रभुः ।
निःसामान्यगुणैर्भुवि प्रसमरैः प्रालेयशैलोज्ज्वलैः
यस्याद्भे कवभोक्तिमो मुनिपतेर्धैर्यं मतं सर्वतः ॥ १९ ॥

(Pārśvanātha caritra noticed in Peterson 3, p. 160.)

The same verse is quoted almost verbatim in the Kāvya-prakāśa-saṁketa by Māṇikyacandra Sūri, noticed in Peterson 3, p. 321.

2 For Nemicandra, see also Peterson 4, p. lxxi.

3 See Dr. R. G. Bhandarkar's Report, 1883-84, p. 122.

4 Udayaprabha Sūri, who was the successor of Haribhadra Sūri through Vijayasena Sūri, in his Dharmābhyudaya-mahākāvya, noticed by Peterson in his 3rd Report, pp. 16-19, writes:—

आनन्दसूरिरिति [तस्य बभूव] शिष्यः
पूर्वोऽपरोऽमरचन्द्रसूरिः ।
धर्मद्विपस्य दशनाविव पापदर्प-
वीरदणौ जयति यौ विमलौ विभातः ॥ २ ॥
प्रज्ञाप्रकर्षपयोनिधिमन्दराद्रि-
शुभ्रांशुभौ किमनयोः स्तुमहे महिम्नः
बाल्येऽपि निर्दलितवादिगजौ जगाद
यौ व्याघ्रसिंहशिशुकाविति सिद्धराजः ॥ ३ ॥

5 For further particulars of Ānanda Sūri and Amaracandra Sūri see Peterson 4, p. vii.

logicians who are referred to by the Hindu logician Gaṅgeśa Upādhyāya in his Tattva-cintāmaṇi under *Siṁha-vyāghrī-lakṣaṇa* of Vyāpti.

Haribhadra Sūri (about 1168 A.D.).

110. We find mention of at least two S'vetāmbara Jaina authors bearing the name Haribhadra Sūri. One died [1] in Saṁvat 535 or 478 A.D., while the other, who was a pupil of Ānanda Sūri and Amaracandra Sūri of the Nāgendragaccha, lived about Saṁvat 1225 or 1168 A.D.[2] It is this second Haribhadra Sūri who was called "Kalikāla-Gautama."[3] He must have been an eminent logician if we suppose him to be the author [4] of the **Saḍdarśana-samuccaya**, the **Daśavaikālika-niryukti-ṭīkā**, the **Nyāya-praveśaka-sūtra** and the **Nyāyāvatāra-vṛtti.** There are

---

1 पंचसए पणतीए विक्कमकालाओ झत्ति अत्थमिओ ।
हरिभद्दसूरिसूरो निब्बुओ दिसउ सिवसुक्खं ॥ १०० ॥

(Gacchotpatti-prakīrṇaka quoted in the Gāthāsāhasrī noticed in Peterson 3, p. 284.)

2 Klatt refers to Bühler's Sukṛtasaṁkīrtana, pp. 24-25 ; see Peterson 4, pp. cxxxix, cxl.

3 सिद्धान्तोपनिषन्निषण्णहृदयो धीजन्मभूमिस्ततो
पट्टे श्रीहरिभद्रसूरिरभवत्सारश्चिणामग्रणीः ।
मान्त्वा ग्रन्थमनाथयेरतिचिरात्सिद्धप्रख्यानतः
सन्तुष्टैः कलिकालगौतम इति ख्यातिर्वितेने गुणैः ॥ ५ ॥

(Dharmābhyudaya-mahākāvya by Udayaprabha Sūri noticed in Peterson 3, Appendix I, p. 18.)

4 In the concluding lines of the Daśavaikālika-niryukti-ṭīkā it is stated that the author of that work was one Haribhadra Sūri who was a *dharmaputra* of *Yākinī*. A similar description of Haribhadra the author of Ṣaḍdarśana-samuccaya is found in the opening sentences of Guṇaratna's commentary on that work (dated about 1409 A.D.). The Caturviṁśati-prabandha by Rājaśekhara Sūri composed in Saṁvat 1405 or 1348 A.D. makes a like reference to Haribhadra, the author of Nyāyāvatāra-vṛtti. Now the *dharmaputra* of *Yākinī* is generally held to be a surname of the first Haribhadra Sūri whose disciples were Haṁsa and Paramahaṁsa, as is evident from Prabhācandra Sūri's Prabhāvaka-caritra dated about 1277 A.D.

In the Gacchotpatti-prakaraṇa, Gāthā-sāhasrī, Vicāra-sāra-prakaraṇa, Vicārāmṛta-saṁgraha, Tapāgacchapaṭṭāvalī, Kharataragaccha-paṭṭāvalī, etc., Haribhadra Sūri I. is stated to have flourished in Saṁvat 535 or 478 A.D.

Now the Nyāyāvatāra which is alleged to have been commented on by Haribhadra Sūri I. was itself composed about 533 A.D. (that is, after 478 A.D.), and Dharmakīrti, whose logical doctrines have been referred to in the Ṣaḍdarśana-samuccaya, lived about 650 A.D. These facts prove that Haribhadra the author of Nyāyāvatāra-vṛtti and Ṣaḍdarśana-samuccaya lived after 650 A.D.

strong grounds for supposing that the Ṣaḍdarśana-samuccaya was not the work of the first Haribhadra Sūri, as it refers in the chapter on the Bauddhadarśana to the views of such authors as Dignāga, Dharmakīrti,[1] and others who flourished long after the 5th century A.D. The six systems (Ṣaḍdarśana) treated by him are (1) Bauddha, (2) Naiyāyika, (3) Sāṁkhya, (4) Jaina, (5) Vaiśeṣika and (6) Jaiminiya.

111. Haribhadra Sūri is often described [2] as having protected the word of the Arhats like a mother by his 1,400 works. He is said to have used the word *viraha* (separation or sorrow) as his mark in the last verse of each of his works. He was by birth a Brāhmaṇa and was chaplain to king Jitāri whose capital was

---

Dr. Jacobi in his letter, dated the 21st October 1907, writes to me that "Haribhadra used the word *viraha* in the Samaraiccakahā, which is alluded to by Siddharṣi who wrote in 905 A.D."

Regarding the dates of the Ṣaḍdarśana-samuccaya, etc., he observes :—These are "unanimously ascribed to the first Haribhadra," "whose date. I believe, with Prof. Leumann, to have been wrongly referr d to the Saṁvat era instead of the Valabhi or *Gupta era*, which commenced in 319 A.D."

According to Dr. Jacobi, therefore, the Ṣaḍdarśana-sammuccaya, etc., were written by the first Haribhadra Sūri, who died in 535 Gupta Saṁvat or 854 A.D.

Dr. Jacobi's theory removes many of our difficulties, yet it is far from being conclusive, as the Jaina authors very seldom used the Gupta era. Moreover, it is inexplicable why Vācaspati Miśra and Udayanācārya did not refer to such an excellent compendium of Indian philosophy as the Ṣaḍdarśana-samuccaya if it existed as early as the 9th or 10th century A.D. I am therefore inclined to believe that Haribhadra Sūri II was the author of the Ṣaḍdarśana-samuccaya, Nyāyāvatāra-vṛtti, etc., while the Samaraiccakahā and other treatises might be the works of the first Haribhadra Sūri.

But I must confess that the modern Jaina Paṇḍitas such as Munis Dharmavijaya and Indravijaya firmly believe that the author of all these works was the first Haribhadra Sūri who, according to them, flourished in 535 Vikrama Saṁvat, or 478 A.D.

प्रत्यक्षं कल्पनापोढमभ्रान्तं तत्र बुध्यताम् ।
त्रिरूपाल्लिङ्गतो लिङ्गिज्ञानं त्वनुमानसंज्ञितम् ॥

(Ṣaddarśana-samuccaya, chapter on Bauddha-darśana, p. 38, edited by Dr. Suali).

This verse refers without doubt to the definition of *Pratyakṣa* and *Anumāna* given by Dharmakīrti who lived about 650 A.D.

2 Klatt in his "Paṭṭāvali of the Kharataragaccha" in the Ind. Ant., Vol. XI, Sept. 1882, p. 247 ; also Peterson 3, p. 35. Also :

स्तौमि श्रीहरिभद्रं तं येनार्हद्गीर्जरज्जरा ।
चतुर्दशप्रकरणशत्यापोष्यत मातृवत् ॥ १९ ॥

Amarasvāmicarita by Muniratna Sūri noticed in Peterson 3, p. 91.

Chittore near the Citrakūṭa hill.[1] He was instructed in the Jaina doctrine by Jinabhaṭa. Two of his pupils, named Haṁsa and Paramahaṁsa, are said to have left him as missionaries of the Jaina faith, and to have been slain in the Bhoṭa country (Tibet) by the fanatical Buddhists whom they sought to convert. The sorrow caused by the death of these two pupils is said to have been symbolised in the word *viraha.*

112. It is generally supposed that Haribhadra Sūri, whose pupils were killed in Tibet, was the first author of that name. But there will be no inconsistency if we suppose him to be the second Haribhadra Sūri, for the religious intercourse between India and Tibet was more frequent in the 12th century A.D. than in the 5th century, when Tibet had scarcely emerged into the ken of history.

RATNAPRABHA SŪRI (1181 A.D.).

113. Ratnaprabha Sūri, who belonged to the S'vetāmbara sect, was a logician of repute, being the author of a light commentary (*laghu-ṭikā*) on the Pramāṇa-naya-tattvālokālaṅkāra called **Syādvāda-ratnāvatārikā**[2] in which are quoted the views of the Buddhist logicians Arcaṭa (q. v.) and Dharmottara (q. v.)

114. While in Broach at the Aśvavabodhatirtha in Saṁvat 1238 or 1181 A.D., he wrote another work called Upadeśamālā-vṛtti[3] to please Bhadreśvara Sūri and in payment of the debt he owed to Vijayasena Sūri, the brother of Bhadreśvara. There he gives his spiritual descent in the Vṛhadgaccha as follows: (1) Municandra Sūri; (2) Deva Sūri; (3) Bhadreśvara Sūri and (4) Ratnaprabha Sūri.[4]

---

1 *Vide* Introduction to Ṣaḍdarśanasamuccaya published in the Chowkhamba series, Benares.

2 प्रमाणे च प्रमेये च बालानां बुद्धिसिद्धये ।
किञ्चिद् वचनचातुर्य्यचापलायेयमादधे ॥
प्रमेयरत्नकोटीभिः पूर्णो रत्नाकरो महान् ।
तथावतारमात्रेण इत्येतस्याः कृतार्थता ॥

(Syādvāda-ratnāvatārikā, Muni Dharmavijaya's MSS., p. 99). A part of the Syādvāda-ratnāvatārikā has been printed and published in the Benares Jaina Yaśovijaya series.

3 श्रीरत्नप्रभसूरिभिः शुभकृते श्रीदेवसूरिप्रभोः ।
शिष्यैः सेयमकारि सन्मदकृते वृत्तिर्विशेषार्थिनाम् ॥
विक्रमाद्वसुलोकार्के (१२३८) वर्षे माघे समर्थिता ।
एकादश्यामथवापि सार्द्धं पञ्चशतं तथा ॥

(Upadeśamālā-vṛtti, noticed in Peterson 5, p. 124).

4 For other particulars of Ratnaprabha Sūri, *vide* Peterson 4, p. cii. Compare also Weber II, p. 922, note 7.

MALLIṢEṆA SŪRI (1292 A.D.).

115. He belonged to the Nagendra Gaccha of the S'vetāmbara sect, and was the author of the **Syādvādamañjarī**, a commentary on Hemacandra's Vītarāga-stuti or Dvātriṁśikā. The Syādvāda-mañjari contains an exposition of the *Pramāṇa*, *Saptabhaṅginaya*, etc., and criticises Akṣapāda's theories of *Pramāṇa*, *Chala*, *Jāti*, *Nigrahasthāna*, etc. The doctrines of the Sāṁkhya, Aulūkya, Jaiminīya, Bhaṭṭapāda, Vedānta, Yogācāra, Mādhyamika, Cārvāka, etc., have also been his favourite subjects of attack. At the close of his work Malliṣeṇa describes himself as a pupil of Udayaprabha Sūri and as having composed the work in S'aka 1214 or A.D. 1292.[1]

RĀJAŚEKHARA SŪRI (1348 A.D.).

116. Rājaśekhara Sūri, or Malladhāri S'rī Rājaśekhara Sūri, belonged to the S'vetāmbara sect and was the author of the **Ratnāvatārīkā-pañjikā**,[2] a sub-commentary on the **Pramāṇa-naya-tattvālokālaṅkāra**, as also of two other works called Syādvāda-kalikā and Caturviṁśatiprabandha.[3] He is also the author of a Pañjikā (commentary) on the Nyāya-kandalī of the Hindu philosopher S'rī-dhara. He studied the Nyāya-kandalī under teacher Jinaprabha,[4] and is said to have lived in Saṁvat 1405 or 1348 A.D.[5]

JÑĀNA CANDRA (1350 A.D.).

117. He belonged to the S'vetāmbara sect and was the author of a gloss on the Ratnāvatārikā called the **Ratnāvatārikā-ṭippana**, which discusses many abstruse points of logic and criticises the

---

1 श्रीमल्लिषेणसूरिभिरकारि तत्पदगगनदिनमणिभिः ।
वृत्तिरियं मनुरविमितशकाब्दे दीपमहसि शनौ ॥ १ ॥
(Syādvādamañjarī, p. 220, printed in the Benares Chowkhamba Sanskrit Series, and edited by Dāmodara Lal Gosvāmi.)

2 A part of the Ratnāvatārikā-pañjikā has been printed and published in the Benares Jaina Yaśovijaya series.

3 This work has been published by Hira Lal Haṁsarāja at Jāmanagara in Kathiwar.

4 श्रीमज्जिनप्रभविभोरधिगत्य न्यायकन्दलीं किञ्चित् ।
तस्यां विवृतिलवमहं करवै स्वपरोपकाराय ॥
(Nyāyakandali of Sridhara with the Pañjikā of Rājaśekhara noticed in Peterson 3, p. 273; cf. also Peterson 3, pp. 28-29.)

5 *Vide* Weber II, p. 1207.

views of Dignāga [1] and others. He composed this work [2] under orders from his preceptor Rājaśekhara Sūri, who flourished in 1348 A.D. Jñāna Candra's date may approximately be fixed at about 1350 A.D.

GUṆARATNA (1409 A.D.).

118. Guṇaratna belonged to the Tapāgaccha of the S'vetāmbara sect, and was the distinguished author of a commentary on the Ṣaḍdarśana-samuccaya [3] called **Saḍdarśana-samuccaya-vṛtti** or **Tarka-rahasya-dīpikā** in which the Nyāya (logic) along with other systems has been lucidly explained. He also wrote the Kriyā-ratna-samuccaya.

119. He is mentioned by Ratna-śekhara Sūri in the S'rāddha-pratikramaṇa-sūtra-vṛtti composed in Saṁvat 1496 or A.D. 1439.[4] In that work Guṇaratna is mentioned as a pupil

---

[1] तेनान्यापोढविषयाः प्रोक्ताः सामान्यगोचराः ।
शब्दाश्च बुद्धयश्चैव वस्तुन्येषामसम्भवात् ॥
अस्य व्याख्या तेनाचार्य्ये दिग्नागेन
अन्यापोढविषयाः ... प्रोक्ताः ॥

Jñānacandra's Ratnāvatārikā-ṭippana, chap. I, p. 7, published in Yaśovijaya-granthamālā of Benares.

[2] रत्नाकरावतारिकां वरटिप्पनं तत्
ज्ञानेन्दुरल्पतरधीः स्वमतिः प्रवृत्त्यै ।
तच्छिष्यको रचितवान् मलधारिपूज्य-
श्रीराजशेखरगुरोश्च निदेशमाप्य

Quoted from the MSS. of Ratnākarāvatārikā-ṭippanaka, lent to me by Muni Dharmavijaya. A part of this work has been printed and published in the Benares Jaina Yaśovijaya series.

[3] Ṣaḍdarśana-samuccaya with Vṛtti, edited by Dr. Suali, is being published by the Asiatic Society of Bengal. There is another commentary on Saddarśanasamuccaya called Laghuvṛtti by Maṇibhadra. It has been published in the Chowkhamba series.

[4] The S'rāddha-prati-kramaṇa-sūtra-vṛtti by Ratnaśekhara Sūri, has been noticed in Peterson 3, pp. 226-227, whence the following lines are quoted :—

विख्याततपेत्याख्या जगति जगच्चन्द्रसूरयोऽभूवन् ।
श्रीदेवसुन्दरगुरूत्तमाश्च तदनुक्रमाद्विदिताः ॥ १ ।
पञ्च च तेषां शिष्यास्तेष्वाद्या ज्ञानसागरा गुरवः । २
कुलमण्डना द्वितीयाः श्रीगुणरत्नास्तृतीयाश्च ॥ ३ ॥

of Devasundara, who attained the exalted position of Sūri at Aṇahillapattana in Saṁvat 1420 or A.D. 1363.[1] Guṇaratna must, therefore, have lived between A.D. 1363 and A.D. 1439. Devasundara Sūri, teacher of Guṇaratna, was a contemporary of Muni-sundara Sūri, the famous author of the Gurvāvalī[2] composed in Saṁvat 1466 or A.D. 1409. Guṇaratna himself says that his Kriyāratna-samuccaya[3] was composed in Saṁvat 1466 or A.D. 1409.

120. Guṇaratna, in his elaborate commentary (*Vṛtti*) on the Ṣaḍdarśana-samuccaya, has mentioned S'auddhodani, Dharmottarācārya, Arcaṭa, Dharmakīrti, Prajñākara, Kamalaśīla, Dignāga, and other Buddhist authors, as well as Tarkabhāṣā, Hetubindu, Arcaṭa-tarkaṭīkā, Pramāṇa-vārtika, Tattvasaṁgraha, Nyāyabindu, Nyāyapraveśaka, and other Buddhist works on logic, etc., in the chapter on the Bauddha system. Mention has also been made, in the chapter on the Nyāya, of such Hindu logicians as Akṣapāda, Vātsyāyana, Udyotakara, Vācaspati, Udayana, Srīkaṇṭha, Abhayatilakopādhyāya, Jayanta, and of such works as Nyāya-sūtra, Nyāyabhāṣya, Nyāyavārtika, Tātparyaṭīkā, Tātparyapariśuddhi, Nyāyālaṅkāra, Nyāyālaṅkāravṛtti, etc. The Nyāya-sāra of Bhā-sarvajña and the eighteen commentaries on it such as Nyāyabhūṣaṇa, Nyāyakalikā, Nyāyakusumāñjali, etc., have also been mentioned.

षड्दर्शनवृत्तिक्रियारत्नसमुच्चयविचारनिचयसृजः ।
येषां श्रीगुरुवर्याः प्रसादतोऽब्दे षडङ्गविश्वमिते ।
श्रीरत्नशेखरगणिर्वृत्तिमिमामसृजत कृतितुष्टे ॥ १

1 *Vide* Dr. Klatt on the Paṭṭāvalī of the Kharataragaccha in the Ind. Ant., Vol. XI, September 1882, pp. 255-256; cf. also Weber II, p. 884; and Dr. R. G. Bhandarkar's Report, 1883-84, p. 157.

2 रसरसमनुमितवर्षे १४६६ मुनिसुन्दरसूरिणा कृता पूर्वम् ।
मध्यस्थैरवधार्य्या गुर्वावलीयं जयश्रीदा ॥ ९९ ॥

(Gurvāvalī, Jaina-Yaśovijaya granthamālā series, p. 109).

3 काले षड्रसपूर्व १४६६ वत्सरमिते श्रीविक्रमार्काद्गते
गुर्वादेशवशाद्विमृश्य च सदा स्वान्योपकारं परम् ।
ग्रन्थं श्रीगुणरत्नसूरिरतनोत् प्रज्ञाविहीनोऽप्यमुं
निर्हेतूपकृतिप्रधानजननैः शोध्यस्त्वयं धीधनैः ॥ ९२ ॥

(Kriyāratna-samuccaya, Jaina Yaśovijaya granthamālā series, p. 309).

DHARMA-BHŪṢAṆA (ABOUT 1600 A.D.).

121. A Digambara author who wrote the **Nyāya-dīpikā** about 300 years ago. He has been mentioned in the Tarkabhāsā [1] by Yaśovijaya Gaṇi.[2]

122. The Nyāya-dīpikā begins with a salutation [3] to Arhat Vardhamāna. It is divided into three chapters (*Prakāśa viz.*, (1) general characteristics of valid knowledge, *pramāṇa-sāmānya-lakṣaṇa*, (2) perception, *pratyakṣa*, and (3) indirect knowledge, *parokṣa*, including recollection, *smṛti*, recognition, *pratyabhijñāna*, argumentation, *tarka*, inference, *anumāna*, tradition, *āgama*, and the method of comprehending things from particular standpoints, *naya*.

123. The technical terms of logic have been defined and minutely examined and the views of other logicians, specially of the Buddhists, have been severely criticised. There are references to Sugata, Saugata, Bauddha, Tāthāgata, Mīmāṁsaka, Yauga, Naiyāyika, Bhāṭṭa, Prābhākara, Dignāga, Samanta Bhadra, Akalaṅka Deva, Śālikā Nātha, Jainendra, Syād vāda-vidyāpati, Māṇikya Nandi Bhaṭṭāraka, Kumāra Nandi Bhaṭṭāraka, Udayana and others. The following works are also mentioned :—Prameya-kamala-mārtaṇḍa, Rājavārtika, Ślokavārtika, Ślokavārtika-bhāṣya Tattvārtha-sūtra, Tattvārtha-bhāṣya, Tattvārtha-śloka-vārtika, Āptamīmāṁsā-vivaraṇa, Nyāyaviniścaya, Pramāṇa-nirṇaya, Pramāṇa-parīkṣā, Parīkṣāmukha, Nyāyabindu, etc.

YAŚOVIJAYA GAṆI (1680 A.D.).

124. Yaśovijaya [4] belonged to the Śvetāmbara sect and was the famous author of **Nyāya-pradipa**, **Tarkabhāṣā**, **Nyāya rahasya**, **Nyāyāmṛta-taraṅgiṇī**, **Nyāya-khaṇḍa-khādya**, Anekānta Jaina-mata-vyavasthā, Jñānabindu-prakaraṇa, etc. He also wrote a commentary on the Digambara work Aṣṭasāhasrī

---

[1] This work has been printed in Kolhāpura.

[2] इत्थं वा ज्ञाननिवर्तकत्वेन तर्कस्य प्रामाण्यं धर्मभूषणोक्तं सत्येव तत्र मिथ्याज्ञानरूपे व्यवच्छेद्ये संगच्छते ।

Yaśovijaya's Tarkabhāṣā, leaf 10, MSS. lent to me by Munis Dharmavijaya and Indravijaya.

[3] श्रीवर्द्धमानमर्हन्तं नत्वा बालप्रबुद्धये ।
विरच्यते मितस्पष्ट सन्दर्भन्यायदीपिका ॥ १ ॥

(Nyāyadīpikā, chap. I).

[4] For other particulars about Yaśovijaya see Peterson 6, p. xiv. For his works see the Jaināgama List published in Bombay.

called **Aṣṭasāhasrī-vṛtti**. The Tarkabhāṣā begins with a salutation to Jina.[1] It consists of three chapters, *viz.* (1) Valid knowledge, *pramāṇa*, (2) Knowledge from particular standpoints, *naya*, and (3) Imposition, *niḥkṣepa*. He occasionally discusses *vyāptigraha*, or the means of establishing the universal connection between the middle term and the major term.

125. He is descended from Hiravijaya, the well-known Sūri of Akbar's time (no. 58 of the Tapāgaccha paṭṭāvali). He ascended heaven in Saṁvat 1745 or A.D. 1688 at Dabhoi, in modern Baroda State. To perpetuate his memory there has been established at Benares a college called Jaina Yaśovijaya-pāṭhaśālā under the auspices of which the scred Jaina works are being published in a series called Jaina Yaśovijaya-granthamālā.

---

[1] ऐन्द्रवृन्दनतं नत्वा जिनं तत्त्वार्थदेशिनम्
प्रमाणनयनिक्षेपैस्तर्कभाषां तनोम्यहम्
(Tarkabhāṣā, chap. I).

BOOK II.

The Buddhist Logic.

CHAPTER I.

THE OLD BUDDHIST REFERENCES TO LOGIC.

BUDDHA GAUTAMA (623 B.C.—543 B.C.).

1. The Buddhists maintain that their religion is eternal. It was taught at different cycles by sages called Buddhas (the Enlightened Ones) or Tathāgatas (those who have realised the truth). In the present cycle, called *Mahā-bhadra-kalpa* (the very blessed cycle), four Buddhas are said to have already appeared, *viz.*, Krakucchanda, Kanaka Muni, Kāśyapa and Gautama, while the fifth, *viz.*, Maitreya, is yet to be born.[1]

2. Of the past Buddhas the last, *viz.*, Buddha Gautama, otherwise called Śākya Muni, was born at Kapilavastu (modern Nigliva in the Nepal Terai) in 623 B.C., and attained *nirvāṇa* at Kuśinagara (modern Kuśinārā near Gorakhpur) in 543 B.C.[2] He passed almost his whole life in Magadha (modern Behar). He is regarded by modern scholars as the real founder of Buddhism, while his predecessors are considered as purely mythical.

ORIGIN OF THE PĀLI BUDDHIST LITERATURE (543 B.C.—76 B.C.).

3. Buddha Gautama is said to have delivered his teachings in the Māgadhī or Pāli language. On his death these teachings were rehearsed by the Buddhist monks in three councils[3] held

---

1 *Vide* Hardy's Manual of Buddhism, second edition, pp. 88—91.

2 The exact date of Buddha is unknown. The date given here is according to the Mahāvaṁsa, the Pāli chronicle of Ceylon. The date of Buddha's nirvāṇa is placed by European scholars between 470—480 B.C. Cf Dr. Fleet's article on "The Date of Buddha's Death" in the Journal of the Royal Asiatic Society of Great Britain and Ireland, January, 1904.

3 For an account of the first and second councils, *vide* Vinaya Piṭaka, Culla Vagga, 11th and 12th Khandhakas, translated by Rhys Davids and

at Rājagṛha, Vaiśāli and Pāṭaliputra under the patronage of kings Ajātaśatru, Kālāśoka and Aśoka about the year 543 B.C., 443 B.C. and 255 B.C.[1] respectively. The texts of the teachings as discussed and settled in these councils form the sacred scripture of the Buddhists. This scripture is called in Pāli *Tepiṭaka* or *Piṭakattaya* and in Sanskrit *Tripiṭaka* or *Piṭaka-traya* which signifies 'Three Baskets.' It consists of the Sermon Basket (Sutta Piṭaka), Discipline Basket (Vinaya Piṭaka) and the Metaphysical Basket (Abhidhamma Piṭaka), each of which embodies a large number of distinct works.

4. The monks assembled in the First Council, that is in the Council of Kāśyapa in 543 B.C., were called (1) Theras, and the scripture canonised by them was called Theravāda. Subsequently ten thousand monks of Vaiśālī having violated certain rules of the Theravāda were, by the decision of the Second Council in 443 B.C., expelled from the community of the Theras. These excluded priests were called (2) Mahāsāṅghikas who were the first heretical sect of the Buddhists. They made certain additions and alterations in the Theravāda. Afterwards within two hundred years from the *nirvāṇa* of Buddha 14 other heretical sects[2] arose, *viz.*, (3) Gokulika, (4) Ekabbohārika, (5) Paññatti, (6) Bāhulika, (7) Cetiya, (8) Sabbatthi, (9) Dhammaguttika, (10) Kassapīya, (11) Saṅkantika, (12) Sutta, (13) Himavata, (14) Rājagiriya, (15) Siddhatthika, (16) Pubbaseliya, (17) Aparaseliya and (18) Vajiriya.

5. Just at the close of the Third Council about 255 B.C., the teachings of Buddha as canonised by the Theras in the form of the *Tepiṭaka* were carried[3] by Mahinda, son of Emperor Aśoka, to the island of Ceylon where they were perpetuated by priests in oral tradition. They are said to have been committed to writing[4] for the first time in Ceylon in the reign of Vaṭṭagāmaṇi during 104-76 B.C. Besides the *Tepiṭaka* there

---

Oldenberg, S.B.E. series, vol. XX, pp. 370, 386. For an account of the third council as also of the first and second, *vide* Wijesiṁha's translation of the Mahāvaṁsa, chapter V, pp. 25—29, as also chapters III and IV.

[1] As to the dates of the 1st and 2nd Councils I follow the Pāli Mahāvaṁsa. The date of the 3rd Council is in accordance with modern researches. Aśoka ascended the throne in 272 B.C. (*Vide* Vincent A. Smith's Aśoka, p. 63), and it was in the 17th year of his reign that the third Council took place (*vide* Wijesiṁha's Mahāvaṁsa, p. 29).

[2] For a discussion about the variant names and subdivisions of these sects, *vide* Wijesiṁha's Mahāvaṁsa, part I, chapter V, p. 15; and Dr. Rhys Davids' "Schools of Buddhist Belief" in the Journal of the Royal Asiatic Society of Great Britain and Ireland, 1892, pp. 1-37.

[3] *Vide* the Mahāvaṁsa, chapter XII.

[4] *Vide* the Mahāvaṁsa, chapter XXXIII. Cf. also Dr. Alwis's Lecture on the Pali Language in the Journal of the Pali Text Society, London, 1883, p. 42.

were numerous other works written in Pāli which have immensely added to the bulk of the Pāli literature.

LOGIC TOUCHED ON IN THE PĀLI LITERATURE.

6. In the *Tepiṭaka*—nay in the whole Pāli literature—there is not a single treatise on Logic. This is not at all a matter of surprise, for, according to the Pāli works, our knowledge (called in Pāli : *Viññāṇa* and in Sanskrit : *Vijñāna*) has arisen from *Avidyā*[1] or cosmic blindness, and is therefore a mere illusion. Such being the character of our knowledge, it cannot form the subject-matter of Logic, the sole function of which consists in laying down criteria for determining real or valid knowledge.

7. The only topic bearing upon Logic which has been touched on in the Pāli works, is the division of knowledge into six kinds. In the Tepiṭaka[2] knowledge (*Viññāṇa*[3]) has been classified as (1) ocular (*cakkhu-viññāṇaṁ*), (2) auditory (*sota-viññāṇaṁ*), (3) olfactory (*ghāna-viññāṇaṁ*), (4) gustatory (*jivhā-viññāṇaṁ*), (5) tactual (*kāya-viññāṇaṁ*) and (6) mental (*mano-viññāṇaṁ*). But this classification has not been carried far enough to lay the foundation of a Logic that deserved the name of science.

8. In the Tepiṭaka there are, however, occasional references to a class of men who were called *Takki* (in Sanskrit : *Tarkin* or *Takkika* (in Sanskrit : *Tārkika*)—that is, those versed in reasoning. It is not known whether these men were Buddhists, Jainas or Brāhmaṇas, perhaps they were recruited from all communities. They were not logicians in the proper sense of the term but they appear to me to have been sophists who indulged in quibble and casuistry.

THE Brahma-jāla-sutta (543 B.C.—255 B.C.).

9. In the **Brahma-jāla-sutta**, which forms a part of the Digha Nikāya of the Sutta Piṭaka and was rehearsed in the three Buddhist Councils during 543 B.C.—255 B.C.,[4] mention

---

[1] *Avidyā* (cosmic blindness) forms the first link in the chain of *Paticca samuppāda* explained in the Vinaya Piṭaka, Mahāvagga, Pathama Khandhaka; translated by Rhys Davids and Oldenberg, S.B.E. series, vol. III, pp. 73—75.

[2] *Vide* the Aṅguttara Nikāya III, 61. 8, edited by Dr. Morris in the Pāli Text Society series of London. *Vide* also the Dhammasaṅginī, and compare Paricchedа IV of the Abhidhammatthasaṅgaha which, though not included in the Tepiṭaka, sums up the topics of the Abhidhamma Piṭaka.

[3] *Viññāṇa* is translated as knowledge or consciousness, such as *cakkhu-viññāṇa* signifies ocular knowledge or eye-consciousness.

[4] "Hofrath Dr. Bühler, in the last work he published, expressed the

is made of those Śramaṇas and Brāhmaṇas who were *Takki* and *Vimaṁsi* and indulged in *Takka* and *Vimaṁsā*. Buddha speaks of them thus :—

"In this case, brethren, some recluse or Brāhmaṇa is addicted to *logic* [sophism] and *reasoning* [casuistry]." He gives utterance to the following conclusion of his own, beaten out by his *argumentations* and based on his *sophistry*: "The soul and the world arose without a cause." [1]

This passage refers, in my opinion, to a sophist rather than to a teacher of Logic.

The **Udāna** (543 B.C.—255 B.C.).

10. Again, in the **Udāna,** which is included in the Khuddaka Nikāya of the Sutta Piṭaka and is supposed to have been rehearsed in the three Buddhist Councils during 543 B.C.—255 B.C., we read :—

"As long as the perfect Buddhas do not appear, the *Takkikas* [sophists] are not corrected nor are the Sāvakas: owing to their evil views they are not released from misery."[2]

This passage leaves no doubt that the *Takkikas* were sophists.

The **Kathāvatthuppakaraṇa** (about 255 B.C.

11. The **Kathāvatthuppakaraṇa,** a work of the Abhidhammapiṭaka, composed by Moggaliputta Tissa at the Third Bud-

---

opinion that these books, as we have them in the Pāli, are good evidence, certainly for the fifth, probably for the sixth, century B.C."

—Rhys Davids' Preface to the Dialogues of the Buddha, p. XX.

[1] The Brahma-jāla-sutta 1—32 included in Dialogues of the Buddha translated by Rhys Davids, London, p. 42.

Dr. Rhys Davids translates *Takki* (*Tarki*) and *Vimaṁsi* (*Mimāṁsi*) as "addicted to *logic* and *reasoning*." But the expression may also be rendered as "addicted to *sophism* and *casuistry*."

The original Pāli runs thus :—

Idha, bhikkhave, ekacco samaṇo vā brāhmaṇo vā *takki* hoti *vimaṁsi*. So *takka*-pariyāhataṁ *vimaṁsā*nucaritaṁ sayaṁ-paṭibhānaṁ evam āha : "Adhicca-samuppanno attā ca loko cāti."

—The Brahma-jāla-sutta 1—32 included in the Dīgha Nikāya, p. 29, edited by T. W. Rhys Davids and J. E. Carpenter, London.

[2] The original of this passage runs as follows : —

Yāva sammā sambuddhā loke n'uppajjanti, na *takkikā* sujjhanti na c'āpi sāvakā, duddiṭṭhī na dukkhā pamuccare'ti.

—Udānaṁ, vi, 10, edited by Paul Steinthal in the Pāli Text Society series, London.

dhist Council during the reign of Aśoka about 255 B.C.,[1] mentions *patiññā* (in Sanskrit: *pratijñā*, proposition), *upanaya* (in Sanskrit, too: *upanaya*, application of reason), *niggaha* (in Sanskrit: *nigraha*, humiliation or defeat), etc.,[2] which are the technical terms of Logic. Though Moggaliputta Tissa has not made any actual reference to Logic, his mention of some of its technical terms warrants us to suppose that that science in some shape existed in India in his time about 255 B.C.

THE **Milinda-pañha** *alias* THE **Bhikṣu-sūtra** (ABOUT 100 A.D.).

12. The only Pāli work in which an explicit reference to Logic called *Nīti* (or *Nyāya*) occurs is the **Milinda-pañha** otherwise known as the **Bhikṣu-sūtra**, which was composed about 100 A.D.[3] It was translated into Chinese under the Eastern Tsin dynasty A.D. 317—420.[4] In the Chinese collection of the Indian books it is designated as the **Nāgasena-Bhikṣu-sūtra**. This work contains questions of Milinda (the Greek King Menander of Bactria) and replies of Bhikṣu Nāga Sena on various abstruse matters. In it Milinda who was versed in Logic (*Nīti* or *Nyāya*) is thus described :—

---

1 Aśoka ascended the throne of Magadha in 272 B.C. (*vide* Vincent A. Smith's Aśoka, p. 63). In the seventeenth year of his reign the Third Buddhist Council took place (Wijesiṁha's Mahāvaṁsa, p. 29).

2 *Niggaha-catukkaṁ* is the name of a section of the first chapter of the Kathāvatthuppakaraṇa. *Upanaya-catukkaṁ* is the name of another section of that work. A passage, in which the terms *paṭiññā* and *niggaha* occur, is quoted below :—

No ca mayaṁ tayā tattha hetāya paṭiññāya hevaṁ paṭijānantā hevaṁ niggahetabbo (Kathāvatthuppakaraṇa, Siamese edition, p. 3, kindly lent to me by Anagārika H. Dharmapāla).

In the commentary on the above passage even *chala* (fraud), which is another technical term of Logic, has been used. *Cf.*

Evaṁ tena, chalena niggaho āropito idāni tass'eva paṭiññāya dhammena samena attavāde jayaṁ dassetuṁ anulomanaye pucchā sakavādissa attano nissāya paṭiññāṁ paravādissa laddhiya okāsaṁ adatvā. . . .

(Kathāvatthuppakaraṇa-aṭṭhakathā, published by the Pali Text Society of London, p. 13).

It is evident from the opening passages of the Kathāvatthuppakaraṇa-aṭṭhakathā that Moggaliputta Tissa discussed in the Kathāvatthuppakāraṇa only those doctrines—Buddhistic and heretic—which had originated after the First and Second Buddhist Councils. From this statement may we not draw the conclusion that the technical terms of Logic which he has used were unknown before the Second Buddhist Council ?

3 For discussions about date *vide* Rhys Davids' Introduction to "the Questions of King Milinda" in the S. B. E. series, vol. xxxv.

4 *Vide* Bunyiu Nanjio's Catalogue of the Chinese Tripiṭaka, No. 1358.

"Many were the arts and sciences he knew—holy tradition and secular law: the Sāṁkhya, Yoga, *Nyāya* and Vaiśesika systems of philosophy; arithmetic; music; medicine; the four Vedas, the Purāṇas, and the Itihāsas; astronomy, magic, *causation* and spells; the art of war; poetry; conveyancing—in a word, the whole nineteen.

As a disputant he was hard to equal, harder still to overcome; the acknowledged superior of all the founders of the various schools of thought. And as in wisdom so in strength of body, swiftness, and valour there was found none equal to Milinda in all India. He was rich, too, mighty in wealth and prosperity, and the number of his armed hosts knew no end ... The king, who was fond of wordy disputation, and eager for discussion with *casuists, sophists*, and gentry of that sort, looked at the sun (to ascertain the time), and then said to his ministers."[1]

13. The following dialogue[2] between Milinda and Nāga Sena is quoted to show what was thought to be the proper mode of carrying on debate in the days of those notable persons:—

"The King said: 'Reverend Sir, will you discuss with me again?'

'If your Majesty will discuss as a scholar (Paṇḍita), well; but if you will discuss as a king, no.'

'How is it then that scholars discuss?'

'When scholars talk a matter over with one another then is there a winding up, an unravelling; one or other is convicted of error, and he then acknowledges his mistake, distinctions are drawn, and contra distinctions; and yet thereby they are not angered. Thus do scholars, O King, discuss.'

'And how do kings discuss?'

'When a king, Your Majesty, discusses a matter, and he advances a point, if any one differ from him on that point, he is apt to fine him, saying: "Inflict such and such a punishment upon that fellow!" Thus, Your Majesty, do kings discuss.'

'Very well. It is as a scholar, not as a king, that I will discuss. Let Your Reverence talk unrestrainedly, as you would with a brother, or a novice, or a lay disciple, or even with a servant. Be not afraid!'

ORIGIN OF THE MAHĀYĀNA (ABOUT 78 A.D.).

14. At the opening of the Christian era the north-western part of India was invaded by the Turuṣkas or Scythians. Kaniṣka,[3] who was one of their chiefs, conquered Kāśmīra,

[1] Taken from Rhys Davids' translation of the Milinda-pañha called "the Questions of King Milinda" in S. B. E. series, vol. xxxv, pp. 6-7.

Nyāya is an equivalent for the original *Nīti, causation* for *Hetu, casuists* for *Lokāyata* and *sophists* for *Vitaṇḍa.*

Nīti may mean "polity," but placed between Yoga and Vaiśeṣika it cannot but signify *Nyāya.*

[2] Vide Rhys Davids' Questions of King Milinda in the S. B. E. series, vol. xxxv, p. 46.

[3] In the Tangyur, Mdo, vol. Gi, there is *Mahārāja-Kanika-lekha*, which is a letter addressed by Maticitra to King Kaniska. Hwen-thsang in the 7th Century A.D. records a prophecy of Buddha that 400 years after his nirvāṇa Kaniṣka would be born: *vide* Beal's Buddhist Records of the Western World, vol. I, p. 99. The same prophecy is mentioned by Fa-hian about 399 A.D., showing thereby that Kaniṣka was regarded as historical even at that time. According to Tibetan books such as the

Palhava and Delhi, and is said to have founded the era called *Śakābda* in 78 A.D. He accepted the Buddhist faith and established a new system of Buddhism called *Mahāyāna*,[1] the Great Vehicle. The old system of Buddhism as promulgated in the Pāli Tepiṭaka was henceforth nicknamed *Hīnayāna*, the Little Vehicle. The *Mahāyāna* gradually spread to Nepal, Tibet, Mongolia, China, Japan, Corea, etc., while the *Hīnayāna* continued in Ceylon and thence spread to Burmah, Siam, etc. In India both the systems prevailed.

ORIGIN OF THE SANSKRIT BUDDHIST LITERATURE (ABOUT 78 A.D.).

15. Under the patronage of Kaniṣka a council[2] was held at Jālandhara under the superintendence of Pārśva (or Pūrṇaka) and Vasu Mitra. It consisted of 500 monks who composed in Sanskrit three works explanatory of the Pāli *Tepiṭaka*, *viz.*, Sūtra Upadeśa of the Sutta Piṭaka, Vinaya Vibhāṣā of the Vinaya Piṭaka and Abhidharma Vibhāṣā of the Abhidhamma Piṭaka. These three works written in Sanskrit were the earliest canonical books of the Mahāyāna School.

16. It must not, however, be supposed that there had been no Buddhist books written in Sanskrit before Kaniṣka held his council. As a fact Kaniṣka thought it expedient to introduce Sanskrit as the medium of Buddhistic communication seeing that there had already existed many valuable Buddhist books in that language. For instance, the Abhidharma-vibhāṣā, or rather the Abhidharma-mahāvibhāṣā-śāstra, which was compiled

---

Sum-paḥi-choṣ-byuṅ, Kaniṣka flourished in 33 B.C., that is, 400 years after the nirvāṇa of Buddha which is said to have taken place in 433 B.C. Dr. J. F. Fleet holds that Kaniṣka founded the Vikrama era in 58 B.C. (*vide* Traditional Date of Kaniṣka in the Journal of the Royal Asiatic Society of Great Britain and Ireland, October 1906). Dr. R. G. Bhandarkar places Kaniṣka at the last quarter of the 3rd century A.D., as appears from "A peep into the early history of India" in the Journal of the Bombay Branch of the Royal Asiatic Society for 1897-98, p. 396. Vincent A. Smith places Kaniṣka in 125 A.D., while Sylvain Lévi assigns him an earlier date of 50 A.D. (*vide* J.R.A.S., January 1905, pp. 52-53). But Mr. Beal, Mr. Lassen, Professor Kern and others adopt the view that the Śaka era dates from Kaniṣka in 78 A.D.

1 *Vide* Takakusu's I-tsing, p. XXV; also Satis Chandra Vidyābhusana's Mahāyāna and Hīnayāna in the Journal of the Royal Asiatic Society of Great Britain and Ireland, January 1900.

2 An account of this council is given by Rai Sarat Chandra Das, C.I.E., in an article named "Some Historical facts connected with the rise and progress of Mahāyāna School of Buddhism, translated from the Sum-paḥi-choṣ-byuṅ" in the Journal of the Buddhist Text Society of Calcutta, vol. I, part III, p. 18. *Vide* also Watters' "On Yuan Chwang," vol I, p. 275; and also Monier Williams' Buddhism, pp. 68-69.

at the council of Kaniṣka was a mere commentary on Kātyāyani-putra's Abhidharma-jñāna-prasthāna-śāstra.[1] This last is a Sanskrit work explanatory of the Pāli Abhidhamma Piṭaka. It was composed 300 years after the nirvāṇa of Buddha or 100 years before the time of Kaniṣka. Though Kaniṣka was not thus the first founder of the Sanskrit Buddhist literature, it cannot but be acknowledged that it was he, who for the first time proclaimed Sanskrit as the language of the Buddhist Canon. Since his time there have been composed innumerable Buddhist works in Sanskrit of which nine called the *Nava Dharmas*[2] are specially worshipped by the Mahāyāna Buddhists.

Logic Mentioned in the Sanskrit Buddhist Literature.

17. None[3] of the works composed during or before the time of Kaniṣka has come down to us in its Sanskrit original, and I have had no opportunity of examining the Chinese or Tibetan version of the same. I cannot, therefore, say whether there is any mention of Logic in those works. But we have before us a very large collection of Sanskrit Buddhist works composed after the time of Kaniṣka. Many of these works, such as some of the *Nava Dharmas*, contain references to Logic, and several works are even replete with logical discussions.

The **Lalitavistara** (before 250 A.D.).

18. The **Lalitavistara**, which is one of the *Nava Dharmas*, was translated into Chinese in 221-263 A.D.[4] The Sanskrit original of it must have been prepared in India before that

---

[1] *Vide* Bunyiu Nanjio's Catalogue of the Chinese Tripiṭaka, nos. 1263, 1273 and 1275. Regarding the authorship of Abhidharma-mahāvibhāṣā, or simply Mahāvibhāṣā, *vide* Takakusu in the Journal of the Royal Asiatic Society of Great Britain and Ireland, January 1905, p. 159.

[2] The *Nava Dharmas* or Nine Sacred Works are :—

(1) Aṣṭa-sāhasrikā Prajñāpāramitā, (2) Gaṇḍa-vyūha, (3) Daśa-bhūmīśvara, (4) Samādhi-rāja, (5) Laṅkāvatāra, (6) Saddharma-puṇḍarīka, (7) Tathāgata-guhyaka, (8) Lalitavistara and (9) Suvarṇa-prabhāsa.

Vide Hodgson's Illustrations of the Literature and Religion of the Buddhists, p. 19.

[3] Dr. Rhys Davids in his Buddhist India, p. 316, observes that the three works composed at the Council of Kaniṣka are extant in European libraries.

[4] The Lalitavistara was translated into Chinese four times. The first and third translations were lost by 730 A.D. The first was prepared under the Han dynasty A.D. 221-263, the second under the Western Tsin dynasty A.D. 265-316, the third under the earlier Suṅ dynasty A.D. 420-479, and the fourth under the Thāṅ dynasty A.D. 683. *Vide* Bunyiu Nanjio's Catalogue of the Chinese Tripiṭaka, nos. 159 and 160.

time. In this work Logic, under the name of *Hetu-vidyā*,[1] is mentioned along with the Sāṁkhya, Yoga, Vaiśeṣika, etc., in all of which the Bodhisattva (Buddha Gautama) is said to have acquired distinction.

Eighteen Sects of the Buddhists.

19. In article 4 we have found that within 200 years after the *nirvāṇa* of Buddha there arose in India 17 heretical sects besides the orthodox priesthood called the Theras. In course of time some of these sects disappeared while new ones grew up, the result being that at the time of Kaniṣka, about 78 A.D., the Buddhists had already been divided into 18 sects[2] grouped into four classes as follows:—

I. Ārya Sarvāstivāda (1) Mūla Sarvāstivāda (2) Kāśyapīya (3) Mahiśāsaka (4) Dharma-guptīya (5) Bahuśrutīya (6) Tāmraśāṭīya (7) Vibhajyavādin II. Ārya Sammitīya (8) Kurukullaka (9) Āvantika (10) Vātsiputrīya	Belonging to the *Vaibhāṣika* School of Philosophy.
III. Ārya Mahāsāṁghika (11) Pūrva-śaila (12) Apara-śaila (13) Haimavata (14) Lokottaravādin (15) Prajñaptivādin IV. Ārya Sthavira (16) Mahāvihāra (17) Jetavanīya, and (18) Abhayagirivāsin.	Belonging to the *Sautrāntika* School of Philosophy.

All the sects mentioned above belonged to the *Hīnayāna* though later on they joined the *Mahāyāna* too.

---

1 निर्घण्टौ निगमे पुराणे इतिहासे वेदे व्याकरणे निरुक्ते शिक्षायां छन्दसि यज्ञकल्पे ज्योतिषि सांख्ये योगे क्रियाकल्पे वैशेषिके वैशिके अर्थविद्यायां बार्हस्पत्ये आश्चर्ये आसुरे मृगपक्षिरुते हेतुविद्यायां जतुयन्त्रे ...... सर्वत्र बोधिसत्त्व एव विशिष्यते स्म ॥

Lalitavistara, edited by Dr. Rājendra Lal Mitra in the Bibliotheca Indica series, Calcutta, Chapter XII, p. 179.

2 *Vide* the Journal of the Buddhist Text Society of Calcutta, vol. I,

FOUR SCHOOLS OF THE BUDDHIST PHILOSOPHY.

20. The philosophical views of the sects mentioned above were gradually formulated into two schools, *viz.*, the (1) *Vaibhāṣika* and (2) *Sautrāntika*. The Mahāyāna sect of the Buddhists founded by Kaniṣka established two other schools of philosophy, *viz.*, the (3) *Mādhyamika* and *Yogācāra*. So there were altogether four schools of philosophy, two of the *Hīnayāna* and two of the *Mahāyāna*.[1]

21. *Vaibhāṣika* was a later appellation of the philosophy of the Sarvāstivāda (Pali : Sabbatthivāda) sect[2] who, as their name implies, admitted the reality of the world—internal and external. The fundamental philosophical work of this sect is Kātyāyanī-putra's Abhidharmajñāna-prasthāna-śāstra,[3] or simply Jñāna-prasthāna-śāstra, composed 300 years after the *nirvāṇa* of Buddha. The next work of this sect is the Abhidharma-mahāvibhāṣā-śāstra[4] or simply Vibhāṣā, compiled at the council of Kaniṣka about 78 A.D. It is from this *Vibhāṣā* that the name *Vaibhāṣika*[5] was derived. *Vibhāṣā* means "commentary" and the *Vaibhāṣika* philosophy seems to have been so called because it was based on the commentaries rather than on the original texts of the teachings of Buddha. Saṅghabhadra's Nyāyānusāra-śāstra,[6] otherwise called Kosa-kāraka-śāstra, composed about 489 A.D.,[7] is a most learned work of the *Vaibhāṣika* philosophy.

---

part III, p. 18; Takakusu's I-tsing, pp. xxiii, xxiv and xxv; Rhys Davids' article in the Journal of the Royal Asiatic Society of Great Britain and Ireland, 1891, p. 411, and 1892, pp. 1-37; Rockhill's Buddha, p. 181 f; Tāranātha's Geschichte des Buddhismus von Schiefner, pp. 270-274; and Wijesiṁha's Mahāvaṁsa, part I, Chapter V, p. 15.

1 *Vide* Beal's Buddhist Records of the Western World, vol. I, pp. 121, 139 n; and Takakusu's I-tsing, p. xxii.

2 *Vide* Takakusu's I-tsing, p. xxi. The Ārya Saṁmitīyas, at any rate their subclass called the Vātsiputrīyas, were also followers of the Vaibhāṣika philosophy. The Hindu philosopher Vācaspati Miśra in his Nyāya vārtika-tātparyaṭikā 3-1-1 quotes the opinions of the Vaibhāṣikas who were called Vātsīputras.

3 This work exists in Chinese and Tibetan: *vide* Bunyiu Nanjio's Catalogue of the Chinese Tripiṭaka, nos. 1273, 1275.

4 This work, too, exists in Chinese and Tibetan: *vide* Bunyiu Nanjio's Catalogue of the Chinese Tripiṭaka, nos. 1263, 1264.

5 Compare the explanation of *Vaibhāṣika* given by the Hindu philosopher Mādhavācārya in his Sarvadarśana-saṁgraha, chapter on Bauddha-darśana, translated by Cowell and Gough, second edition, p. 24. *Vide* also Satis Chandra Vidyābhūṣana's "Mādhyamika School" in the Journal of the Buddhist Text Society of Calcutta for 1895, part II, p. 4.

6 This work exists in Chinese and Tibetan; *vide* Bunyiu Nanjio's Catalogue of the Chinese Tripitaka, no. 1265.

7 *Vide* Bunyiu Nanjio's Catalogue of the Chinese Tripitaka, Appendix II, no. 95. For Saṅgha-bhadra, *vide* also Hwen-thsang's Travel in Beal's Buddhist Records of the Western World, vol. I, pp. 193-194.

22. The name *Sautrāntika*[1] was derived from *Sūtrānta*, called in Pāli *Suttanta*, meaning "original text." The *Sautrāntika* philosophy seems to have been so called because it was based on the original text of the teachings of Buddha rather than on the commentaries thereon. The text on which the *Sautrāntika* philosophy was based belonged to the sect of Ārya Sthaviras, called in Pāli Theras, who held the First Council in 543 B.C., and possibly also to the sect of the Mahāsāṁghikas[2] who were the first dissenters in 443 B.C. The philosophical principles of this school are said to have been formulated in Kāśmīra[3] during the reign of Kaniṣka about 78 A.D. by a sage named Dharmottara or Uttara-dharma.[4] But the Chinese pilgrim Hwen-thsang, who visited India early in the 7th century A. D., states that the renowned teacher Kumāralabdha[5] of Takṣaśilā (Taxila in the Punjab) was the founder of the *Sautrāntika* school and wrote several very valuable treatises on it. He is supposed to have lived about 300 A.D. as he was a contemporary of Nāgārjuna (q. v.), Ārya Deva (q. v.) and Aśvaghoṣa. There was another very famous teacher named S'rilabdha[6] who wrote *Vibhāṣā-śāstra* (or commentary on a work) of the *Sautrāntika* school. Hwen-thsang saw in Ayodhyā the ruins of a Saṅghārāma where S'rilabdha resided.

Mention of Logic in the Works of these Schools.

23. As none of the old works belonging to the *Vaibhāṣika* or *Sautrāntika* school has yet become accessible to us, I cannot state whether there is any mention of Logic in those works. But there are ample references to Logic in the works of the *Mādhyamika* and *Yogācāra* schools, short accounts of which are given below.

---

1 Compare the explanation of the term *Sautrāntika* given by the Hindu philosopher Mādhavācārya in the Sarvadarśana-saṁgraha, chapter on Bauddha-darśana, translated by Cowell and Gough, second edition, p. 26. *Vide* also Satis Chandra Vidyābhūsana's "Mādhyamika School" in the Journal of the Buddhist Text Society of Calcutta for 1895, part II, p. 4.

Vide Rhys Davids' Buddhist India, p. 168, and Beal's Fahian and Sungyun, p. 143.

2 *Vide* Watters "On Yuan Chwang," vol. II, p. 161.

3 *Vide* the Journal of the Buddhist Text Society of Calcutta, vol. I, part III, pp. 18, 19; and Tārānātha's Geschichte des Buddhismus von Schiefner, p. 59.

4 For the Dhammuttariya sect, *vide* Wassilief's Buddhism, p. 233; and Mahāvaṁsa, part I, chapter V, p. 15, Wijesiṁha's foot-note.

5 *Vide* Beal's Buddhist Records of the Western World, vol. II, p. 302; and Tārānātha's Geschichte des Buddhismus von Schiefner, p. 78, where Kumāra-lābha stands for Kumāra-labdha.

6 *Vide* Beal's Buddhist Records of the Western World, vol. I, pp. 225, 226; and Tārānātha's Geschichte des Buddhismus von Schiefner, p. 67.

Ārya Nāgārjuna (about 300 A.D.).

24. The name *Mādhyamika* was derived from *madhyama*, meaning the middle. The *Mādhyamika* philosophy was so called because it avoided two extremes, *i.e.*, advocated neither the theory of absolute reality, nor that of total unreality, of the world, but chose a *middle path*,[1] inculcating that the world had only a conditional existence. The founder of this school was Nāgārjuna or rather Ārya Nāgārjuna, who was born at Vidarbha (modern Berar) in Mahākośala,[2] during the reign of King Sadvāha or Sātavāha[3] [of the Andhra dynasty].[4] He passed many of his days in meditation in a cave-dwelling of the S'rī-parvata,[5] that bordered on the river Krishnā. He was a pupil of S'araha and is said to have converted a powerful king, named Bhoja Deva,[6] to Buddhism.

---

[1] Compare—

अतो भावाभावान्तद्वयरहितत्वात् सर्वस्वभावानुत्पत्तिलक्षणा शून्यता मध्यमा प्रतिपन्मध्यमो मार्ग इत्युच्यते ॥

——Mādhyamikā Vṛtti published by the Buddhist Text Society of Calcutta, chapter XXIV, p. 185.

Compare the explanation of the term *Mādhyamika* given by the Hindu philosopher Mādhavācārya, in the Sarvadarśana-saṁgraha, chapter on Bauddha darśana, translated by Cowell and Gough, second edition, p. 24; and also Satis Chandra Vidyabhusana's History of the Mādhyamika Philosophy of Nāgārjuna in the Journal of the Buddhist Text Society of Calcutta, 1897, part IV, pp. 7-20.

[2] *Vide* Hwen-thsang's Travel in Beal's Buddhist Records of the Western World, vol. II, Book VIII, p. 97, and Book X, p. 210; Watters' "On Yuan Chwang," vol. II, pp. 201-202; and Wassiljew quoted by Schiefner in the Geschichte des Buddhismus, p. 301.

[3] Sadvāha is the same as Sātavāha, which is a general name of the kings of the Andhra dynasty.—*Vide* Dr. R. G. Bhandarkar's Early History of the Dekkan, second edition, pp. 25-37.

Nāgārjuna wrote an instructive letter to Sātavāha[na], whose private name in Chinese was Sh'-yen-töh-cia. This letter is called Ārya Nāgārjuna Bodhisattva Suhṛllekha. It was translated into Chinese in 434 A.D. An English translation of this letter has appeared in the Journal of the Pali Text Society of London, 1883, pp. 71-75.

[4] The Andhra kings ruled the northern portion of the Madras Presidency and the whole of Kaliṅga, and overthrew the Kanva dynasty in northern India about 31 B.C. They remained powerful up to 436 A.D. They were Buddhists, and it was by them that the magnificent marble stūpa at Amarāvatī was erected.—*Vide* Sewell's Lists of Antiquities in Madras, vol. II. pp. 141-146.

[5] For an account of S'rī-parvata or S'rī-śaila see Hwen-thsang's Life, Introduction, p. xi, by Beal; Tārānātha's Geschichte des Buddhismus von Schiefner, p. 84; Wilson's Mālatī-Mādhava, act I; and Satis Chandra Vidyabhusana's Notes on Ratnāvalī, pp. 27-29.

[6] *Vide* Tārānātha's Geschichte des Buddhismus von Schiefner, pp. 66, 69-73.

25. Nāgārjuna is said to have lived four hundred years[1] after the *nirvāṇa* of Buddha, that is, in 33 B.C. But he does not appear to me to have so early a date as he was one of the early patrons or founders of the university of Nālandā,[2] which had not, perhaps, come into existence in the 1st century B.C., and was insignificant[3] even at 399 A.D., when the Chinese pilgrim Fa-hian came to visit India. Nāgārjuna is stated by Lama Tārānātha to have been a contemporary of King Nemi Candra, who is supposed to have reigned about 300 A.D.[4] The

---

[1] It is prophesied in the Mañju-śrī-mūla-tantra (called in Tibetan Ḥjam-ḍpal-ṛtsa-ṛgyuḍ) that :—

དེ་བཞིན་གཤེགས་པ་ང་འདས་ནས།
ལོ་ནི་བཞི་བརྒྱ་ལོན་པ་ན།
དགེ་སློང་ཀླུ་ཞེས་དེ་ཙ་བོད་འབྱུང་།
བསྟན་པ་ལ་ནི་དད་ཅིང་ཕན།།

(Quoted in the Introduction to Śeṣ-rab-ṣdoṅ-bu published in Calcutta).

"Four hundred years after Buddha's departure from the world there will appear a Bhikṣu, named Nāgārjuna, who will do good to the believers in the doctrine."

It should be noted that according to some books of Tibet, Buddha was born in 514 B.C., lived 81 years and attained *nirvāṇa* in 433 B.C. Nāgārjuna, who was born 400 years after the *nirvāṇa*, must, at this calculation, be placed in 33 B.C.

[2] *Vide* Tārānātha's Geschichte des Buddhismus von Schiefner, pp. 66, 69-73.

[3] Fahian describes Nālandā as a mere village Nā-lo: *vide* Beal's Travels of Fahian and Sungyun, p. 111.

[4] According to Lama Tārānātha, Nāgārjuna was a contemporary of King Nemi Candra, whose genealogy is thus traced :—

Akṣa Candra
|
Jaya Candra
|
Nemi Candra
} Ruled in Aparāntaka.

Phaṇi Candra
|
Bhaṁśa Candra
|
Śāla Candra
|
Candra Gupta
} Ruled in Magadha.

The six kings, beginning with Akṣa Candra to Śāla Candra, are stated to have been weak and insignificant, while Candra Gupta, the seventh king,

latest date that can be assigned to Nāgārjuna is 401 A.D.,[1] when his biography was translated into Chinese by Kumārajīva.

26. Nāgārjuna's **Mādhyamika-kārikā** is the first work of the *Mādhyamika* philosophy. In it he has occasionally referred to certain technicalities of Logic, such as the fallacy of *Sādhya-sama*[2] (*petitio principii*) in chapter IV. He was the author of several other works[3] on the *Mādhyamika* philosophy, such as the (1) **Yukti-ṣaṣṭikā kārikā** or sixty memorial verses on argumentation, (2) **Vigraha-vyavartanī kārikā**, or memorial verses on conquering disputes, and (3) **Vigraha-vyavartanī vṛtti** or a commentary on the Vigraha-vyavartanī kārikā.[4] In these works he has, as the titles indicate, largely employed the methods of Logic[5] to establish the abstruse conclusions of the *Mādhyamika* philosophy.

Ārya Deva (about 320 A.D.).

27. Deva[6] or rather Ārya Deva was the next writer on the *Mādhyamika* philosophy. He is otherwise known as Karṇaripa,

---

is described as having been very powerful. This Candra Gupta, who "did not take refuge in Buddha," may be the same who founded the Gupta era in 319 A.D. The reigns of his predecessors were very short. Nemi Candra may be assigned to about 300 A.D.—Cf. Tārānātha's Geschichte des Buddhismus von Schiefner, pp. 80-83.

[1] *Vide* Bunyiu Nanjio's Catalogue of the Chinese Tripiṭaka, Appendix I, No. 3.

[2] The Mādhyamika-kārikā with the vṛtti of Candra Kīrti has been published by the Buddhist Text Society of Calcutta; the work is being republished in the St. Petersburg Buddhist Text series under the editorship of Professor De La Vallee Poussin. The following verse refers to the fallacy of *Sādhyasama*:—

विग्रहे यः परीहारं कृते शून्यतया वदेत् ।
सर्वं तस्यापरिहृतं समं साध्येन जायते ॥

(Mādhyamika-kārikā, chapter IV).

[3] For an account of some of the works on the Tantra by Nāgārjuna, *vide* Satis Chandra Vidyabhusana's Introduction to the Sragdharā-stotra in the "Bibliotheca Indica" series. For the latest researches in the medical works of Nāgārjuna, see Dr. Palmyr Cordier's "Introduction A L'Etude des Traites Medicaux Sanscritas" printed in Hanoi, 1903; and for his hymns such as **धर्मधातुस्तव, निरुपमस्तव** etc., *vide* Tangyur, Bstod-pa, vol. *Ka*.

[4] For an account of these works, *vide* the article "Indian Logic as preserved in Tibet, No. 3," by Satis Chandra Vidyabhusana in the Journal of the Asiatic Society of Bengal, new series, vol. III, No. 7, 1907. For the philosophical works of Nāgārjuna, see Bunyiu Nanjio's Catalogue of the Chinese Tripitaka, Appendix I, no. 3.

[5] The Nyāya-dvāra-tarka-śāstra, as noticed in Bunyiu Nanjio's Catalogue of the Chinese Tripiṭaka, Nos. 1223, 1224, is not a work of Nāgārjuna but of Dignāga.

[6] *Vide* Bunyiu Nanjio's Catalogue of the Chinese Tripiṭaka, Appendix

Kāṇa Deva, Nīla-netra and Piṅgala-netra. He was born in Southern India and was an eminent disciple of Nāgārjuna. According to Hwen-thsang,[1] he visited the countries of Mahākośala, Srughna, Prayāga, Coḷa and Vaiśālī, in all of which he won great renown by defeating the Tīrthikas and preaching the true doctrines of Buddha. According to Lama Tārānātha,[2] Deva resided for a long time in Nālandā, where he was a Paṇḍita. He flourished during the reign of Candra Gupta, whose date is supposed to be about 320 A.D.[3] The latest date that can be assigned to Deva is 401 A.D.,[4] when his biography was translated into Chinese by Kumārajīva. He wrote numerous works on the *Mādhyamika* philosophy, such as the **Śataka-śāstra, Bhrama-pramathana-yukti-hetu-siddhi,**[5] etc., all of which bear evidences of his knowledge of Logic.

LOGIC OF THE YOGĀCĀRA SCHOOL (ABOUT 300-500 A.D.).

28. The word *Yogācāra* is compounded of *yoga* meaning 'meditation' and *ācāra* meaning 'practice.' The *Yogācāra*[6] or the contemplative system was so called because it emphasised the practice of meditation as means of attaining *Bhūmis*[7] or the seventeen stages of Buddhistic Perfection. The chief dogma established in it is *ālaya-vijñāna*,[8] the basis of conscious states,

I, No. 4; and Watters' "On Yuan Chwang," vol. I, p. 321, vol. II, pp. 225-226.

[1] *Vide* Beal's Buddhist Records of the Western World, vol. I, Book IV, pp. 186-190, Book V, p. 231; vol. II, Book X, pp. 210, 227, Book XII, p. 302, Book VIII, pp. 98-102.

[2] *Vide* Lama Tārānātha's Geschichte des Buddhismus von Schiefner, pp. 83-86 and 93.

[3] *Vide* foot-note 4, p. 69.

[4] *Vide* Bunyiu Nanjio's Catalogue of the Chinese Tripiṭaka, Appendix I, No. 4.

[5] *Vide* Satis Chandra Vidyabhūsana's "Indian Logic as preserved in Tibet No. 3" in the Journal of the Asiatic Society of Bengal, new series, vol. III, No. 7, 1907.

[6] The *Yogācāra* philosophy is generally known in China, Tibet and Nepal as *Yogācārya*. For an account of this system, *vide* Watters' "On Yuan Chwang," vol. I, p. 356; Dr. Schlagintweit's Buddhism quoted in the Journal of the Buddhist Text Society of Calcutta for 1895, part II, Appendix IV.

Compare explanation of the word *Yogācāra* given by the Hindu Philosopher Mādhavācārya in the Sarvadarśana-saṁgraha, chapter on Bauddha darśana, translated by Cowell and Gough, second edition, p. 24. *Vide* also Satis Chandra Vidyabhusana's "The Mādhyamika School" in the Journal of the Buddhist Text Society of Calcutta, 1895, part II, p. 4.

[7] *Vide* Dharma-saṁgraha, LXIV and LXV, edited by Max Müller and Wenzel.

[8] For an explanation of *ālaya-vijñāna*, see Satis Chandra Vidyabhusana's note on p. 2 of the Laṅkāvatāra Sūtra, Calcutta Buddhist Text Society's edition, and also see p. 45 of the same work.

which is the same as our 'ego' or 'soul.' It is not known who was the founder of the *Yogācāra* school, but in the Tibetan and Chinese books the Laṅkāvatāra Sūtra, Mahāsamaya Sūtra, Bodhisattva-caryā-nirdeśa and the Sapta-daśabhūmi-śāstra-yogācārya have been named as the prominent old works of the system.[1]

THE Laṅkāvatāra Sūtra (ABOUT 300 A.D.).

29. The Laṅkāvatāra Sūtra[2] is a very sacred work as it is one of the *Nava Dharmas.* The exact date of it is unknown, beyond the fact that it was translated into Chinese in 443 A.D.[3] The approximate date seems to be 300 A.D., for, it existed at or before the time of Ārya Deva who mentions it.[4] This work speaks in a prophetic style of the *Naiyāyikas* (dialecticians) and *Tārkikas* (logicians). Thus in chapter II of the work Mahāmati asks Buddha :—

"Say how in the time to come *Naiyāyikas* will flourish ?"[5]

---

1 *Vide* Section Mdo of the Tangyur ; Lama Tārānātha's Geschichte des Buddhismus von Schiefner, p. 111 f ; Bunyiu Nanjio's Catalogue of the Chinese Tripitaka, Appendix I, No. 1; Beal's Buddhist Records of the Western World, vol. I, p. 226, vol. II, pp. 220, 275 ; and Watters' "On Yuan Chwang," vol. I, p. 371.

2 The Sanskrit original of this work is being published by the Buddhist Text Society of Calcutta under the editorship of Rai Sarat Chandra Das, C.I.E., and Dr. Satis Chandra Vidyabhusana. The work also exists in Chinese and Tibetan. Hwen-thsang mentions the Laṅkāvatāra, *vide* Beal's Buddhist Records of the Western World, Book XI, p. 251.

Vide an account of the Laṅkāvatāra Sūtra by Satis Chandra Vidyabhusana in the Journal of the Royal Asiatic Society of Great Britain and Ireland, 1906.

3 *Vide* Bunyiu Nanjio's Catologue of the Chinese Tripiṭaka, nos. 175, 176 and 177.

4 *Vide* Bunyiu Nanjio's Catalogue of the Chinese Tripiṭaka, nos. 1259, 1260 and Appendix I, no. 4.

5 The Sanskrit original runs as follows :—

नैयायिकाः कथं ब्रूहि भविष्यन्ति अनागताः ।

(Laṅkāvatāra Sūtra, Asiatic Society of Bengal's MSS., chapter II, leaf 11).

The Tibetan version runs thus :—

སྨྲེ་བ་རྣམས་ཀྱང་ཇི་ལྟ་བུར།

མ་འོངས་དུས་ན་འབྱུང་བ་གསུངས།།

(Kangyur, Mdo, vol. V, Asiatic Society of Bengal's xylograph).

" How is *tarka* (reasoning or argumentation) corrected, and how is it carried on ?"[1]

Again in chapter X of the work we read :—

" Whatever is produced is destructible : this is the conclusion of the *Tārkikas*."[2]

MAITREYA (ABOUT 400 A.D.).

30. The date of the Mahāsamaya-sūtra [3] is not known. The Bodhisattva-caryā-nirdeśa was translated into Chinese during 414-421 A.D. and the Sapta-daśa-bhūmi-śāstra-yogācārya in 646-647 A.D. The author of these two works was Maitreya [4] (called in Chinese ' Mirok '), who lived 900 years after the nirvāṇa of Buddha, that is about 400 A.D.[5] He is reported by Hwen-thsang to have communicated the materials of three Buddhist treatises to Ārya Asaṅga while the latter was residing in a monastery in Ayodhyā.[6] In the **Sapta-daśa-bhūmi-śāstra-yogācārya** [7] Maitreya has discussed certain topics of Logic, a

---

1 कथं हि शुध्यते तर्कः कथं तर्कः प्रवर्तते ।

(Laṅkāvatāra Sūtra, chapter II, leaf 11, A.S.B. MSS.)

ཇི་ལྟར་རྟོག་གེ་རྣམ་དག་འགྱུར།
རྟོག་གེ་ཅི་ཡི་སླད་དུ་འབྱུང་།།

(Kangyur, Mdo, vol. V.)

2 कृतकस्य विनाशः स्यात् तार्किकाणामयं नयः ।

(Laṅkāvatāra Sūtra, chapter X, leaf 143, A.S.B. MSS.)

བྱས་ན་རྣམ་པར་འཇིག་པར་འགྱུར།།
འདི་ནི་རྟོག་གེ་ཅན་གྱི་ཚུལ།།

(Kangyur, Mdo, vol. V.)

3 *Vide* Dr. Schlagintweit's Buddhism quoted in the Journal of the Buddhist Text Society of Calcutta, 1895, part II, Appendix IV, p. 16.

4 *Vide* Bunyiu Nanjio's Catalogue of the Chinese Tripiṭaka, Appendix I, No. 1.

5 *Vide* " Hindu Logic as preserved in China and Japan," by Dr. Sugiura, p. 30.

6 *Vide* Watters' " On Yuan Chwang," Vol. I, pp. 355—56. The three treatises are :—Saptadaśabhūmiśāstra-yogācārya, Sūtrālaṅkāraṭīkā and Madhyānta vibhāga śāstra.

7 It is perhaps this work which is called *Yoga* by Dr. Sugiura, *vide* its Chinese version Yuka Ron, Book XV.

short account of which is given below from the researches of Dr. Sugiura.[1]

31. Maitreya mainly discussed the practical questions of Logic as is evident from the titles of some of the chapters of his work, *viz.*: (1) Of Kinds of Debate, (2) Of Occasions of Debate, (3) Of the Attributes of the Debator, (4) Of Defeat, etc. But occasionally there was mixed in with the discussions some Pure Logic too. A thesis [*pratijñā*], according to Maitreya, is to be supported by a reason [*hetu*] and two examples [*dṛṣṭānta*]. Validity of the reason and of the examples requires that they be based either (1) on fact [*pratyakṣa*], (2) on another inference [*anumāna*], or (3) on holy saying [*āgama*]. Analogy or Comparison [*upamāna*] is omitted. The form of reasoning is illustrated as follows :—

1. Sound is non-eternal,
2. Because it is a product,
3. Like a pot, but not like ether [*ākāśa*],
4. A product like a pot is non-eternal,
5. Whereas, an eternal thing like ether is not a product.

Ārya Asaṅga (about 450 A.D.).

32. Asaṅga,[2] called in Chinese Mucak, was born in Gāndhāra (modern Peshwar). He was at first an adherent of the Mahīśāsaka[3] sect and followed the *Vaibhāṣika* philosophy of the *Hīnayāna*. Later on he became a disciple of Maitreya and adopted the *Yogācāra* philosophy of the *Mahāyāna*. He is said to have lived for some years as a paṇḍita in Nālandā.[4] He lived about 450 A.D.[5] The latest date that can be assigned to him is 531 A.D.,[6] when one of his works, called the Mahāyāna-samparigraha-śāstra, was translated into Chinese. Hwen-thsang in the 7th century A.D. saw the ruins of *Saṅghārāmas* in Kauśāmbi and Ayodhyā, where Asaṅga resided for some years.[7] He wrote 12 works, most of which still exist in Chinese and Tibetan versions.[8]

---

[1] *Vide* "Hindu Logic as preserved in China and Japan," p. 30.

[2] *Vide* Hwen-thsang's Travel in Beal's Buddhist Records of the Western World, Vol. I, pp. 98, 227 and 236.

[3] *Vide* Watters' "On Yuan Chwang," Vol. I, p. 357.

[4] *Vide* Tārānātha's Geschichte des Buddhismus von Schiefner, p. 122.

[5] Asaṅga is approximately placed at 450 A.D. as he was the eldest brother of Vasubandhu (q.v.) who lived about 480 A.D.

[6] *Vide* Bunyiu Nanjio's Catalogue of the Chinese Tripiṭaka, Appendix I, No. 5.

[7] *See* Beal's Buddhist Records, Vol. I, pp. 98, 227, 236.

[8] *Vide* Bunyiu Nanjio's Catalogue of the Chinese Tripiṭaka, Appendix I, no. 5.

33. Dr. Sugiura [1] has ascertained from Chinese sources that Asaṅga treated Logic in the tenth volume of Genyo, in which he simply reproduced the conclusions of his master Maitreya, and also in the sixteen volumes of Zaschuh, in which he showed a slight originality. Asaṅga's form of reasoning, which is somewhat different from Maitreya's, is given below :—

1. Sound is non-eternal,
2. Because it is a product,
3. Like a pot (but not like ether) ;
4. Because a pot is a product it is non-eternal ; so is sound, as it is a product :
5. Therefore we know sound is non-eternal.

Here we find that Asaṅga made some improvement on the form of syllogism adopted in the Logic of his master. The basis of Maitreya's inference, so far as it related to the connection between "produced-ness" and "non-eternality," was a mere analogy founded upon a single instance. This connection (between "produced-ness" and "non-eternality" in the case of the pot) might be accidental. Asaṅga emphasised the essential connection between "produced-ness" and "non-eternality" by saying "Because a pot is a product, it is non-eternal." In so doing he appealed not merely to an instance but to a *law*.

VASUBANDHU (ABOUT 480 A.D.).

34. Vasubandhu,[2] called in Chinese Seish, was born in Gāndhāra (modern Peshwar), where a tablet to his memory was seen by Hwen-thsang in the 7th century A.D. His father's name was Kauśika. He began his career as a *Vaibhāṣika* philosopher of the Sarvāstivāda sect, but was later converted by his eldest brother Asaṅga to the *Yogācāra* school of the *Mahāyāna*. He passed many years of his life in Śākala, Kauśāmbi and Ayodhyā, in the last of which places he died at the age of eighty years. He was a friend of Manoratha, a master of the Vaibhāṣika Śāstra, who flourished in the middle of the thousand years after the *nirvāṇa* of Buddha, that is before 500 A.D. He was a contemporary of another *Vaibhāṣika*

The original Sanskrit text of Asaṅga's Vajracchedikā has been published in the Anecdota Oxoniensia edited by Professor Max Müller.

[1] *Vide* "Hindu Logic as preserved in China and Japan" by Dr. Sugiura, p. 31.

[2] *Vide* Hwen-thsang's Travel in Beal's Buddhist Records of the Western World, Vol. I, pp. 98, 105, 172, 193, 225, 236; and Watters' "On Yuan Chwang," Vol. I, p. 210.

teacher, named Saṅghabhadra, who lived about 489 A.D.[1] So we may approximately fix the date of Vasubandhu at about 480 A.D. His biography[2] was translated from Sanskrit into Chinese during 557-569 A.D. Vasubandhu was the author of a large number of very valuable works[3] including the **Tarka-śāstra**, which consists of three chapters and is perhaps the first regular Buddhist work on Logic. This work was translated into Chinese in 550 A.D. The Chinese version still exists, while the Sanskrit original has been long lost. The work appears to have been translated into Tibetan too, but my persistent efforts to discover the Tibetan version were unsuccessful.

35. Dr. Sugiura[4] from Chinese sources has ascertained that in the 7th century A.D., while Hwen-thsang was in India, he saw three other books on Logic attributed to Vasubandhu, which are called in Chinese **Ronki**, **Ronshiki** and **Ronshin**, respectively. In the Ronki, quoted by Kwei-ke, Vasubandhu maintained that a thesis can be proved by two propositions only, and that, therefore, the necessary parts in a syllogistic inference are only three[5] (i.e. *pakṣa* or minor term, *sādhya* or major term

---

[1] Saṅghabhadra translated Vibhāṣā-vinaya into Chinese in 489 A.D. *Vide* Bunyiu Nanjio's Catalogue of the Chinese Tripiṭaka, Appendix II, No. 95.

Mr. Takakusu, in a very learned article on Paramārtha's Life of Vasubandhu and the date of Vasubandhu published in the Journal of the Royal Asiatic Society of Great Britain and Ireland, January 1905, says that Saṅghabhadra, contemporary of Vasubandhu, was the translator of the Samantapāsādikā of Buddhaghoṣa into Chinese in 488 A.D.

[2] *Vide* Bunyiu Nanjio's Catalogue of the Chinese Tripiṭaka, Appendix I, No. 6. The statement that there was an older translation of the life of Vasubandhu by Kumārajīva A.D. 401-409 but that it was lost in 730 A.D., cannot be accepted without further testimony. Takakusu says that "some Catalogues mention by mistake that such a work was then in existence": *vide* Journal of the Royal Asiatc Society of Great Britain and Ireland, January 1905, p. 39.

[3] *Vide* Bunyiu Nanjio's Catalogue of the Chinese Tripiṭaka, Appendix I, No. 6.

[4] *Vide* Dr. Sugiura's "Hindu Logic as preserved in China and Japan," p. 32.

[5] The Jaina logician Siddhasena Divākara probably refers to Vasubandhu, when he says that according to some logicians *antarvyāpti* (internal inseparable connection) consisting of *pakṣa* or minor term, *sādhya* or major term and *hetu* or middle term is quite enough in establishing a thesis, and that dṛṣṭānta or example is altogether useless. Siddhasena Divākara writes:—

अन्तर्व्याप्त्यैव साध्यस्य सिद्धेर्बहिरुदाहृतिः ।
व्यर्था स्यात्तदसद्भावेऽप्येवं न्यायविदो विदुः ॥ २० ॥

(Nyāyāvatāra of Siddhasena Divākara, edited by Satis Chandra Vidyabhusana and published by the Indian Research Society of Calcutta).

and *hetu* or middle term). But it is to be regretted that these three logical works are lost, and we cannot know how far the theory of syllogism was developed in them. The work in Chinese from which alone we can know anything of his Logic is his polemic against heresies (**Nyojits-ron**).[1] In this book he gives the following form of reasoning :—

1. Sound is non-eternal,
2. Because it is a product of a cause,
3. Things produced by a cause are non-eternal like a pot, which is produced by a cause and is non-eternal ;
4. Sound is an instance of this (kind),
5. Therefore sound is non-eternal.

---

[1] Is this the same work as the Tarka-śāstra already referred to ?

CHAPTER II.

SYSTEMATIC BUDDHIST WRITERS ON LOGIC (500—1200 A.D.).

LOGIC DISTINGUISHED FROM PHILOSOPHY.

36. In the previous chapter we have seen that from the origin of Buddhism in the 6th century B.C. to its expansion into four philosophical schools in the 4th century A.D., there were no systematic Buddhist works on Logic, but only a few stray references to that science in the works on philosophy and religion. During 400—500 A.D., Maitreya, Asaṅga and Vasubandhu handled Logic, but their treatment of it was merely incidental, being mixed up with the problems of the *Yogācāra* and *Vaibhāṣika* schools of philosophy. Vasubandhu's three works [1] on Pure Logic mentioned by Hwen-thsang are now lost and consequently their merits cannot be judged. With 500 A.D. began a period when Logic was completely differentiated from general philosophy, and a large number of Buddhist writers gave their undivided attention to that branch of learning. Dignāga is the earliest known writer of this period.

37. ĀCĀRYA DIGNĀGA—FATHER OF MEDIÆVAL LOGIC.

[Flourished in Andhra, modern Teliṅgāna in the Madras Presidency, about 500 A.D.]

The likeness of Dignāga reproduced in the next page is taken from the Tibetan Tangyur (M̱do, Ce, folio 1) which was put in its present form by the celebrated Lama Bu-ṣton, who passed the last days of his life at the monastery of Sha-lu, twelve miles south-east of Tashi-lhun-po. Bu-ṣton, who lived early in the fourteenth century A.D.,[2] must have copied the likeness from some earlier specimen, which was taken to Tibet during her intercourse with India between 600 A.D. and 1200 A.D.

A peculiarity of this likeness is its cap. In the early Buddhist Church monks were not allowed to wear any head-dress (*vide* the Pātimokkha rules of the Vinaya Piṭaka). With the introduction of Mahāyāna in the first century A.D. by Kaniṣka, a great change was effected in the dress of monks, and caps of various shapes were invented. The hat worn here is called Panchen-shwa-ḏmar [3] or "Paṇḍita's red cap," with a pointed

---

[1] *Vide* Book II, Chapter I, under the head "Vasubandhu."
[2] *Vide* Sarat Chandra Das's Tibetan Dictionary, p. 870.
[3] *Vide* Waddell's Lamaism, pp. 194—196.

peak and long lappets. The lappets of the cap were lengthened in proportion to the rank of the wearer.

It is not known when the "Paṇḍita's cap" was first introduced. It is said to have been taken to Tibet in 749 A.D. by S'ānta Rakṣita. "Paṇḍita" was a degree which was conferred by the Vikramaśilā University on its successful candidates. It is not known what title the University

བསྟན་འགྱུར་མདོ་ཆེ་གཅིག།

སློབ་དཔོན་ཕྱོགས་གླང་ལ་ན་མོ།།

versity of Nālandā conferred on its distinguished students. Perhaps in that university, too, the title "Paṇḍita" was recognised, and "Paṇḍita's cap" was possibly a distinctive badge of the scholars of that famous university where Dignāga distinguished himself in philosophical controversies.

The woollen *shawl* worn here is indicative of the fact that after Buddhism had spread into cold climes, monks like Brahmanic sages were allowed to put on suitable warm clothes. There is also in the palms of the image a thunderbolt called in Sanskrit *Vajra* and in Tibetan *Dorje*, which is a remover of all evils. The halo round the head of the image indicates that Dignāga was a saint.

Life of Dignāga (about 500 A.D.).

38. Dignāga or rather Ācārya Dignāga is called in Tibetan Phyogs-glaṅ. He[1] was born in a Brāhmaṇa family in Siṁhavaktra near Kāñcī, modern Conjeeveram in the Madras Presidency. By Nāgadatta, a Paṇḍita of the Vātsīputrīya sect, he was admitted to the religious system of that sect and attained erudition in the *Tripiṭaka* of the *Hīnayāna*. Afterwards he became a disciple of Ācārya Vasubandhu with whom he studied all the Piṭakas of the *Mahāyāna* and *Hīnayāna*. He miraculously saw the face of Mañjuśrī, the Buddhist god of learning, from whom he received inspiration in the Law (Dharma). A few years later he was invited to Nālandā (*Vide* appendix A) where he defeated Brāhmaṇa Sudurjaya and other Tīrtha dialecticians and won them to the doctrine of Buddha. Since he had refuted chiefly the Tīrtha controversialists he was called the "Bull in discussion" (Sanskrit: Tarkapuṅgava, and Tibetan: Ṛtsod-pahi-khyu-mchog). He travelled through Orissa and Mahārāṣṭra to the south, meeting the Tīrtha controversialists in discussions. At Mahārāṣṭra he is said to have resided frequently in the Ācāra's Monastery.[2] At Orissa he converted Bhadra Pālita, Treasury-minister of the king of the country, to Buddhism. He was a man of vast learning and wisdom, and practised during his life-time twelve tested virtues. He is said to have died in a solitary wood in Orissa.

39. Dignāga must have lived before 557—569 A.D.[3] when two of his works were translated into Chinese. The early limit

---

1 This account of Dignāga is taken from Lama Tārānātha's Geschichte des Buddhismus von Schiefner, pp. 130—135. Lama Tārānātha also relates that Dignāga frequently resided in Orissa in a cavern of a mountain called Bhoraśilā where he used to give himself up to contemplation. He was specially versed in incantation formulas. It is stated that the stem of a myrobalan tree called Muṣṭiharītakī in the garden of Bhadra Pālita in Orissa entirely withered, but it revived in seven days after Dignāga had uttered incantation for its restoration. For a fuller account of Dignāga *vide* Satis Chandra Vidyabhusana's "Dignāga and his Pramāṇa-samuccaya" in the Journal of the Asiatic Society of Bengal, Vol I, No. 9, 1905.

2 *Vide* Watters' On Yuan Chwang, Vol. II, p. 122.

3 *Vide* Bynyiu Nanjio's Catalogue of the Chinese Tripiṭaka, App. 1, No. 10, where Dignāga is called Jina. The Chinese name of Dignāga has been wrongly rendered as Jina by Japanese writers as well as Rev. Beal.

of his date in 480 A.D. when his teacher Vasubandhu lived. Dignāga flourished possibly about 500 A.D. when the Buddhist kings of the Pallava [1] dynasty ruled the eastern coast of Southern India.

40. We have already seen that Dignāga travelled in Nālandā, Orissa, Mahārāṣṭra and Dakṣiṇa (Madras) entering everywhere into disputes with controversialists. He attacked his opponents as frequently as he was attacked by them. His whole life was passed in giving blows and receiving counter-blows. On account of this love of discussion he was, during his life-time, called the "Bull in discussion" (*Tarka-puṅgava*).[2] Even his death did not terminate the great intellectual war in which he had been engaged: though he could no longer offer any violence, his opponents continued to fall upon him with force. Mark the volleys on his dead body coming from no mean warriors! Kālidāsa,[3] the prince of poets, warns his poem to avoid the "rugged hand" (*sthūla-hasta*) of Dignāga. Udyotakara,[4] the eminent logician, calls Dignāga "a quibbler" (*Kutārkika*). Vācaspati Miśra [5] describes him as "an erring one" (*bhrānta*) and speaks of his "blunders" (*bhrānti*). Mallinātha [6] compares him with a "rock" (*adrikalpa*). Kumārila Bhaṭṭa and Pārtha-sārathi Miśra [7] turn their arrows against him. The

---

1 On the downfall of the Andhras in 436 A.D., the Pallavas rose to power. They were in their turn driven out of their northern possessions, the kingdom of Veṅgi, by Kubja Viṣṇuvardhana of the Eastern Chalukya dynasty. During 552—580 A.D., Kāñcī, the capital of the Pallava kings, was captured by Vikramāditya I. of the Western Chalukya dynasty. *Vide* Sewell's Lists of Antiquities, Madras, Vol. II, pp. 141,146,148, 149 and 211, 212.

2 *Vide* Lama Tārānātha's Geschichte des Buddhismus von Schiefner, p. 134.

3 *Vide* Meghadūta, Pūrva-megha, verse 14.

4 यदक्षपादः प्रवरो मुनीनां
शमाय शास्त्रं जगतो जगाद ।
कुतार्किकाज्ञाननिवृत्तिहेतुः
करिष्यते तस्य मया निबन्धः ॥

Udyotakara's Nyāya-vārtika, Introductory stanza, p. 1, in the Bibliotheca Indica series. Compare also Nyāya-vārtika, 1-1-4, pp. 43—44; 1-1-5, p. 52; 1-1-6, pp. 60—61; 1-1-7, p. 63, etc.

5 *Vide* Vācaspati Miśra's Nyāya-vārtika-tātparya-ṭīkā, edited by Gangadhara Sastri, 1-1-1, pp. 1, 31; 1-1-4, pp. 76—77, 97—98, 102; 1-1-5, p. 102; 1-1-6, p. 135, etc.

6 Mallinātha's commentary on verse 14 of the Meghadūta, Pūrva-megha.

7 *Vide* Pārtha-sārathi's gloss on 59—60. Anumānapariccheda of Kumārila Bhaṭṭa's vārtika on the 5th Sūtra of Jaimini.

Vedāntins and Jainas[1] were not inactive in their hostility. Even Dharmakīrti[2] the Buddhist sage attempted to oppose him. Dignāga must have been a very strongly built man, both physically and mentally, otherwise he could hardly have lived for a single day under assaults from so many sides. Those of his works which still exist enable us somehow to measure his strength and his weakness.

DIGNĀGA'S **Pramāṇa-samuccaya.**[3]

41. The **Pramāṇa-samuccaya** is one of the grandest literary monuments of Dignāga. It is said to have been composed while he was residing on a solitary hill near Veṅgi in Andhra[4] (modern Teliṅgāna) in the Madras Presidency. Seeing

---

[1] *Vide* the works of Prabhācandra and Vidyānanda referred to in the J.B.B.R.A.S., Vol. XVIII, p. 229. The Digambara Jaina logician Dharmabhūṣaṇa, in controverting the Vaiśeṣika doctrine of *Sāmānya*, generality, quotes in support of his own conclusion the following verse of Dignāga :—

न याति न च तत्रासे न पश्चादस्ति नांशवत् ।
जहाति पूर्व्वं नाधारमहो व्यसनसन्ततिः ॥
इति दिग्नागदूषितदूषणगणप्रसरप्रसङ्गात्

(Quoted in Dharmabhūṣaṇa's Nyāya-dīpikā, Chap. III).

The same verse has been quoted in a little altered form by the Hindu philosopher Mādhavācārya as follows :—

न याति न च तत्रासीदस्ति पश्चान्न चांशवत् ।
जहाति पूर्व्वं नाधारमहो व्यसनसन्ततिः ॥

(Sarvadarśana saṁgraha, chapter on Bauddhadarśana).

[2] *Vide* the head " Dharmakīrti " which follows.

[3] The account of the composition of the Pramāṇa-samuccaya given here is taken from Lama Tārānātha's Geschichte des Buddhismus von Schiefner, pp. 132, 133 ; and the Tibetan Pag-sam-jon-zang edited by Rai Sarat Chandra Das, Bahadur, C.I.E., pp. 62, 75, 100 and LXVII.

[4] *Vide* Hwen-thsang's Travel in Beal's Buddhist Records of the Western World, Vol. II, pp. 218, 219 and 220 where the Chinese term for Dignāga is wrongly rendered as Jina. Hwen-thsang gives the following account of the composition of the Pramāṇa-samuccaya :—" When Dignāga began to compose a useful compendium [presumably the Pramāṇa-samuccaya] for overcoming the difficulties of the Hetuvidyā-śāstra, the mountains and valleys shook and reverberated ; the vapour and clouds changed their appearance, and the spirit of the mountain appeared before him, asking him to spread abroad the śāstra (Hetuvidyā). Then the Bodhisattva (Dignāga) caused a bright light to shine and illumine the dark places. Surprised at this wonder, the king of the country (Andhra) came near him and asked whether he was entering into *nirvāṇa*. When the king spoke of the infinite bliss of *nirvāṇa* Dignāga resolved to enter into it. Mañ-

that the Śāstras on Dialectics written earlier by him remained scattered about, he resolved to collect them. Accordingly, putting together fragments from particular works, he engaged himself in compiling in verse a compendium called the Pramāṇa-samuccaya. While he was writing the opening lines the earth trembled and all the places were filled with light and a great tumult was audible. A Brāhmaṇa named Īśvara-kṛṣṇa[1] surprised at this wonder came to Ācārya Dignāga, and finding that he had gone out to collect alms, wiped out the words he had written. Dignāga came and rewrote the words and Īśvara-kṛṣṇa wiped them out again. Dignāga wrote them a third time and added: "Let no one wipe this out even in joke or sport, for none should wipe out what is of great importance; if the sense of the expression is not right, and one wishes to dispute on that account, let him appear before me in person." When after Dignāga had gone out to collect alms, the Brāhmaṇa again came to wipe out the writings he saw what was added and paused. The Ācārya returning from his rounds for meal met the Brāhmaṇa: they began controversy, either staking his own doctrine. When he had vanquished the Tīrtha (Brāhmaṇa) several times and challenged him to accept the Buddhist doctrine, the Tīrtha scattered ashes pronouncing incantations on them, and burnt all the goods of the Ācārya that happened to lie before him; and when the Ācārya was kept back by fire the Tīrtha ran away. Thereupon Dignāga reflected that since he could not work the salvation of this single individual, he would not be able to work that of others. So thinking he was on the point of giving up his purpose of compiling the Pramāṇa-samuccaya when the Bodhisattva Ārya Mañjuśrī miraculously appeared before him in person and said:—

Dignāga and Īśvara-kṛṣṇa.

"Son, refrain, refrain: the intellect is infected by arguing with mean persons Please know that when you have demonstrated it this Śāstra cannot be injured by the host of Tīrthas. I undertake to be your spiritual tutor till you have attained the

---

juśrī, the god of learning, knowing his purpose was moved with pity. He came to Dignāga and said: "Alas! how have you given up your great purpose, and only fixed your mind on your own personal profit, with narrow aims, giving up the purpose of saving all." Saying this he directed him to explain the Yogācāryabhūmi-śāstra and Hetuvidyā-śāstra. Dignāga receiving these directions, respectfully assented and saluted the saint. Then he gave himself to profound study and explained the Hetuvidyā-śāstra and the Yoga discipline.

[1] Īśvarakṛṣṇa here referred to was very probably the author of the Sāṁkhya kārikā.

stage of perfection. In later times this śāstra will become the sole eye of all the śāstras." [1]

So saying Mañjuśrī disapppeared and Dignāga resumed his work and completed the Pramāṇa-samuccaya.

42. The Pramāṇa-samuccaya [2] is a Sanskrit work written in *anuṣṭubh* metre. The Sanskrit original of it is lost but a Tibetan translation still exists. The translation was prepared by an Indian sage named Hema Varma (in Tibetan: G̱ser-gyi-go-cha) and a Tibetan interpreter named Dad̲-pah̲i-śes̲-rab in the monastery of Ses̲-pah̲i-d̲ge-gnas̲. It occupies folios 1—13 of the Tangyur, section M̲do, volume Ce. [3] In Tibetan it is called Tshad̲-mah̲i-m̲do-kun-las̲-b̲tus̲-pa (=Pramāṇa-sūtra-samuccaya) or briefly Tshad̲-ma-kun-las̲-b̲tus̲-pa (=Pramāṇa-samuccaya) signifying a compilation of aphorisms on Pramāṇa, valid knowledge. It begins thus:—" Bowing down before Sugata—the teacher and protector—who is *Pramāṇa* incarnate, and benefactor of the world, I, for the sake of expounding Pramāṇa (valid knowledge), put together here various scattered matters, compiled from my own works." [4] In the closing lines

---

1 བུ་མ་བྱེད་མ་བྱེད་སྐྱེ་བོ་དམར་དང་འཕྲད་ལས་བློ་གྲོས་ངན་སྐྱེ་སྟེ། ཁྱོད་ཀྱི་བསྟན་ནས་འཆོས་འདི་ལ་མུ་སྟེགས་ཚོགས་ཀྱིས་གནོད་མི་ནུས་པར་ཤེས། ཁྱོད་ཀྱིས་ས་མ་ཐོབ་ཀྱི་བར་དུ་དགེ་བའི་བཤེས་སྲུང་འགྱུར་གྱི། ཕྱི་མའི་དུས་སུ་བསྟན་བཅོས་ཀུན་གྱི་མིག་གཅིག་ཏུ་ནི་འདི་འགྱུར་རོ།།

Pag-sam-jon-zang, edited by Rai Sarat Chandra Das, Bahadur, C.I.E., p. 101.

2 Probably the same as "The Sāstra on the grouped inferences," *vide* Takakusu's I-tsing, p. 167.

3 The volume Ce of the Tangyur, section M̲do, was put at my disposal by the India Office, London, through Mr. Thomas.

ཚད་མར་གྱུར་པ་འགྲོ་ལ་ཕན་པར་བཞེད།
སྟོན་པ་བདེ་གཤེགས་སྐྱོབ་ལ་ཕྱག་འཚལ་ནས།
ཚད་མ་སྒྲུབ་ཕྱིར་རང་གི་གཞུང་ཀུན་ལས།
བཏུས་ཏེ་སྣ་ཚོགས་འཐོར་རྣམས་འདིར་གཅིག་བྱ།།

(Tangyur, M̲do, Ce, folio 1).

it is stated that "Dignāga, the subduer of controversialists in all regions and the possessor of elephantine strength, compiled this from his own works." [1]

43. It is divided into six chapters which are named respectively: (1) Perception (Sanskrit: *Pratyakṣa*, Tibetan: M̱ṅon-sum); (2) Inference for one's own self (Sanskrit: *Svārthānumāna*, Tibetan: Raṅ-don-gyi-ṟje-ḏpag); (3) Inference for the sake of others (Sanskrit: *Parārthānumāna*, Tibetan: G̱shan-gyi-don-gyi-ṟje-ḏpag); (4) Three characteristics of the Middle Term (Sanskrit: *Tri-rūpa-hetu*, Tibetan: Tshul-sum-gtan-tshigs̱) and Rejection of Comparison (Sanskrit: *Upamāna-khaṇḍana*, Tibetan. Ḏpe-daṅ-ḏpe-ḻtar-ṣnaṅ-pa); (5) Rejection of Credible Word or Verbal Testimony (Sanskrit: *Śabdānumānanirāsa*, Tibetan: S̱gra-ṟje-ḏpag-min); and (6) Parts of a syllogism (Sanskrit: *Nyāyāvayava*, Tibetan: Rigs̱-paḫi-yan-lag).

Perception.

44. Dignāga does not give any formal definition of Perception, which is well known as the knowledge of objects derived through the channels of the senses. But he describes Perception as that which is freed from illusory experiences and is unconnected with name, genus, etc.[2] Suppose a man in the twilight mistakes a rope for a snake: his experience of the snake is merely illusory

---

[1] ཕྱོགས་རྣམས་ཀུན་གྱི་ཕས་ཀྱི་རྒོལ་བ་རྣམས། །
འཇོམས་པར་བྱེད་ལ་གླང་པོ་ཡི་སྟོབས་ལྡན་པ། །
ཕྱོགས་ཀྱི་གླང་པོ་ཡི་གཞུང་ཀུན་ལས་བཏུས་པ། །
(Tangyur, M̱do, Ce, folio 13).

[2] In chapter I of the Pramāṇa-samuccaya, Dignāga describes Perception as follows:—

མངོན་སུམ་རྟོག་པ་དང་བྲལ་བ། །
མིང་དང་རིགས་སོགས་མི་བསྲེས་པའོ། །

The Sanskrit equivalents for those two lines are as follows:—

प्रत्यक्षं कल्पनापोढं
नामजात्याद्यसंयुतम् ॥
(Pramāṇa-samuccaya, chapter I).

The first of these lines has actually been quoted, and Dignāga's whole theory of Perception severely criticised, by the Hindu logician Udyotakara in his Nyāya-vārtika, 1-1-4.

and is not, according to Dignāga, an act of Perception. Dignāga contends that Perception is also not connected with name, genus, etc. Suppose I see a cow. This cow, which I see, is a peculiar one. Its infinite peculiarities can only be realised by me who have seen it. If I proceed to indicate this cow to other persons by saying that I saw a cow which is named Dittha or which is red, etc., I can only convey to those persons the idea of a cow of a certain class, that is, a cow possessing the common characteristics of a class of cows, but can never express to them the individual cow which I saw. Hence it follows that (a result of) Perception cannot be properly expressed by name, genus, etc. But very different is the case with inference. Knowledge derived through inference is general, and can be well expressed by name genus, etc., whereas that derived through Perception is particular, and is incapable of being properly communicated to others by name, genus, etc.

Dignāga criticises Vātsyāyana.

45. In the chapter on Perception Dignāga has criticised the Hindu logician Vātsyāyana, who concluded that the mind (*manas*) was a sense-organ, because it was accepted as such in several systems of philosophy, and the view was not opposed in the Nyāya-sūtra according to the maxim "if I do not oppose a theory of my opponent [1] it is to be understood I approve of it." Dignāga criticises this maxim of Vātsyāyana saying: "if silence proved assent it was useless for the Nyāya-sūtra to mention other sense-organs." [2]

---

[1] Vātsyāyana writes :—

मनस इन्द्रियभावाच्च वाच्यं लक्षणान्तरमिति। तन्त्रान्तरसमाचाराच्चैतत् प्रत्येतव्यमिति परमतमप्रतिषिद्धमनुमतमिति हि तन्त्रयुक्तिः।

(Nyāyabhāṣya, 1-1-4).

[2] Dignāga writes :—

བཀག་པ་མེད་ཕྱིར་ཐོབ་ཞེ་ན།
དབང་པོ་གཞན་གྱི་སྒྲ་དོན་མེད།།

(Pramāṇa-samuccaya, chapter I).

The Sanskrit originals of the lines are as follows :—

अनिर्देशादुपात्तं चेत्
अन्येन्द्रियरुतं वृथा ॥

(Pramāṇa-samuccaya, chapter I).

These two lines have been quoted and criticised by the Hindu logician Vācaspati Miśra in his Nyāya-vārtika-tātparya-ṭīkā, 1-1-4.

46. In chapter II of the Pramāṇa-samuccaya, Dignāga mentions the views of some logicians who from smoke, which is the middle term, infer *fire* which is inseparably connected with it, and also of others, who from smoke infer the connection between it and the hill which is the minor term. He argues against the first-mentioned logicians saying that if they infer *fire* from smoke they gain no new knowledge from this inference, for it is already known that smoke is inseparably connected with fire. His argument against the other logicians is that they are not able to infer the *connection*, for connection implies two things, whereas here only one thing, *viz.*, the hill, is visible, but the other, *viz.*, fire, is not visible. What then do we really infer from smoke? Dignāga says it is not fire nor the connection between it and the hill, but it is the *fiery* hill that is inferred.[1]

Inference.

What Dignāga meant to say is:—

The Nyāya-sūtra distinctly mentions the eye, ear, nose, tongue and touch as sense-organs, but says nothing as to whether the mind (*manas*) is a sense-organ or not. The presumption from this silence is that the mind is not a sense-organ according to the Nyāya-sūtra.

But Vātsyāyana, the famous Hindu commentator on the Nyāya-sūtra interprets the silence in a quite different way, concluding therefrom that the mind (*manas*) is a sense-organ according to the Nyāya-sūtra.

Dignāga contends "if silence was a proof of assent why did the Nyāya-sūtra not remain silent regarding the other five sense-organs too?"

[1] Dignāga writes:—

རྟགས་ནི་འཁྲུལ་བ་མེད་པའི་ཕྱིར།
ཁ་ཅིག་ཆོས་གཞན་དཔོག་ཅེས་ཟེར།
ཆོས་དང་ཆོས་ཅན་གྲུབ་པའི་ཕྱིར།
ཁ་ཅིག་འབྲེལ་བ་འདོད་པ་ཡིན།
ཆོས་ལ་རྟགས་ནི་གྲུབ་ཅེ་ན།
གཞན་དེས་ཅི་ཞིག་དཔག་པར་བྱེད།
ཅི་སྟེ་ཆོས་ཅན་ལ་དེ་ཉིད།
ཅི་ཕྱིར་རྗེས་སུ་དཔོག་མི་བྱེད།
འབྲེལ་པ་ལ་ཡང་གཉིས་པོ་མེད།

47. In chapter III, Dignāga says that an Inference for the sake of others consists in making explicit a matter which was inferred by one's own self.[1] In chapter IV, he rejects Comparison as a separate source of knowledge. He says that when we recognise a thing through Perception of a similar thing, we really perform an act of Perception. Hence Comparison or Recognition of Similarity is not a separate source of knowledge, but is included in Perception.[2] In chapter V, he rejects "Credible Word" or "Verbal Testimony" as a separate source of knowledge. He asks: "what is the significance of a Credible Word? Does it mean that the person who spoke the word is credible or the fact he averred is credible?" "If the person," continues Dignāga, "is credible, it is a mere infer-

Comparison and Verbal Testimony rejected.

དེ་ལྡན་ལ་ནི་དྲུག་པ་བྲོས།
བརྗོད་མིན་དོན་གྱིས་གཟུང་བར་འགྱུར།
འདི་ལ་རྟགས་དང་འབྲེལ་མ་ཡིན།

(Pramāṇa-samuccaya, chapter II).

The Sanskrit originals of these lines are as follows :—

केचिद् धर्म्मान्तरं मेयं लिङ्गस्याव्यभिचारतः ।
संबन्धं केचिदिच्छन्ति सिद्धत्वाद्धर्म्मधर्म्मिणोः ॥
लिङ्गं धर्म्मे प्रसिद्धं चेत् किमन्यत् तेन मीयते ।
अथ धर्म्मिणि तस्यैव किमर्थं नानुमेयता ॥
संबन्धेऽपि द्वयं नास्ति षष्ठी श्रूयते तद्वति ।
अवाच्योऽनुग्रहीतत्वान्नचासौ लिङ्गसंगतः ॥

(Pramāṇa-samuccaya, chapter II).

The Hindu logician Vācaspati Miśra has quoted and criticised these lines in the Nyāya-vārtika-tātparya-ṭīkā, 1-1-5.

[1] Dignāga writes :—

གཞན་གྱི་དོན་གྱི་རྗེས་དཔག་ནི།
རང་གིས་མཐོང་དོན་གསལ་བྱེད་ཡིན།
དེ་ལ་དཔག་བྱ་བསྟན་པ་ནི།།

(Pramāṇa-samuccaya, chapter III).

[2] *Vide* a very interesting discussion on it in the Nyāya-vārtika, 1-1-6, where the Hindu logician Udyotakara defends the Nyāya-sūtra and the Nyāya-bhāṣya from the attacks of Dignāga.

ence. On the other hand if the fact is credible, it is a case of Perception." Hence Dignāga concludes that Credible Word or Verbal Testimony is not a separate source of knowledge, but is included in Perception and Inference.[1]

Dignāga's Nyāya-praveśa.

48. The **Nyāya-praveśa**[2] or rather "Nyāya-praveśo-nāma pramāṇa-prakaraṇa" is another excellent work on Logic by Dignāga. The Sanskrit original is lost. There exists a Tibetan translation of it which extends over folios 183—188 of the Tangyur, section Mdo, volume Ce. The translation was prepared by the great Kāśmīrian Paṇḍita Sarvajña-śrī Rakṣita and the Sākya monk Grags-pa-rgyal-mtshan-dpal-bzaṅ, in the great Sa-skya monastery of Western Tibet. The work in Tibetan is called Tshad-ma-rigs-par-hjug-pahi-sgo signifying the "Door of Entrance to Logic." It opens thus :—

"Demonstration and refutation together with their fallacies are useful in arguing with others ; and Perception and Inference together with their fallacies are useful for self-understanding ; seeing these I compile this S'āstra."[3]

Parts of a Syllogism.[4]

49. Some of the subjects discussed in the work are noticed below :—

---

1 *Vide* Udyotakara's rejoinder in the Nyāya-vārtika 1-1-7.

2 I consulted the Nyāya-praveśa from the volume Ce of the Tibetan Tangyur which was placed at my disposal by the India Office, London. I have also brought a copy of the Nyāya-praveśa from the monastery of Labrang in Sikkim which I visited in May 1907. This is probably the same as "Nyāya-dvāra-śāstra" : *Vide* Takakusu's I-tsing, p. 186, and Bunyiu Nanjio's Catalogue of the Chinese Tripiṭaka, Nos. 1223 and 1224. Cf. Dr. Sugiura's "Hindu Logic as preserved in China and Japan," pp. 36, 60, where Saṅkara Svāmin's Nyāya-prāveśa-tarka-śāstra is noticed.

3 སྒྲུབ་པ་དང་ནི་སུན་འབྱིན་ཉིད།
ལྟར་སྣང་བཅས་པ་གཞན་རྟོགས་ཕྱིར།
མངོན་སུམ་དང་ནི་རྗེས་སུ་དཔག།
ལྟར་སྣང་བཅས་པ་བདག་རིག་ཕྱིར།
ཅེས་པ་བསྟན་བཅོས་བསྡུས་པའོ།།

(Nyāya-praveśa).

4 In Tibetan : Rigs-pahi-yan-lag (རིགས་པའི་ཡན་ལག) and in Sanskrit : Nyāyāvayava (न्यायावयव) ।

Reasoning, according to the Nyāya-praveśa, is carried on by means of a minor term, a major term, a middle term and two examples. The minor term is also called the subject (in Sanskrit: *pakṣa* or *dharmin*, and in Tibetan phyogs̲ or chos̲-can). The major term is otherwise called the predicate (in Sanskrit: *sādhya* or *dharma*, in Tibetan: b̲sgrub-par-bya or chos̲). The middle term is also called the reason or mark (in Sanskrit: *hetu*, *liṅga* or *sādhana*, in Tibetan: gtan-tshigs̲ or b̲sgrub-par-byed̲). The example (called in Sanskrit: *dṛṣṭānta*, in Tibetan: d̲pe-b̲rjod̲) is of two kinds, *viz.*, (1) homogeneous (in Sanskrit: *sādharmya*, in Tibetan: chos̲-m̲thun-pa) and (2) hetrogeneous (in Sanskrit: vaidharmya, in Tibetan: chos̲-mi-m̲thun-pa).

Form of a Syllogism.

50. The form of reasoning is as follows:—

(1) This hill is fiery,

(2) Because it has smoke,

(3) All that has smoke is fiery like a kitchen and whatever is not fiery has no smoke like a lake.

Here 'hill' is the minor term, 'fiery' the major term, 'smoke' the middle term, 'kitchen' a homogeneous example and 'lake' a hetrogeneous example.

Thesis.

51. A minor term and a major term linked together constitute a proposition, *e.g.*

The *hill* (minor term) is *fiery* (major term).

A proposition which is offered for proof is a Thesis.

The Fallacies of Thesis.[1]

52. There are certain types of thesis which cannot stand the test of proof and are therefore fallacious.

The following theses are fallacious:—

(1) A thesis incompatible with perception, such as: "sound is inaudible."

(2) A thesis incompatible with inference, such as: "A pot is eternal."

(Really "A pot is non-eternal because it is a product.")

(3) A thesis incompatible with the public opinion, such as: "Man's head is pure, because it is the limb of an animate being." (Or money is an abominable thing. I or some men like me may say "money is an abominable thing," but the world does not say so).

---

[1] In Tibetan: phyogs̲-ltar-s̲naṅ (ཕྱོགས་ལྟར་སྣང་); in Sanskrit: pakṣābhāsa (पक्षाभास)।

(4) A thesis incompatible with one's own belief or doctrine, such as : A Vaiśeṣika philosopher saying " sound is eternal."

(5) A thesis incompatible with one's own statement such as : " My mother is barren."

(6) A thesis with an unfamiliar minor term, such as : The Buddhist speaking to the Sāṁkhya, " Sound is perishable." (Sound is a subject well known to the Mīmāṁsaka, but not to the Sāṁkhya).

(7) A thesis with an unfamiliar major term, such as : The Sāṁkhya speaking to the Buddhist, " The soul is animate."

(8) A thesis with both the terms unfamiliar, such as : The Vaiśeṣika speaking to the Buddhist, " The soul has feelings as pleasurable, etc."

(The Buddhist neither deals with the soul nor with its feelings).

(9) A thesis universally accepted, such as : "Fire is warm." (This thesis cannot be offered for proof as it is accepted by all.

Three Characteristics of the Middle Term.[1]

53. The Middle Term (Hetu) must possess three characteristics, *viz.* :—

(1) The whole of the minor term (pakṣa) must be connected with the middle term, *e.g.*

> Sound is non-eternal,
> Because it is a product,
> Like a pot but unlike ether.

In this reasoning "product" which is the middle term includes the whole of " sound " which is the minor term.

(2) All things denoted by the middle term must be homogeneous with things denoted by the major term, *e.g.*

> All things produced are non-eternal as a pot.

(3) None of the things heterogeneous from the major term must be a thing denoted by the middle term, *e.g.*

> No non-non-eternal (that is, no eternal) thing is a product, as ether.

54. If we suppose the minor term or subject to be 'S,' the middle term or reason to be 'R,' and the major term or predicate to be 'P,' then the above-mentioned three characteristics of the middle term may be symbolically set forth as follows :—

(1) All S is R.
(2) All R is P.
(3) No R is non-P.

---

[1] Called in Tibetan : Gtan-tshigs-ni-tshul-gsum (གཏན་ཚིགས་ནི་ཚུལ་གསུམ) and in Sanskrit : Liṅgasya trairūpyam (लिङ्गस्य त्रैरूप्यम्) ।

Now, the negative aspect of the middle term, *viz.*, no R is non-P only confirms the truth conveyed by one of the positive aspects, *viz.*, all R is P. Hence we may put aside the negative aspect, and exhibit the positive aspects as follows :—

(1) All S is R.
(2) All R is P.

Again, in the above instance 'R' and 'P' may be taken in their whole extent or partially. So the two positive aspects mentioned above may be fully exhibited as follows :—

(1) (*a*) All S is all R.
(*b*) All S is some R.
(2) (*a*) All R is all P.
(*b*) All R is some P.

Combining aspect (1) and aspect (2) together we find that a syllogism may be of any one of the following forms :—

(1) All S is all P (conclusion):
Because All S is all R,
All R is all P.
(2) All S is some P (conclusion) :
Because All S is all R,
All R is some P.
(3) All S is some P (conclusion) :
Because All S is some R,
All R is all P.
(4) All S is some P (conclusion):
Because All S is some R,
All R is some P.

Hence we find that Dignāga admits only two conclusions, *viz.*
All S is all P, and
All S is some P.

Relative extension of the Middle Term and the Major Term.

55. The second and third of the characteristics mentioned above indicate the relative extension of the middle term and major term. They show that the middle term is universally or inseparably connected with the major term. This universal or inseparable connection between them is called in Sanskrit *Vyāpti* and in Tibetan *Khyab* which was, as far as I find, first discovered by Dignāga.

Supposing that the middle term or reason is R, and the major term or predicate is P, the connection between the two terms may be symbolically set forth as follows :—

(1) All R is all P, and
(2) All R is some P.

56. Owing to the violation of one or more of the three characteristics, there occur Fallacies of the Middle Term which may be of fourteen kinds as follows :—

Fallacies of the Middle Term.[1]

A. The *unproved* (Sanskrit : Asiddha, Tibetan : Ma-grub) which occurs :

(1) When the lack of truth of the middle term is recognised by both the parties, *e.g.*

Sound is non-eternal,
Because it is *visible.*

(Neither of the parties admits that sound is visible).

(2) When the lack of truth of the middle term is recognised by one party only, *e.g.*

Sound is evolved,
Because it is a *product.*

(The Mīmāṁsakas do not admit that sound is a product).

(3) When the truth of the middle term is questioned, *e.g.*

The hill is fiery,
Because there is *vapour.*

(Vapour may or may not be an effect of fire and may or may not be connected with it otherwise).

(4) When it is questioned whether the minor term is predicable of the middle term, *e.g.*

Ether is a substance,
Because it has qualities.

(It is questioned whether ether has qualities).

B. The *uncertain* (Sanskrit : Aniścita, Tibetan : Ma-ṅes-pa) which occurs :

(5) When the middle term is too general, abiding equally in the major term as well as in the opposite of it, *e.g.*

Sound is eternal,
Because it is *knowable.*

(The 'knowable' is too general because it abides in the eternal as well as the non-eternal. This is a fallacy of being too general, called in Sanskrit : *Sādhāraṇa* and in Tibetan : *Thun-moṅ*).

(6) When the middle term is not general enough, abiding neither in the major term nor in its opposite, *e.g.*

---

[1] In Tibetan : G̱tan-tshigs-ḻtar-s̱naṅ (གཏན་ཚིགས་ལྟར་སྣང་) and in Sanskrit : Hetvābhāsa (हेत्वाभास) ।

Sound is eternal,
Because it is audible.

(This is a fallacy of being not general enough, called in Sanskrit: *Asādhāraṇa*, and in Tibetan: Thun-moṅ-ma-yin).

(7) When the middle term abides in some of the things homogeneous with, and in all things heterogeneous from, the major term, *e.g.*

Sound is not a product of effort,
Because it is *non-eternal.*

(The non-eternal abides in some of the things which are not products of effort, such as lightning, and abides in all things which are not non-products of effort).

(8) When the middle term abides in some of the things heterogeneous from, and in all things homogeneous with, the major term, *e.g.*

Sound is a product of effort,
Because it is non-eternal.

(The non-eternal abides in some of the things which are not products of effort, as lightning, and abides in all things which are products of effort).

(9) When the middle term abides, in some of the things homogeneous with and in some heterogeneous from, the major term, *e.g.*

Sound is eternal,
Because it is incorporeal.

(Some incorporeal things are eternal as ether, but others are not as intelligence).

(10) When there is a non-erroneous contradiction, that is, when a thesis and its contradictory are both supported by what appear to be valid reasons, *e.g.*

The Vaiśeṣika speaking to the Mīmāṁsaka:

"Sound is non-eternal,
Because it is a product."

The Mīmāṁsaka speaking to the Vaiśeṣika:

"Sound is eternal,
Because it is always audible."

(Both of the reasonings are correct, but as they lead to contradictory conclusions they are classed as *uncertain*).

C. The contradictory (Sanskrit: Viruddha, Tibetan: Ḫgal-wa) which occurs:

(11) When the middle term is contradictory to the major term, *e.g.*

Sound is eternal,
Because it is a product.

(Product is inconsistent with eternal).

(12) When the middle term is contradictory to the implied major term, *e.g.*

The eyes, etc., are serviceable to some being,
Because they are made of particles,
Like a bed, seat, etc.[1]

(Here the major term "serviceable to some being" is ambiguous, for, the apparent meaning of 'some being' is 'the body,' but the implied meaning of it is 'the soul.' Though things 'made of particles' are serviceable to the body, they are not, according to the Sāṁkhya, serviceable to the soul which is attributeless. Hence there is contradiction between the middle term and the implied major term).

(13) When the middle term is inconsistent with the minor term, *e.g.*

Sāmānya (generality) is neither substance, quality, nor action;
Because it depends upon one substance and possesses quality and action.
(*Sāmānya* or generality does not depend upon one substance, etc.)

(14) When the middle term is inconsistent with the implied minor term, *e.g.*

Objects are stimuli of action;
Because they are apprehended by the senses.
("Objects" is ambiguous meaning (1) things and (2) purposes. The middle term is inconsistent with the minor term in the second meaning).

Dignāga's theory of examples. Examples converted to universal proposition.

57. An example before the time of Dignāga served as a mere familiar case which was cited to help the understanding of the listner, *e.g.*

The hill is fiery,
Because it has smoke,
Like a kitchen (example).

Asaṅga (q.v.) made the example more serviceable to reasoning, but Dignāga converted it into a universal proposition, that

---

[1] This example may lead us to presume that the author of Nyāya-praveśa knew Īśvara Kṛṣṇa's Sāṁkhya-kārikā which is the oldest of the works on Sāṁkhya philosophy that have come down to us.

is a proposition[1] expressive of the universal or inseparable connection between the middle term and the major term, *e.g.*

The hill is fiery ;
Because it has smoke ;
All that has smoke is fiery as a kitchen (homogeneous example).

The above example is homogeneous. A heterogeneous example is thus given :—

Whatever is not fiery has no smoke as a lake.

Fallacies of the homogeneous example.[2]

58. Examples have already been stated to be of two kinds, *viz.*, 1. Homogeneous and 2. Heterogeneous. Each of these kinds becomes fallacious under certain circumstances. Fallacies of the homogeneous example are the following :—

(1) An example not homogeneous with the middle term, *e.g.*

Sound is eternal,
Because it is incorporeal,
That which is incorporeal is eternal as the atoms.

(The atoms cannot serve as an example because they are not incorporeal. This is called a fallacy of the Excluded Middle Term).

(2) An example not homogeneous with the major term, *e.g.*

Sound is eternal,
Because it is incorporeal,
That which is incorporeal is eternal as intelligence.

(Intelligence cannot serve as an example because it is not eternal. This is called a fallacy of the Excluded Major Term).

(3) An example homogeneous with neither the middle term nor the major term, *e.g.*

---

[1] The universal proposition, that is, the proposition expressive of the universal relation between the middle term and the major term, serves as the major premise in a syllogism of the celebrated Greek logician Aristotle. It was long unknown in India. Dignāga's discovery of the universal proposition marks a new era in the history of Indian Logic and shows a great development of the principle of induction first apprehended by Asaṅga in India.

[2] Called in Tibetan: Chos-mthun-dpe-ltar-snaṅ-wa (ཆོས་མཐུན་དཔེ་ལྟར་སྣང་བ) and in Sanskrit: Sādharmya-dṛṣṭāntābhāsa (साधर्म्य-दृष्टान्ताभास)।

Sound is eternal,
Because it is incorporeal,
That which is incorporeal is eternal, as a pot.

(The pot cannot serve as an example because it is neither incorporeal nor eternal. This is called a fallacy of the Excluded Middle and Major Terms).

(4) A homogeneous example showing a lack of universal connection between the middle term and the major term, *e.g.*

This person is passionate,
Because he is a speaker,
Whoever is a speaker is passionate, as a certain man in Magadha.

(Though a certain man in Magadha may be both speaker and passionate, there is nevertheless no universal connection between being a speaker and being passionate. This is a fallacy of Absence of Connection called in Sanskrit: Ananvaya, in Tibetan: Rjes-su-hgro-wa-med).

(5) A homogeneous example showing an inverse connection between the middle term and the major term, *e.g.*

Sound is non-eternal,
Because it is a product of effort,
Whatever is non-eternal is a product of effort, as a pot.

(The pot cannot serve as an example because though it is both non-eternal and a product of effort, the connection between the major term and the middle term has been inverted, *i.e.*, all products of effort are non-eternal; but all non-eternals are not products of effort. This is a fallacy of Inverse Connection called in Sanskrit: Viparītānvaya, in Tibetan: Rjes-su-hgro-wa-phyin-ci-log-pa).

Fallacy of the heterogeneous example.[1]

59. Fallacies of the heterogeneous example are the following :—

(6) An example not heterogeneous from the opposite of the middle term, *e.g.*

Sound is eternal,
Because it is incorporeal,
Whatever is non-eternal is not incorporeal, as intelligence.

---

[1] Called in Tibetan: Chos-mi-mthun-dpe-ltar--snan-wa (ཆོས་མི་མཐུན་དཔེ་ལྟར་སྣང་བ) and in Sanskrit: Vaidharmya-dṛṣṭāntābhāsa (वैधर्म्य-दृष्टान्ताभास)।

(Intelligence is non-eternal, yet incorporeal. This is a fallacy of Included Middle Term in a heterogeneous example).

(7) An example not heterogeneous from the opposite of the major term, *e.g.*

Sound is eternal,
Because it is incorporeal,
Whatever is non-eternal is not incorporeal, as atoms.

(The atoms are not incorporeal yet they are eternal. This is a fallacy of Included Major Term in a heterogeneous example).

(8) An example heterogeneous from neither the opposite of the middle term nor the opposite of the major term, *e.g.*

Sound is eternal,
Because it is incorporeal,
Whatever is non-eternal is not incorporeal, as a pot.

(A pot is neither eternal nor incorporeal. This is called a fallacy of Included Middle and Major Terms in a heterogeneous example).

(9) A heterogeneous example showing an absence of disconnection between the middle term and the major term, *e.g.*

This person is passionate,
Because he is a speaker,
Whoever is non-passionate is not a speaker, as a piece of stone.

(This is called a fallacy of Absence of Disconnection of a heterogeneous example).

(10) A heterogeneous example showing an absence of inverse disconnection between the middle term and the major term, *e.g.*

Sound is non-eternal,
Because it is a product,
Whatever is non-product is not non-eternal, as ether.

The example should be inverted as:

Whatever is non-non-eternal, *i.e.*, eternal, is not a product, as ether. This is called a fallacy of Inverted Negation of a heterogeneous example.

60. All the three kinds of fallacies—of the Thesis, Middle Term and Example—are fallacies of reasoning. Refutation (called in Sanskrit: Dūṣaṇa and in Tibetan: Sun-ḥbyin) consists in finding out in the reasoning of the opponent any one of the fallacies aforementioned. Fallacy of Refutation (called in

Sanskrit: Dūṣaṇābhāsa and in Tibetan: Sun-ḥbyin-ltar-snaṅ-wa) consists in alleging a fallacy where there is no fallacy at all.

Perception and Inference and their Fallacies.

61. Perception and Inference are the two kinds of valid knowledge for one's own self. Perception (called in Sanskrit: Pratyakṣa, and in Tibetan: Mṅon-sum) is knowledge derived through the senses. It is free from illusory experiences and is not connected with name, genus, etc. Inference called in Sanskrit: Anumāna and in Tibetan: Rjes-su-dpag is the knowledge of objects derived through a mark (Tibetan: Rtags) or middle term which has three characteristics. There are Fallacies of Perception as well as of Inference (called respectively Pratyakṣābhāsa and Anumānābhāsa in Sanskrit, and Mṅon-sum-ltar-naṅ and Rjes-dpag-ltar-snaṅ in Tibetan).

DIGNĀGA'S Hetu-cakra-hamaru.

62. The **Hetu-cakra-hamaru**[1] is another small treatise on Logic by Dignāga. The Sanskrit original is lost, but a Tibetan translation is preserved in the Tangyur, section Mdo, folios 193-194. The Tibetan translation was prepared by the sage Bodhisattva of Za-hor and the Bhikṣu Dharmāśoka. The work in Tibetan is called Gtan-tshigs-kyi-ḥkhor-lo-gtan-la-dwab-pa, signifying "the Wheel of Reasons put in order." It begins thus:—

"Bowing down to the Omniscient One (Buddha), who has destroyed the net of errors, I explain the system of three characteristics of the Reason (or Middle Term)."[2]

In this work Dignāga has analysed all nine possible relations between the middle and the major terms and has found that there

---

[1] I brought a copy of the Tibetan version of the Hetu-cakra-hamaru from the monastery of Labrang in Sikkim which I visited in June 1907. This work is probably the same as the Hetu-dvāra-śāstra: *vide* Takakusu's I-tsing, p. 187.

[2] འཁྲུལ་པའི་དྲ་བ་འཇོམས་མཛད་པའི།
ཐམས་ཅད་མཁྱེན་ལ་ཕྱག་འཚལ་ནས།
གཏན་ཚིགས་ཚུལ་གསུམ་ཁོ་བོ་ཡི།
གཏན་ལ་དབབ་པ་བཤད་པར་བྱ།།

(Hetu-chakra-hamaru).

are among them two relations which conform to the three characteristics of the middle term already laid down, and the remaining seven relations are at variance with those characteristics. Accordingly he has concluded that only two relations are valid as will be evident from the annexed diagram.

OTHER WORKS OF DIGNĀGA.

Pramāṇa-samuccaya-vṛtti.

65. The **Pramāṇa-samuccaya-vṛtti** is a commentary on the Pramāṇa-samuccaya by Dignāga himself. The Sanskrit original of this work is lost, but there exists a Tibetan translaton [1] which extends over folios 13—96 of the Tangyur, section Mdo, volume Ce. The Tibetan translation was prepared, at the command of king Rigs-ldan-rgyal-po, by the famous Indian sage Vasudhara Rakṣita, who was as it were the crest-gem of logicians, and the Tibetan interpreter Sha-ma-dge-bsñen-siṅ-rgyal. In Tibetan it is called Tshad-ma-kun-las-btus-pahi-hgrel-wa. It is divided into six chapters corresponding to those of the Pramāṇa-samuccaya itself. At the end of the work it is stated that "led on by the command of Mañjunātha (the god of learning), Dignāga the great dialectician of sharp intellect wrote this śāstra which is as deep as the ocean."

66. There is another translation of the **Pramāṇa-samuccaya-vṛtti** in Tibetan extending over folios 96—180 of the Tangyur, section Mdo, volume Ce. It was prepared by the Indian sage Hema Varma (called in Tibetan Gser-gyi-go-cha) and the Tibetan interpreter Dad-pa-śes-rab in the monastery of S'i-wahi-dge-gnas.

Pramāṇa-śāstra-praveśa.

67. **Pramāṇa-śāstra-praveśa** [2] is another work by Dignāga It was translated into Chinese by the Chinese interpreter Tha-sam-tsan. The Chinese version was translated into Tibetan by the Chinese scholar Dge-śes-siṅ-gyaṅ and the Tibetan monk Ston-gshon in the Saskya monastery of Western Tibet. The Sanskrit original of the work appears to be lost, but the Tibetan version still exists. It consists of folios 188—193 of the Tangyur, section Mdo, volume Ce. In Tibetan the work is called Tshad-mahi-bstan-bcos-rig-pa-la-hjug-pa signifying "An Entrance to the Science of Logic."

---

[1] I have consulted the Tibetan xylograph of this work in the possession of the India Office, London.

[2] I have consulted the Tibetan xylograph of this work in the possession of the India Office, London.

Ālambana-parīkṣā.

68. The **Ālambaṇa-parīkṣā** [1] is another work by Dignāga. The Sanskrit original of this work appears to be lost, but there exists a Tibetan translation which consists of one folio only (folio 180) of the Tangyur, section Mdo, volume Ce. The work in Tibetan is called Dmigs-pa-brtag-pa signifying "An Examination of the Objects of Thought." It begins with an invocation to Buddha and all Bodhisattvas.

Ālambaṇa-parīkṣā-vṛtti.

69. The **Ālambaṇa-parīkṣā-vṛtti** [2] is a commentary on the Ālambaṇa-parīkṣā by Dignāga himself. The Sanskrit original of this work appears to be lost, but there exists a Tibetan version which is embodied in the Tangyur, section Mdo, volume Ce, folios 180—182. The work in Tibetan is called Dmigs-pa-brtag-pahi-hgrel.

Trikāla-parīkṣā.

70. The **Trikāla-parīkṣā** [3] is a work by Dignāga. The Sanskrit original of this work appears to be lost, but there exists a Tibetan version in the Tangyur, section Mdo, volume Ce, folios 182—183. This version was prepared by the great Paṇḍita Śāntakara Gupta and the interpreter-monk Tshul-hkhrims-rgyal-mtshan. The work in Tibetan is called Dus-gsum-brtag-pa signifying "An Examination of Three Times."

Śaṅkara Svāmin (about 550 A.D.).

71. Śaṅkara Svāmin,[4] as it appears from Chinese records, was a pupil of Dignāga. He seems to have been a native of Southern India. Logic is said to have been handed down by Dignāga through Śankara Svāmin and ten other masters to Śīlabhadra, who was the head of the Nālandā University, and the favourite teacher of the Chinese pilgrim Hwen-thsang in

---

1 I have consulted the Tibetan xylograph of this work as contained in the India Office, London. This is probably the same as "Ālambaṇa-pratya ya-dhyāna-śāstra": *vide* Bunyiu Nanjio's Catalogue of the Chinese Tripiṭaka, No. 1173, and Takakusu's I-tsing, p. 188.

2 I have consulted the xylograph of this work as contained in the India Office, London.

3 I have consulted the Tibetan xylograph of this work as contained in the India Office, London. This work is probably the same that is called by Takakusu "The Śāstra on the Meditation of the Three Worlds": *vide* Takakusu's I-tsing, p. 187. The "worlds" is evidently a mistake for "times."

4 *Vide* Dr. Sugiura's Hindu Logic as preserved in China and Japan, pp. 36, 37.

635 A.D. According to the Chinese Tripiṭaka S'aṅkara S᠆ was the author of a work called **Nyāya-praveśa Tarka-śā᠆** which was translated into Chinese by Hwen-thsang in 647 A.. This work seems to be different[2] from the "Nyāya-praveśa" or more fully the "Nyāya-praveśo nāma pramāṇa-prakaraṇa" which, as we have seen, is ascribed by the Tibetans to Dignāga.

DHARMAPĀLA (ABOUT 600—635 A.D.).

72. Dharmapāla,[3] a logician, was a native of Kāñcīpura in Drāviḍa (modern Conjeeveram in Madras). He was the eldest son of a great minister of the country. From his childhood he exhibited much cleverness, and as he was a young man the king and queen of the country condescended to entertain him at a feast. In the evening of that day his heart was oppressed with sorrow, and assuming the robes of a Buddhist recluse he left home, and applied himself with unflagging earnestness to learning. He was admitted into the University at Nālandā (*vide* Appendix A) in which he acquired great distinction. Subsequently he became the head of the University. He must have retired from Nālandā before 635 A.D., when Hwen-thsang visited it, and found that S'īlabhadra had succeeded him in the headship of the University. Dharmapāla conjointly with Bhartṛhari composed a Beḍā vṛtti on Pāṇini's grammar.

73. He was a follower of the Yogācāra philosophy and was the author of several works such as (1) Ālambaṇa-pratyaya-dhyāna-śāstra-vyākhyā; (2) Vidvāmātra-siddhi-śāstra-vyākhyā; and (3) S'ata-śāstra-vaipulya-vyākhyā which was translated into Chinese in 650 A.D. Hwen-thsang, who visited India in 629 A.D., found in Kauśāmbī the ruins of a monastery where Dharmapāla had refuted the arguments of the heretics.

ĀCĀRYA S'ĪLABHADRA (635 A.D.).

74. S'īlabhadra[4] belonged to the family of the king of Samataṭa (Bengal), and was of the Brāhmaṇa caste. He was a pupil

---

[1] *Vide* Bunyiu Nanjio's Catalogue of the Chinese Tripitaka, no. 1216, and Appendix I, No. 13.

[2] The Tibetans do not know Sankara Svāmin at all. The Chinese pilgrim I-tsing, who visited India during 671—695, speaks of Dignāga and Dharmakīrti, but does not mention Sankara Svāmin. Even Hwen-thsang in his Travel does not mention him.

[3] *Vide* Beal's Buddhist Records of the Western World, vol. I, p. 237; vol. II, pp. 110—223, 229 and 230. *Vide* also Takakusu's I-tsing, p. lvii, and Bunyiu Nanjio's Catalogue of the Chinese Tripiṭaka, Appendix I, No. 16.

[4] *Vide* Beal's Buddhist Records of the Western World, vol. II, p. 110; and Takakusu's I-tsing, p. 181.

of Dharmapāla at the Nālandā University (*vide* Appendix A) of which subsequently he became the head. The Chinese pilgrim Hwen-thsang was his pupil[1] in 635 A.D. S'īlabhadra was a great logician and master of śāstras.

Ācārya Dharmakīrti (about 635—650 A.D.).

75. The excellent Dharmakīrti,[2] called in Tibetan Chos-grags, according to the accounts of all earlier sages, was born in the south in the kingdom of Cūḍāmaṇi.[3] Since, however, there is now no country by that name, and since on the other hand all the orthodox and heterodox alike name Trimalaya as the birth-place of Dharmakīrti, it is to be accepted that in olden times Trimalaya was called the kingdom of Cūḍāmaṇi. His father was a Tīrtha of the Brāhmaṇa caste, Parivrājaka Korunanda by name. Endowed from childhood up with a very keen intellect he attained to great skill in the fine arts, in the Vedas and Vedāṅgas, in the art of healing, in grammar, and in all the theories of the Tīrthas. When only sixteen or eighteen years old, he was already deeply versed in the philosophy of the Tīrthas. Occasionally he attended lectures of the Buddhists, and realised that the teachings of Buddha were without faults. There grew up in him a strong inclination towards Buddhism. He donned the dress of a Buddhist Upāsaka (devotee). When the Brāhmaṇas inquired the reason of this he praised the excellence of Buddhism for which he was out-casted. Thereupon he came to Madhyadeśa[4] (Magadha), was received into the Saṅgha (priesthood) by Ācārya Dharmapāla, attained to great learning in the three Piṭakas, and knew in all 500 sūtras and dhāraṇīs by heart.

76. Dharmakīrti desiring to become acquainted with the

---

[1] *Vide* Takakusu's I-tsing, p. xlv.

[2] This account is taken from Lama Tārānātha's Geschichte des Buddhismus von Schiefner, pp. 175—185.

[3] Cūḍāmaṇi is probably the same as Coḍa or Chola country in the Eastern Deccan. As a fact Dharmakīrti was born in the Deccan: *Vide* article 82 under Pramāṇa-vārtika kārikā.

[4] In Tibetan literature Madhya-deśa signifies Magadha (Behar). But Manu defines Madhya-deśa as the country lying between the Himalayas on the north, the Vindhya mountains on the south, Prayāga in the east, and the river Sarasvatī on the west:

हिमवद्विन्ध्ययोर्मध्यं यत् प्राग् विनशनादपि ।
प्रत्यगेव प्रयागाच्च मध्यदेशः प्रकीर्त्तितः ॥

(Manusaṃhitā 2: 21).

In this connection *vide* a very learned article named "Note on the Middle Country of Ancient India" by Rhys Davids in the Journal of the Royal Asiatic Society, January 1904.

secret doctrine of the Tīrtha system, donned a slave-attire and went southward. On inquiring who was versed in the Tīrtha system, he was informed that the Brāhmaṇa Kumārila was an incomparable master of the same. The assertion that Kumārila was an uncle of Dharmakīrti is unsupported by Indian authority. Kumārila had received a large fortune from his king, owned many rice-fields, five hundred male slaves and five hundred female slaves and many hundred men. When Dharmakīrti after entering their service performed the work of fifty slaves indoors and outdoors, Kumārila and his wife were satisfied. They allowed him to hear the secret doctrines. Obtaining knowledge of the secret teaching from Kumārila, he left his house. With the wages which he received from Kumārila for his special services he gave a great feast to the Brāhmaṇas in the night of his departure.

77. Thereupon he challenged the followers of the system of Kaṇāda named Kaṇāda Gupta and other followers of the Tīrtha system and entered upon debates with them. The debates lasted for three months, during which he withstood all his opponents and converted many of them to Buddhism. Upon this Kumārila was enraged and appeared with 500 Brāhmaṇas for debate. He proposed the condition that whoever was defeated should be killed. Dharmakīrti who did not desire the death of Kumārila induced the latter to enter upon the condition that whoever was defeated should accept the doctrine of the winner. Putting *Dharma* (doctrine) up as the prize they began the debate, and finally Dharmakīrti was victorious. Kumārila and his 500 followers became followers of Buddha.

78. Dharmakīrti further withstood the Nirgranthas (Jainas), Rāhuvratin and others, who lived within the range of the Vindhya mountains. Returning to Dravali (Drāviḍa?) he challenged by criers those who were ready for debate. The majority of the Tīrthas fled; and some actually confessed that they were not equal to the fight. He re-established all the religious schools that had fallen into decay in that country, and lived in the loneliness of the forest given up to meditation.

79. Dharamkītri towards the end of his life erected a vihāra in the land of Kaliṅga, and after having converted many people to the Law (*Dharma*) passed away. Those of his pupils, who by their lives had become like Brahma, carried him to the cemetery for cremation. Then there fell a heavy rain of flowers, and for seven days the whole country was filled with fragrance and music.

80. This Ācārya (Dharmakīrti) and the Tibetan king Sroṅ-tsan-gam po are said to have been contemporaries, which statement might be accepted as authoritative.

81. From this account it is evident that Dharmakīrti was a pupil of Dharmapāla. As the latter lived in 635 A.D., Dharmakīrti must also have lived about that time. This date agrees well with the statement that Dharmakīrti was a contemporary of the Tibetan king Sron-tsan-gam-po who lived during 627—698 A.D.[1] It seems that in 635 A.D., Dharmakīrti was very young as Hwen-thsang does not mention him. On the other hand I-tsing, who travelled over India during 671—695 A.D., declares eloquently how "Dharmakīrti made further improvement in Logic"[2] after Dignāga. The Brāhmanic logician Udyotakara[3] is attacked by Dharmakīrti. The Mīmāṁsaka Sureśvarācārya,[4] author of the Bṛhadāraṇyaka-vārtika, and the Digambara Jaina Vidyānanda, author of the Aṣṭa-sāhasrikā,[5] have on the contrary criticised the definition of perception (*Pratyakṣa*) as given by Dharmakīrti, who is some times designated by the shorter name Kīrti. Vācaspati Miśra[6] too quotes Dharmakīrti to criticise him.

Pramāṇa-vārtika-kārikā.

82. Dharmakīrti is the author of numerous works on Logic. The **Pramāṇa-vārtika-kārikā** is one of them. A verse[7] of this work was quoted by the Hindu philosopher Mādhavācārya in

---

1 *Vide* Wassilief, p. 54; and Csoma de Koros's Tibetan Grammar, p. 183.

2 Takakusu's I-tsing, p. lviii.

3 *Vide* K. B. Pathak's "Bhartṛhari and Kumārila," *Journal of the Bombay Branch of the Royal Asiatic Society*, 1892, vol. xviii, p. 229.

4 Cf. त्रिष्वेव त्वविनाभावादिति यद्धर्मकीर्तिना ।
प्रत्यज्ञायि प्रतिज्ञेयं हीयेतासौ न संशयः ॥
(Sureśvara's Bṛhadāraṇyaka-vārtika, chap. vi.)

5 Vide *Journal of the Bombay Branch of the Royal Asiatic Society*, vol. xix, 1895—97, p. 56.

6 Cf. यथाह धर्मकीर्तिः—
तस्मान्नार्थे न च ज्ञाने स्थूलाभासस्तदात्मनः ।
एकत्र प्रतिषिद्धत्वाद्बहुष्वपि न सम्भवः ॥
(Vācaspati's Bhāmatī on Vedānta-sūtra 2-2-28).

7 The verse runs thus :—
भेदश्च भ्रान्तिविज्ञानैर्दृश्येतेन्दाविवाद्वये ॥
(Pramāṇa-vārtika-kārikā quoted in Mādhavācārya's Sarvadarśanasaṁgraha, chapter on Bauddha darśana).

the 14th century A.D. The following story [1] is told regarding the composition of this work :—

It is said that Dharmakīrti studied many dialectic śāstras, but his spirit was not satisfied. Once at the house of one Īśvara Sena,[2] a pupil of Dignāga, he heard the Pramāṇa-samuccaya. Having heard it for the first time he at once became as proficient as Īśvara Sena who had minutely studied the work. When he heard it the second time, he became like Dignāga, the author of the work, and when he heard it the third time, he recognised several errors in the work. When he mentioned them to Īśvara Sena, the latter so far from being displeased, told him that he was at liberty to condemn all the mistakes of the work and to prepare a critical commentary on it. With the permission thus received he composed a metrical commentary on the Pramāṇa-samuccaya called the Pramāṇa-vārtika-kārikā.

83. The Sanskrit original of the Pramāṇa-vārtika appears to be lost, but there exists a Tibetan translation [3] of it in the Tangyur, section M̱do, volume Ce, folios 194—258. This translation was prepared by the Indian sage Subhūti-śrī-śānti and the Tibetan interpreter Ḏge-waḥi-ḇlo-groṣ. The work in Tibetan is called Tshaḏ-ma-ṟnam-ḫgrel-gyi-tshig signifying "Memorial Verses explanatory of *Pramāṇa* or Sources of Knowledge." The work is divided into four chapters as follows :—(1) Inference for one's own self (in Tibetan : Raṅ-gi-don-ṟjeṣ-su-ḏpag-pa, in Sanskrit : Svārthānumāna) ; (2) Establishment of *Pramāṇa* (in Tibetan : Tshaḏ-ma-grub-pa, in Sanskrit : Pramāṇa-siddhi) ; (3) Perception (in Tibetan : Mṉon-sum, in Sanskrit : Pratyakṣa) ; and (4) Words for the sake of others (in Tibetan : Ǥshan-gyi-don-gyi-tshig, in Sanskrit : Parārtha-vākya). The work concludes by stating that "it was written by the great sage Śrī Dharmakīrti

---

The Tibetan version of the verse runs as follows :—

རྣམ་ཤེས་འཁྲུལ་བས་ཟླ་བ་གཉིས།།
མེད་པར་ཐ་དད་མཐོང་བ་བཞིན།།

(Pramāṇa-vārtika-kārikā embodied in the Tangyur, M̱do, Ce, folio 239. *Vide* Louis de la Vallée Poussin's Le Bouddhisme d'après les sources brahmaniques, p. 34).

[1] *Vide* Tārānātha's Geschichte des Buddhismus von Schiefner, p. 176.

[2] It seems that Īśvara Sena, in whose house Dharmakīrti heard the Pramāṇa-samuccaya, was not a direct pupil of Dignāga, for, while Dignāga lived about 500 A.D., Dharmakīrti lived about 635 A.D.

[3] I have consulted the copy of this work embodied in the Tangyur of the India Office, London.

who was unrivalled and whose fame filled the entire earth."[1] It is further stated that he was born in the Deccan (in Tibetan: Yul-lho-phyog).

Pramāṇa-vārtika-vṛtti.

84. There was a sub-commentary on the Pramāṇa-vārtika-kārikā called **Pramāṇa-vārtika-vṛtti** by Dharmakīrti himself. The Sanskrit original of this work is lost. There exists, however, a Tibetan translation[2] of it in the Tangyur, Mdo, Ce, folios 420—535. In Tibetan the work is named Tshad-ma-rnam-hgrel-gyi-hgrel-wa. In the concluding lines of the work Dharmakīrti is described as "a great teacher and dialectician, whose fame filled all quarters of the earth and who was, as it were, a lion, pressing down the head of elephant-like debaters."[3]

Pramāṇa-viniścaya.

85. **Pramāṇa-viniścaya** quoted[4] by Mādhavācārya is another work on Logic by Dharmakīrti. The Sanskrit original

---

[1] སྙན་པའི་གྲགས་པས་སའི་སྟེང་མ་ལུས་པ་ཁྱབ་པ། འགྲན་ཟླ་མེད་པའི་མཁས་པ་ཆེན་པོ་དཔལ་ཆོས་ཀྱི་གྲགས་པས་མཛད་པ་རྫོགས་སོ།།

(Pramāṇa-vārtika kārikā).

[2] I have consulted the Tibetan xylograph of this work embodied in the Tangyur of the India Office, London.

[3] རིགས་པ་ཆེན་པོ་སའི་སྟེང་མ་ལུས་པ་ན་སྨྲ་བའི་གླང་པོ་ཆེའི་སྤྱི་བོ་གནོན་པར་མཛད་པའི་སེང་གེ། ཕྱོགས་མ་ལུས་པར་སྙན་པར་གྲགས་པ་ཅན་དཔལ་སློབ་དཔོན་ཆོས་གྲགས་སྦྱར་བ།

(Pramāṇa-vārtika-vṛtti).

[4] The following verses of Pramāṇa-viniścaya were quoted in the Sarvadarśana-saṁgraha, chapter on Bauddha darśana, by the Hindu philosopher Mādhavācārya in the 14th century A.D. :—

नान्योऽनुभाव्यो बुद्ध्यास्ति तस्या नानुभवोऽपरः ।
ग्राह्यग्राहकवैधुर्यात् स्वयं सैव प्रकाशते ॥ (क)
सहोपलम्भनियमाद् अभेदो नीलतद्धियोः ॥ (ख)
अविभागोऽपि बुद्ध्यात्मा विपर्यासितदर्शनैः ।
ग्राह्यग्राहकसंवित्तिभेदवानिव लक्ष्यते ॥ (ग)

(Pramāṇa-viniścaya, chap. I).

of this work appears to be lost, but there exists a Tibetan translation[1] of it in the Tangyur, Mdo, Ce, folios 259—347. The translation was prepared by the Kāśmīrian Paṇḍita Parahita Bhadra and the Tibetan interpreter Blo-ldan-śes-rab in the matchless city of Kāśmīra. The work in Tibetan is called Tshad-ma-rnan-par-ṅes-pa signifying "Determination of Pramāṇa or Sources of Knowledge." The work is divided into three chapters as follows:—(1) System of Perception (in Tibetan: Mṅon-sum-gtan-la-dwab-pa, in Sanskrit: Pratyakṣa-vyavasthā); (2) Inference for one's own self (in Tibetan: Raṅ-gi-don-gyi-rjes-su-dpag-pa, in Sanskrit: Svārthānumāna); and (3) Inference for the sake of others (in Tibetan: Gshan-gyi-don-gyi-rjes-su-dpag-pa, in Sanskrit: Parārthānumāna). In the concluding lines Dharmakīrti is described as a great sage of unrivalled fame born in Southern India.

Prof. Louis de la Vallee Poussin in his "Le Bouddhisme d'après les sources brahmaniques," pp. 32 and 34, identifies the above verses with their Tibetan versions as follows :—

བློ་ཡིས་ཉམས་མྱོང་བྱ་གཞན་མེད།།
དེ་ཡི་མྱོང་བ་གཞན་ཡོད་མིན།།
གཟུང་དང་འཛིན་པ་མེད་པའི་ཕྱིར།།
དེ་ནི་དེ་ལྟར་རང་ཉིད་གསལ།། (ཀ)
ལྷན་ཅིག་དམིགས་པ་ངེས་པའི་ཕྱིར།།
སྔོ་དང་དེ་བློ་གཞན་མ་ཡིན།། (ཁ)
བློ་བདག་རྣམ་པར་དབྱེར་མེད་ཀྱང་།།
མཐོང་བ་ཕྱིན་ཅི་ལོག་རྣམས་ཀྱིས།།
གཟུང་བ་འཛིན་པ་རིག་པ་རྣམས།།
ཐམས་ཅད་དང་བཅས་བཞིན་རྟོགས་འགྱུར།། (ག)

(Pramāṇa-viniścaya, chap. I, embodied in the Tibetan Tangyur, Mdo, Ce, folios 272, 274 and 273 respectively).

[1] I have consulted the Tibetan xylograph of this work embodied in the Tangyur of the India Office, London.

Nyāya-bindu.

86. **Nyāya-bindu** is another excellent work on Logic by Dharmakīrti. The Sanskrit original of this work was discovered among the palm leaf manuscripts preserved in the Jaina temple of S'āntinātha, Cambay, and has been published in the Bibliotheca Indica series of Calcutta by Professor Peterson. There exists a Tibetan translation [1] of the work in the Tangyur, Mdo, Ce, folios 347—355. The work in Tibetan is called Rigs-paḥi-thigs-pa signifying "A Drop of Logic." It is divided into three chapters as follows: (1) Perception (in Tibetan: Mṅon-sum, in Sanskrit: Pratyakṣa); (2) Inference for one's own self (in Tibetan: Bdag-gi-don-gyi-rjes-su-dpag-pa, in Sanskrit: Svārthānumāna); and (3) Inference for the sake of others (in Tibetan: Gshan-gyi-don-rjes-su-dpag-pa, in Sanskrit: Parārthānumāna). Some of the subjects discussed in the work are noted below:—

87. In chapter I, it is stated that all objects of man are accomplished by perfect or valid knowledge. Valid knowledge is of two kinds: (1) Perception (in Sanskrit: Pratyakṣa) and (2) Inference (in Sanskrit: Anumāna). Perception which is knowledge derived through the senses, etc., is described as that which is free from illusory experiences (*kalpanā*) and devoid of confusion (*abhrānta*). Illusory experiences are the experiences of false images which appear real as if they were capable of being addressed and touched, *e.g.*, the shadow of a tree may appear as the tree itself or a rope may appear as a snake. Confusion is engendered by such causes as darkness, quick motion, journey by boat, shaking, etc., for instance, to a man journeying by boat, trees on both banks appear to move. Perception is of four kinds: (1) perception by the five senses; (2) perception by the mind; (3) self-consciousness; and (4) knowledge of a contemplative saint. An object of perception is like itself (sva-lakṣaṇa) while an object of inference is like any one of its class (sāmānya-lakṣaṇa), for instance, a cow which I see is a peculiar one possessing an infinite number of qualities which distinguish it from all cows, whereas a cow which I infer is a general one possessing certain qualities in common with other cows; that is, perception is individual knowledge while inference is general knowledge. According to the proximity or remoteness of an object, perception of it varies. This is the peculiar characteristic of an object of perception, and this characteristic proves the object to be absolutely real (paramārtha-sat), as it

Perception.

---

[1] I have consulted the Tibetan xylograph of the Nyāya-bindu embodied in the Tangyur of the India Office, London, as also the excellent edition of F. J. Sher-batski.

shows that it possesses some practical efficiency, and this characteristic also shows that perception is a source of valid knowledge for it exactly corresponds to the object perceived.

Inference for one's own self.

88. In chapter II, Inference for one's own self (Svārthānumāna) is defined as the knowledge of the inferrible derived through the reason or middle term with its three forms or characteristics. In the instance 'this hill has fire, because it has smoke,' the knowledge of the hill as having fire is derived through smoke which is the reason or middle term. The three forms or characteristics of the reason or middle term are the following :—

(1) The middle term must be connected with the minor term, *e.g.*

The hill has fire,
Because it has smoke,
Like a kitchen but unlike a lake.

In this reasoning there must be 'smoke' on the 'hill.'

(2) The middle term must abide only in cases which are homogeneous with the major term, *e.g.*, in the above reasoning 'smoke' abides in a kitchen which is homogeneous with things that contain fire.

(3) The middle term must never abide in cases which are heterogeneous from the major term, *e.g.*, in the above reasoning 'smoke' does not abide in a lake which is heterogeneous from things that contain fire.

Three kinds of the middle term.

89. The middle term is of three kinds according to the relation which it bears to the major term, thus :—

(1) Identity (in Tibetan : Raṅ-bshin, in Sanskrit : Svabhāva), *e.g.*

This is a tree,
Because it is śiṁśapā.

(2) Effect (in Tibetan : Hbras-bu, in Sanskrit : Kārya), *e.g.*
Here there is fire, because there is smoke.

(3) Non-perception (in Tibetan : Mi-dmigs-pa, in Sanskrit : Anupalabdhi), which is of 11 kinds as follows :—

i. Non-perception of identity (Svabhāvānupalabdhi), *e.g.*
Here is no smoke, because it is not perceived (though smoke is of a nature as to be perceived if existent).

ii. Non-perception of effect (Kāryānupalabdhi), *e.g.*
Here there are no causes of smoke of unobstructed capacity, because there is no smoke here.

iii. Non-perception of the pervader or container (Vyāpakānupalabdhi), *e.g.*

Here there is no Śiṁśapā, because there is no tree at all.

iv. Perception contrary to identity (Svabhāva-viruddhopalabdhi), *e.g.*

There is no cold sensation here because there is fire.

v. Perception of the opposite effect (Viruddha-kāryopalabdhi), *e.g.*

Here there is no cold sensation because there is smoke.

vi. Perception of contrary connection (Viruddha-vyāptopalabdhi), *e.g.*

Even the destruction of the past entity is not certain, because it is dependent on other causes.

vii. Perception contrary to the effect (Kārya-viruddhopalabdhi), *e.g.*

Here there are no causes of cold of unobstructed capacity, because there is fire.

viii. Perception contrary to the container (vyāpakaviruddhopalabdhi), *e.g.*

Here there is no icy sensation, because there is fire.

ix. Non-perception of the cause (Kāraṇānupalabdhi), *e.g.*

There is no smoke, because there is no fire.

x. Perception contrary to the cause (Kāraṇa-viruddhopalabdhi), *e.g.*

Hair on his body does not stand erect, because he sits near a fire.

xi. Perception of effect contrary to its cause (Kāraṇa-viruddha-kāryopalabdhi), *e.g.*

This place does not contain any person on whose body hair stands erect, because there is smoke here.

Inference for the sake of others.

90. In chapter III Inference for the sake of others (Parārthānumāna) is defined as the declaration of the three-formed middle term in words, that is, when the reason is set forth in words with a view to producing a conviction in others, it is said to be an inference for the sake of others.

Inference is a kind of knowledge; and words are here called inference by the attributing of effect to cause, for, though they are not themselves knowledge, they produce it. Inference for the sake of others is of two kinds: (1) direct or homogeneous (in Sanskrit: Sādharmyavat); and (2) indirect or heterogeneous (in Sanskrit: Vaidharmyavat), as follows:—

(*a*) Sound is non-eternal,
Because it is a product,
All products are non-eternal as a pot (direct).

(*b*) Sound is non-eternal,
Because it is a product,
No non-non-eternal *i.e.*, eternal (thing) is a product as ether (indirect).

91. The minor term (Pakṣa) is that to which the relation of the major term is to be proved, as—This hill has fire, because it has smoke. In this reasoning 'hill' is the minor term which is to be proved as having 'fire' which is the major term. A minor term and its corresponding major term combined together, constitute a proposition which, when offered for proof, is called a thesis.

Fallacies of thesis or Pakṣābhāsa.

92. There are four fallacies of the thesis (Pakṣābhāsa).

A thesis is fallacious if it is incompatible with—

(1) Perception, *e.g.* Sound is inaudible;
(2) Inference, *e.g.* Sound is eternal;
(3) Conception, *e.g.* The moon is not *luna* (S'aśi a-candra);
or (4) One's own statement, *e.g.* Inference is not a source of knowledge.

Fallacies of the middle term.

93. It has already been stated that the middle term must possess three characteristics. Fallacies of the middle term (Hetvābhāsa) occur even if one of the characteristics is unproved, uncertain or contradictory, thus—

A. Unproved (asiddha).

(1) Sound is eternal, because it is visible.
(Visibility of sound is admitted by neither party).

(2) Trees are conscious, because they die if their barks are taken off.
(This peculiar kind of death of trees is not admitted by the opponent).

(3) The hill has fire, because it has vapour.
(Vapour as an effect of fire is questioned).

(4) The soul is all-pervading, because it is perceived everywhere.
(It is a matter of doubt whether the soul is perceived everywhere).

B. Uncertain (anaikāntika).

(5) Sound is non-eternal.
Because it is knowable.

(The knowable is too general, because it includes the eternal as well as the non-eternal).

(6) A certain man is omniscient,
Because he is a speaker.

(The reason is not general enough, for speakers are not necessarily either omniscient or non-omniscient).

C. Contradictory (viruddha).

(7) Sound is eternal,
Because it is a product.

(Here 'product' is not homogeneous with 'eternal,' that is, the middle term is opposed to the major term).

(8) Sound is eternal,
Because it is a product.

(Here 'product' is not heterogeneous from 'non-eternal')

Dharmakīrti criticises Digṅāga.

94. The opposition of the middle term to the major term is a kind of contradiction which is admitted by both Digṅāga and Dharmakīrti. Opposition of the middle term to the implied major term (in the event of the major term being ambiguous) is noted by Digṅāga in his Nyāya-praveśa[1] as another kind of contradiction (*Viruddha*). Dharmakīrti in his Nyāyabindu rejects this view saying that this second contradiction is included in the first kind.[2] Digṅāga has in his Nyāya-praveśa treated another kind of fallacy called "non-

---

[1] *Vide* Nyāya-praveśa, Fallacies of the Middle Term, No. 12. This contradiction, *viz.*, the opposition of the middle term to the implied major term (इष्टविघातकृद् विरुद्ध) is called in Tibetan: ཆོས་ཅན་གྱི་ཁྱད་པར་ཕྱིན་ཅི་ལོག་ཏུ་བསྒྲུབ་པར་བྱེད་པ། (Nyāya-praveśa).

[2] तत्र च तृतीयोऽपि इष्टविघातकृद् विरुद्धः । ... स इह कस्मान्नोक्तः अनयोरेवान्तर्भावात् । (Nyāya-bindu, Peterson's edition, Bibliotheca Indica series, chapter III, p. 113).

अयं च विरुद्ध आचार्य्य दिङ्नागेन उक्तः । स कस्माद् वार्त्तिककारेण सता मया नोक्तः । (Nyāyabindu-ṭīkā, Peterson's edition, Bibliotheca Indica series, chapter III, p. 78).

erroneous contradiction"[1] (Viruddhāvyabhicāri), which it rejected by Dharmakīrti in his Nyāyabindu, on the ground that it does not arise in the case of inference, but is based on the scriptures of the two parties engaged in disputation.

Dharmakīrti's Theory of example.

95. In opposition to Dignāga, Dharmakīrti maintains that 'example' is not a part of a syllogism,[2] as it is included in the middle term, *e.g.*

The hill is fiery,
Because it is smoky,
Like a kitchen.

In this reasoning the term 'smoky' includes a 'kitchen' as well as other similar things, hence it is almost unnecessary to cite the example 'kitchen.'

Compare K. B. Pathak's "On the authorship of the Nyāyabindu" in the *Journal of the Bombay Branch of the Royal Asiatic Society*, vol. XIX, p. 51.

1 *Vide* Nyāya-praveśa, Fallacies of the Middle Term, No. 10. This fallacy of 'non-erroneous contradiction' is called in Sanskrit: **विरुद्धा-व्यभिचारी** and in Tibetan: འགལ་བ་ལ་མི་འཁྲུལ་པ (Nyāya-praveśa).

विरुद्धाव्यभिचार्यपि संशयहेतुरुक्तः। स इह कस्मान्नोक्तः अनुमानविषये ऽसम्भवात् । (Nyāyabindu, p. 115).

ननु चाचार्येण विरुद्धाव्यभिचार्यपि संशयहेतुरुक्तः।... क तर्हि चाचार्य-दिङ्नागेन अयं हेतुदोष उक्तः इत्याह। ... तस्मादागमाश्रयमनुमानमाश्रित्य विरुद्धा-व्यभिचार्युक्तः । (Nyāyabindu-ṭikā, p. 84).

Compare also B.B.R.A.S., vol. XIX, p. 49.

2 **त्रिरूपो हेतुरुक्तः। तावतैव अर्थप्रतीतिरिति न पृथग् दृष्टान्तो नाम साधना-वयवः कश्चित्। तेनास्य लक्षणं पृथग् [न] उच्यते गतार्थत्वात्।**

(Nyāyabindu, Peterson's edition, Bibliotheca Indica series, pp. 115—116). Peterson has omitted **न** wrongly as will appear from the Tibetan version which runs as follows :—

གཏན་ཚིགས་ཀྱི་མཚན་ཉིད་གསུམ་སྟོན་པ་དེ་ཙམ་གྱིས་དོན་རྟོགས་པས།
དཔེ་ཞེས་བྱ་བ་སྒྲུབ་པའི་ཡན་ལག་ནི་ལོགས་ཤིག་ཏུ་ཅི་ཡང་མེད་དོ།།
དེས་ན་དེའི་མཚན་ཉིད་ལོགས་ཤིག་ཏུ་མ་བརྗོད་དེ་དོན་གོ་བའི་ཕྱིར།།༡༢༢།།

(Nyāyabindu„ Sherbatski's edition, St. Petersburg, p. 193).

Nevertheless, says Dharmakīrti,[1] the example has this much value that it points out in a particular way what has been expressed in a general form by the middle term: thus, the general expression "all smoky things are fiery" is made more impressive by the particular example 'kitchen' which is smoky as well as fiery.

96. Example is of two kinds: (1) homogeneous and (2) heterogeneous. Fallacies of the homogeneous example occur as follows:—

Fallacies of the homogeneous example.

(1) Sound is eternal,
Because it is incorporeal,
Like action.

(Action cannot serve as an example, because it is not eternal, that is, because it is excluded from the major term).

(2) Sound is eternal,
Because it is incorporeal,
Like atoms.

(Atoms cannot serve as an example, because they are not incorporeal, that is, because they are excluded from the middle term).

(3) Sound is eternal,
Because it is incorporeal,
Like a pot.

(Pot cannot serve as an example, because it is neither eternal nor incorporeal, that is, because it is excluded from both major and middle terms).

(4) This man is passionate,
Because he is a speaker,
Like a person in the street.

(The person in the street cannot serve as an example, as it is questionable whether he is passionate, that is, it involves doubt as to the validity of the major term).

(5) This man is mortal,
Because he is passionate,
Like a person in the street.

(This example involves doubt as to the validity of the middle term, that is, it is questionable whether the person in the street is passionate).

---

[1] ......उक्तम् धर्मेण,......
पुनर्विशेषेण दर्शनीयावुक्तौ। (Nyāyabindu, p. 116).

(6) This man is non-omniscient,
Because he is passionate,
Like a person in the street.

(This example involves doubt as to the validity of both the major and middle terms, that is, it is questionable whether the person in the street is passionate and non-omniscient).

(7) This man is passionate,
Because he is a speaker,
Like a certain person.

(This example is unconnected (*ananvaya*), for there is no inseparable connection between being 'passionate' and being a 'speaker').

(8) Sound is non-eternal,
Because it is a product,
Like a pot.

(This example involves the fallacy of 'connection unshown,' ***apradarśitānvaya*** : the connection should be shown as follows: All products are non-eternal like a pot).

(9) Sound is a product,
Because it is non-eternal,
All non-eternal things are products like a pot.

(The example involves the fallacy of inverted connection, ***viparītānvaya*** ; the real connection should be shown as follows : All products are non-eternal like a pot).

97. Similarly there are nine fallacies of the heterogeneous example.

98. *Refutation* (*Dūṣaṇa*) consists in pointing out in the reasoning of an opponent any one of the fallacies mentioned above. The fallacies or semblances of refutation are the futilities called in Sanskrit *Jāti*.[1]

99. In the concluding lines of the Nyāyabindu it is stated that "Dharmakīrti vanquished the entire Tīrthikas as Śākyamuni had subdued the large army of Māra ; and as the sun dispels darkness, the Nyāyabindu has exterminated the Ātmaka theory (that is, the Tīrthika doctrine)—wonderful ![2]

---

[1] For Jāti *vide* Nyāya-sūtra, Book I, aphorism 58.

[2] ཤཱ་ཀྱ་ཐུབ་པས་བདུད་ཀྱི་སྡེ་བོ་ཆེ ||
ཆོས་ཀྱི་གྲགས་པས་མུ་སྟེགས་མ་ལུས་པ ||

Hetu-bindu-vivaraṇa.

100. The **Hetu-bindu-vivaraṇa** is another excellent work on Logic by Dharmakīrti. The Sanskrit original of this work is lost, but there exists a Tibetan translation [1] in the Tangyur, M̱do, Ce, folios 355—375. The work in Tibetan is called Gtan-tshigs̱-kyi-thigs̱-pa signifying "A Drop of Reason." The work is divided into three chapters as follows :—

(1) Relation of identity between the middle term and the major term (in Tibetan : Raṅ-ḇshin-gyi-gtan-tshigs̱, in Sanskrit : Sva-bhāva-hetu) ; (2) Relation of effect and cause between the middle term and the major term (in Tibetan: H̱bras̱-buḫi-gtan-tshigs̱, in Sanskrit : Kārya-hetu) ; and (3) Relation of negation between the middle term and the heterogeneous major term (in Tibetan : Mi-ḏmigs̱-paḫi-gtan-tshigs̱, in Sanskrit : Anupalabdhi-hetu).

Tarka-nyāya or Vāda-nyāya.

101. The **Tarka-nyāya** or **Vāda-nyāya** is another treatise on Logic by Dharmakīrti. The Sanskrit original of this work is lost, but there exists a Tibetan translation [2] in the Tangyur, M̱do, Ce, folios 384—416. The work in Tibetan is called Ṟtsoḏ-paḫi-rigs̱-pa signifying the "Method of Discussion." The Tibetan translation was prepared by the great Indian sage Jñāna-śrī-bhadra and the Tibetan interpreter-monk Ḏge-waḫi-ḇlo-gros̱. Subsequently the translation was retouched by the great Paṇḍita Dīpaṅkara (of Vikramanīpura in Bengal, born in 980 A.D.) and the interpreter-monk Dar-ma-grags̱.

Santānāntara-siddhi.

102. The **Santānāntara-siddhi** is a philosophical treatise by Dharmakīrti. The Sanskrit original of the work is lost, but there exists a Tibetan version [3] in the Tangyur, M̱do, Ce, folios

---

ཉི་མས་སླག་ཙམ་རིགས་པའི་ཐིགས་པ་ཡིས།།

བདག་གི་བློ་བ་དྲངས་ཕྱུང་ངོ་མཚར་ཉིད།།

(Nyāyabindu).

1 I have consulted the copy embodied in the Tangyur of the India Office, London.

2 I have consulted the work embodied in the Tangyur of the India Office, London.

3 I have consulted the Tibetan version embodied in the Tangyur of the India Office, London.

416—420. The work in Tibetan is called Rgyud-gshan-grub-pa signifying "Proof of the Continuity of Succession."

Sambandha-parīkṣā.

103. The **Sambandha-parīkṣā** is another philosophical treatise by Dharmakīrti. The Sanskrit original of the work is lost, but there exists a Tibetan translation[1] in the Tangyur, Mdo, Ce, folios 375—377. The work in Tibetan is called Hbrel-wa-brtag-pa signifying "Examination of Connection." The Tibetan translation was prepared by the Indian teacher Jñānagarbha and the interpreter Vande-nam-mkhas.

Sambandha-parīkṣā-vṛtti.

104. The **Sambandha-parīkṣā-vṛtti**[2] is a commentary on the Sambandha-parīkṣā by Dharmakīrti himself. The Sanskrit original of the work is lost, but there exists a Tibetan translation in the Tangyur, Mdo, Ce, folios 377—384. The work in Tibetan is called Hbrel-wa-brtag-pahi-hgrel-wa.

Devendrabodhi (about 650 A.D.).

105. Devendrabodhi, called in Tibetan Lha-dwaṅ-blo, was a contemporary of Dharmakīrti,[3] and so lived about 650 A.D. He wrote the following work on Logic :—

106. The **Pramāṇa-vārtika-pañjikā**, called in Tibetan, Tshad-ma-rnam-hgrel-gyi-dkah-hgrel, signifying "An Explanation of Difficulties in the Pramāṇa-vārtika of Dharmakīrti." The Sanskrit original of this work is lost, but there exists a Tibetan translation[4] in the Tangyur, Mdo, Che, folios 1—380. The translation was prepared by the Indian sage Subhūti-śrī and the Tibetan interpreter-monk Dge-wahi-blo-gros.

107. This story[5] is told regarding the composition of the Pramāṇa-vārtika-pañjikā :—

Dharmakīrti chose Devendrabodhi to write a commentary on his Pramāṇa-vārtika. After Devendrabodhi had finished the

---

[1] I have consulted the copy embodied in the Tangyur of the India Office, London.

[2] I have consulted the copy of this work embodied in the Tangyur of the India Office, London.

[3] *Vide* Tārānātha's Geschichte des Buddhismus von Schiefner, pp. 186—187.

[4] I have consulted the work in the monastery of Labrang in Sikkim in 1907.

[5] *Vide* Tārānatha's Geschichte des Buddhismus von Schiefner, pp. 186-187.

commentary for the time and shown it to Dharmakīrti, the latter erased it with water. After he had compiled it a second time, Dharmakīrti burnt it in fire. He then compiled it a third time and gave it to Dharmakīrti with the observation: "Since the majority of men are incompetent and time is fleeting, I have written this commentary for the people of lighter understanding." This time Dharmakīrti allowed the work to exist.

S'ākyabodhi (about 675 A.D.).

108. S'ākyabodhi [1] is stated to have been a pupil of Devendrabodhi. He seems to have lived about 675 A.D. He was the author of the following work :—

109. The **Pramāṇa-vārtika (-pañjikā)-ṭikā**, called in Tibetan: Tshad-ma-rnam-hgrel-gyi-hgrel-bśad, which is an annotation on the Pramāṇa-vārtika-pañjikā of Devendrabodhi. The Sanskrit original of this work appears to be lost, but there exists a Tibetan translation [2] which covers volumes Je and Ñe of the Tangyur, Mdo. The translation was prepared by the interpreter Dge-wahi-blo gros.

Vinīta Deva (about 700 A.D.).

110. Vinīta Deva,[3] called in Tibetan Dul-lha, lived in Nālanda during the time of king Lalita Candra, son of Govi Candra, and Dharmakīrti died during the time of Govi Candra. Vimala Candra, the father of Govi Candra, was married to the sister of Bhartṛhari, who sprang from the ancient royal family of Malwa. Supposing this Bhartṛhari to be identical with the famous grammarian of that name who died in 651—652 A.D.,[4] we may place his contemporary Govi Candra in the middle of the 7th century A.D. This is exactly the time when Dharmakīrti died. Hence we may conclude that Lalita Candra, son of Govi Candra, flourished towards the end of the 7th century A.D. Vinīta Deva, contemporary of Lalita Candra, must also have lived about this time, a view which harmonises with the date of Dharmakīrti on whose works Vinīta Deva wrote commentaries.

Vinīta Deva, who was the famous author of the Samayabhedoparacana-cakra, wrote the following works on Logic :—

---

1 *Vide* Tārānātha's Geschichte des Buddhismus von Schiefner, p. 187.

2 I have consulted this work in the monastery of Labrang in Sikkim in 1907.

3 *Vide* Tārānātha's Geschichte des Buddhismus von Schiefner, pp. 195—198, 272; Pag-sam-jon-zang edited by Sarat Chandra Das, pp. xlviii, 108.

4 *Vide* Takakusu's I-tsing, p. lvii.

111. **Nyāya-bindu-ṭīkā**, called in Tibetan: Rigs-paḥi-thigs-pa-rgya-cher-ḥgrel-wa, which is a detailed commentary on the Nyāyabindu of Dharmakīrti. The Sanskrit original of this work is lost, but a Tibetan translation [1] of it exists in the Tangyur, Mdo, She, folios 1—43. The translation was prepared by the Indian sage Jina Mitra and the interpreter of Shu-chen named Vande-ye-śes-sde.

112. **Hetu-bindu-ṭīkā**, called in Tibetan: Gtan-tshigs-kyi-thigs-pa-rgya-cher-ḥgrel-wa, which is a detailed commentary on the Hetu-bindu of Dharmakīrti. The Sanskrit original of this work appears to be lost, but there exists a Tibetan translation [2] in the Tangyur, Mdo, She, folios 116—205. The translation was prepared by the Indian teacher Prajñā Varma and the interpreter-monk of Shu-chen named Dpal-brtsegs-rakṣita.

113. **Vāda-nyāya-vyākhyā**, called in Tibetan: Rtsod-paḥi-rigs-paḥi-ḥgrel-wa, which is a commentary on the Vāda-nyāya (otherwise called Tarka-nyāya) of Dharmakīrti. The Sanskrit original of this work appears to be lost, but there exists a Tibetan translation [3] in the Tangyur, Mdo, Ze, folios 39—65. The work opens thus: "Who is self-perfected in sweet logical discussion, supreme in patience, affection, charity and self-restraint, and who is the most excellent of logicians—to him (Buddha) bowing down I compose a commentary on the text of Vāda-nyāya."

114. **Sambandha-parīkṣā-ṭīkā**, called in Tibetan Ḥbrel-pa-brtag-paḥi rgya-cher-bśad-pa, which is a copious commentary on the Sambandhaparīkṣā of Dharmakīrti. The Sanskrit original of this work is lost, but there exists a Tibetan translation [4] in the Tangyur, Mdo, Ze, folios 1—24. The translation was prepared by the Indian sage Jñāna-garbha and the Tibetan interpreter Vande-nam-mkhas. The work opens thus:—

"Who is entirely unconnected with the world, and is yet designated as the supreme teacher of it—to him bowing down fully I explain the Sambandha-parīkṣā."

115. **Ālambana-parīkṣā-ṭīkā**, called in Tibetan Dmigs-pa-brtag-paḥi-ḥgrel-bśad, is an annotation on the Ālambana-parīkṣā of Dignāga. The Sanskrit original of this work appears to be lost, but there exists a Tibetan translation [5] in the

---

[1] This work was brought down to Calcutta by the British Mission to Tibet during 1904. I examined it by permission of the Government of India. It is now deposited in the British Museum, London.

[2] I examined this work by permission of the Government of India when it was brought down to Calcutta by the British Mission to Tibet, 1904.

[3] I have consulted the India Office copy.

[4] I have consulted the India Office copy.

[5] I have consulted the India Office copy.

Tangyur, Mdo, Ze, folios 186—200. The translation was prepared by the Indian sage S'ākya-siṁha and the interpreter Vande-dpal-brtsegs of Shu-chen. The work opens thus:—

"Meditating on the merciful Omniscient One, and saluting him by my head, I compose the Ālambana-parīkṣā-ṭīkā."

It ends thus:—

"Here is finished the Ālambana parīkṣā-ṭīkā, which is a clean work of the teacher Vinīta Deva who weighed all sorts of ālambana (objects of thought), and is a lion of speakers confounding the brains of the Tīrthika-elephants."

116. **Santānāntara-siddhi-ṭīkā**, called in Tibetan: Rgyud-gshan-grub-pahi-bgrel-bśad, being a commentary on the Santānāntara-siddhi of Dharmakīrti. The Sanskrit original of this work appears to be lost, but there exists a Tibetan translation [1] in the Tangyur, Mdo, Tshe, folios 1—21. The translation was prepared by the Indian sage Viśuddha-siṁha and the interpreter of Shu-chen named Dpal-rtsegs-rakṣita.

Candra Gomin (about 700 A.D.).

117. Candra Gomin,[2] called in Tibetan: Zla-wa-dge-bsñen, was born in a Kṣatriya family in the east at Vārendra (modern Rajshahye in Bengal). He was endowed with a very keen intellect and acquired distinction in literature, grammar, logic, astronomy, music, fine arts and the science of medicine. Under Ācārya Sthiramati he learnt the Sūtra and Abhidharma Piṭakas of the Buddhist scripture, and was converted to Buddhism by the Vidyādhara Ācārya Aśoka.[3] He had an ardent faith in the Buddhist god Avalokiteśvara and the goddess Tārā.[4] He was offered in marriage a daughter of the king of Nâlendra. Being told that she was named Tārā, which was the name of his tutelary deity, he thinking it improper to accept her hands shrank from her with fear. Upon this the king of Vārendra became angry and put Candra Gomin into a chest which was thrown into the Ganges. The chest was carried down until it stopped at an island at the place where the Ganges flows into the ocean. Candra Gomin with deep reverence offered a prayer to goddess Tārā by whose blessing he got out of the chest. He

---

1 I have consulted the India Office xylograph of the Tibetan version.

2 *Vide* Tāranātha's Geschichte des Buddhismus von Schiefner, pp. 145—146, 148—158; and Pag-sam-jon-zang edited in the original Tibetan by Sarat Chandra Das, Calcutta, pp. 95 96.

3 Ācārya Aśoka was the author of a logical treatise called **Sāmānya-dūṣaṇa-dikprakāśikā**, a short treatise on the refutation of generality, lately recovered from Nepal.

4 For Candra Gomin's "Ārya-Tārā-antarbali-vidhi" *vide* Satischandra Vidyabhusana's Sragdharā-stotra, Introduction, pp. xx, xxi.

resided in the island which was in course of time named Candra-dvīpa[1] or the island of Candra. He as a Buddhist devotee (*upāsaka*) established there stone-images of Avalokiteśvara and Tārā. At first only fishermen settled in the island, but afterwards other people came to live there. Gradually the island became a town.

118. Candra Gomin thereupon went to Ceylon and on his way back found in Southern India in the house of Vararuci, Nāga-S'eṣa's (Patañjali's) Bhāṣya on Pāṇini's grammar. Finding that it contained "many words but few thoughts," he himself composed a commentary on Pāṇini, which was named Candra-vyākaraṇa.[2] Afterwards he came to Nālandā—the store-house of knowledge—and met there Candra-kīrti, the famous commentator on the Mādhyamika Philosophy of Ārya Nāgārjuna. Candra Gomin himself was a follower of the Yogācāra system expounded by Ārya Asanga. While Candra Kīrti and Candra Gomin entered upon philosophical discussions people used to observe[3]: "Alas! the text of Ārya Nāgārjuna is medicine to some but poison to others, whereas the text of invincible Ārya Asaṅga is very ambrosia to all men." It is further stated that into a well at Nālandā Candra Gomin threw the original manuscript of his grammar, thinking that it was not better than the one which Candra Kīrti had written. At that time Tārā and Avalokiteśvara appeared before him saying: "Though Candra Kīrti is overwhelmed with pride as a sage, your work is more useful than all others and will do immense good to the world." They raised the manuscript from the well, which was

---

1 Candra dvīpa is situated in the district of Barisal in South-eastern Bengal at a place where the Padmā, which is a main outlet of the Ganges, falls into the ocean. Vārendra in which Candra Gomin was born is identical with the Rajshahye division in North-eastern Bengal through which the Padmā flows.

2 For Candra-vyākaraṇa *vide* Satis Chandra Vidyabhusana's "Sanskrit works on Literature, Grammar, Rhetoric and Lexicography, as preserved in Tibet" in the *Journal of the Asiatic Society of Bengal*, new series, Vol. iii, No. 2, 1907. The Candra-vyākaraṇa in the original Sanskrit has been printed in Germany.

3 ཀྱི་མ་འཕགས་པ་ཀླུ་སྒྲུབ་གཞུང་།
ལ་ལའི་སྨན་ལ་ལ་ལའི་དུག།
མི་ཕམ་འཕགས་པ་ཐོགས་མེད་གཞུང་།
སྐྱེ་བོ་ཀུན་ལ་བདུད་རྩི་ཉིད། (Pag-sam-jon-zang, p. 96).

thence reputed as "Candra's well" (in Sanskrit: Candra-kūpa and in Tibetan: Tsandraḥi-khron-pa), the water of which was wont to be drunk by people in the belief that thereby their intellect would become sharp. Candra Kīrti was, however, a great admirer of Candra Gomin. When the latter arrived at Nālandā the monks refused to give him a reception, saying that it was not proper for priests to welcome a mere devotee (*upāsaka*). Hearing this Candra Kīrti brought three chariots, two of which were occupied by himself and Candra Gomin respectively, while in the third was placed an image of Mañjuśrī, the Buddhist god of learning. The chariots passed through the town in a great procession attended by the whole body of priests who came really to recite hymns to Mañjuśrī, but apparently to accord a fitting welcome to Candra Gomin.[1]

119. Candra Gomin lived at a time when S'īla, son of Harṣa, reigned. During this time king Siṁha of the Licchavi dynasty reigned in Vārendra. The famous poet Ravi Gupta was a contemporary of Bharṣa, son of Siṁha. S'rī Harṣa seems to be the same as king Harṣa Vardhana who was a contemporary of Hwen-thsang and reigned in 647 A.D. His son S'īla seems, on a rough calculation, to have reigned in 700 A.D., when his contemporary Candra Gomin must also have lived. Jaina Hema Candra Sūri who lived during 1088—1172 A.D., refers to Candra Gomin while Jayāditya,[2] the famous author of the Kāśikā-vṛtti, who died in 661—662 A.D.,[3] does not mention him. This may be explained on the supposition that Candra Gomin lived after Jayāditya, but preceded Hema Candra.

120. Candra Gomin was the author of the following work on Logic: **Nyāyāloka-siddhi**, called in Tibetan: Rigs-pa-grub-paḥi-sgron-ma, signifying "a lamp of logical reasoning." The Sanskrit original of this work appears to be lost, but there exists a Tibetan translation[4] in the Tangyur, Mdo, Ze, folios 200—201. The translation was prepared by Paṇḍita S'rī Sita-prabha and the interpreter-monk Vairocana.

RAVI GUPTA (ABOUT 725 A.D.).

121. Ravi Gupta,[5] called in Tibetan: Ñi-ma-sbas, was born in Kāśmīra. He was a great poet, dialectician and Tāntric

---

1 *Vide* Pag sam-jon-zang, pp. 95-96.

2 *Vide* Professor F. Kielhorn's "Indra Gomin and other grammarians" in the Indian Antiquary, Vol. xv, June 1886, pp. 181, 184.

3 *Vide* Takakusu's I-tsing, p. lvii.

4 I have used the India Office copy.

5 *Vide* Tārānātha's Geschichte des Buddhismus von Schiefner, pp. 146, 147, 243; and Pag-sam-jon-zang, part i, pp. 90, 101, 118, xxxvii.

teacher, who established 12 great religious schools in his native country and Magadha. He was a contemporary of king Bharṣa of Vārendra, and flourished a little later than Candra Gomin, who had lived during the time of Bharṣa's father Siṁha. Ravi Gupta must have lived in the first quarter of the eighth century A.D., for his disciple the famous Tāntric monk Sarvajña Mitra [1] lived in the middle of that century. Ravi Gupta was the author [2] of the following work on Logic:—

122. **Pramāṇa-vārtika-vṛtti**, called in Tibetan: Tshad-ma-rnam-hgrel-gyi-hgrel-pa, which is an annotation on the Pramāṇa-vārtika of Dharmakīrti. The Sanskrit original of this work appears to be lost, but there exists a Tibetan translation [3] in the Tangyur, Mdo, Tshe, folios 132-252.

JINENDRABODHI (ABOUT 725 A.D.).

123. In the Tangyur, Mdo, Re, there is the Tibetan version of a work called **Viśālāmala-vatī-nāma-pramāṇa-samuccaya-ṭīkā**. This version was prepared by the Tibetan interpreter Rdo-rje-rgyal-mtshan with the assistance of Dpal-ldan-blo-gros.

124. The author of the original work was Jinendrabodhi, called in Tibetan Rgyal-dwaṅ-blo-gros, who was a venerable countryman of the Bodhisattva (Dignāga?). He is perhaps the same person who wrote the well-known Nyāsa on the grammar of Pāṇini in the eighth century A.D.

S'ĀNTA RAKṢITA (749 A.D.).

125. S'ānta Rakṣita,[4] called in Tibetan: Shi-wa-htsho, was born in the royal family of Za-hor [in Bengal?]. The exact date of his birth is unknown, but it is stated that he was born at the time of Go Pāla who reigned up to 705 A.D. (*vide* Appendix B) and died at the time of Dharma Pāla who became king in 765 A.D. He followed the Svatantra Mādhyamika school, and was a Professor at Nālandā (*vide* Appendix A). He visited Tibet at the invitation of King Khri-sroṅ-deu-tsan who was born in 728 A.D., and died in 864 A.D. The king, with the assistance of S'ānta Rakṣita, built in 749 A.D. the monastery of Sam-ye [5] in

---

[1] *Vide* Satis Chandra Vidyabhusana's Sragdharā Stotra, Introduction, p. xxx, printed in the Bibliotheca Indica series of Calcutta.

[2] For Ravi Gupta's Ārya-koṣa see Rockhill's Buddha, p. 228; and for his works on Tantra, see Satis Chandra Vidyabhusana's Sragdharā Stotra, Introduction, pp. v-vii.

[3] I have consulted the copy of the India Office, London.

[4] *Vide* Pag-sam-jon-zang edited by Sarat Chandra Das, C.I.E., Calcutta, p. 112.

[5] *Vide* Csoma de Koros's Tibetan Grammar, p. 183; Sarat Chandra Das in the *Journal of the Asiatic Society of Bengal*, 1881, Part I, p. 226: and Waddell's Lamaism, p. 28.

Tibet, modelled after the Odantapura Vihāra of Magadha. Sam-ye was the first Buddhist monastery in Tibet and Śāna Rakṣita was its first abbot. He worked in Tibet for 13 years, that is, until 762 A.D. He was known there under the name of Ācārya Bodhisattva, and was the author of the following works on Logic:—

126. **Vāda-nyāya-vṛtti-vipañcitārtha,** called in Tibetan: Rtsoḏ-paḫi-rigs̱-paḫi-ḫbrel-pa-don-ṟnam-par-ḫbyeḏ-pa, an elaborate commentary on the Vāda-nyāya of Dharmakīrti. The Sanskrit original of this work appears to be lost, but there exists a tibetan translation [1] in the Tangyur, M̱do, Ze, folios 65—186, and in the Tangyur, M̱do, Tshe, folios 21—131. The translation was prepared by the Indian sage Kumāra-śrī-bhadra and the Tibetan interpreter-monks venerable S'es̱-rab and Ḫbro-señ-ḏkar (who was a native of the province of Ḫbro or Dö) in the holy monastery of Ḇsam-yas̱ (Sam-ye). The work opens thus:—

"Who constantly dispersing darkness by the ray of the heap of various pure precious qualities, exerted himself for the sake of obtaining the fruits of desire of various sentient beings and rejoiced to do good to the entire world—to that Mañju-śrī bowing down in reverence, I compose this concise and stainless Vāda-nyāya-vṛtti-vipañcitārtha."

127. **Tattva-saṁgraha-kārikā**, called in Tibetan: De-kho-na-ñid-ḇs̱dus̱-paḫi-tshig-leḫur-ḇyas̱-pa, a work containing memorial verses on a summary of the Tattvas. The Sanskrit original of this work appears to be lost, but there exists a Tibetan translation [2] in the Tangyur, M̱do, H̱e, folios 1—146. The translation was prepared by the Indian Paṇḍita Guṇākara-śrī-bhadra (belonging to the religious circle first instituted by the great king Lalitāditya in the incomparable city of Kāśmīra) and the great Tibetan interpreter the S'ākya monk Lha-ḇla-ma-shi-wa-ḫod in the province of Guge (S.-W. Tibet). The work reviews various systems of philosophy such as the Sāṁkhya, Jaina, etc.[3]

---

[1] I have consulted the xylograph of this work contained in the India Office, London.

[2] I have consulted the work in the monastery of Labrang, Sikkim, which I visited in June 1907. For a detailed account of this work *vide* my "Sāṁkhya Philosophy in the Land of the Lamas" in the *Journal of the Asiatic Society of Bengal*, new series, Vol. iii, No. 8.

[3] The Tattvasaṁgraha herein noticed is quite different from the Tattvasamāsa, a Brāhmaṇic work on the Sāṁkhya philosophy, a manuscript of which is contained in the library of the Asiatic Society of Bengal.

Dr George Bühler, during his explorations of the Bṛhat-jñāna-koṣa in the temple of Pārśva-nātha at Jesalmir, found in 1873 a *Pothi*, consisting of 189 ancient palm-leaves showing the characters of the 12th or 13th century, and bearing on the outside corner the title *Kamala-śīla-tarka*

128. The subject-matter of the work begins thus:—

"From *Pradhāna* (the primordial matter or nature) possessed of entire powers all sorts of effects are produced."

(*vide* Dr. G. Bühler's correspondence with Rai Sarat Chandra Das, Bahadur, C.I.E., published in the *Journal of the Buddhist Text Society of Calcutta*, Vol. i, part ii, p. x). The real name of the work, according to Dr. Bühler, is *Tarka-saṁgraha*. Now, this Tarkasaṁgraha is nothing but Tattvasaṁgraha of S'ānta Rakṣita with the commentary, by Kamala S'īla. The introductory part (*Maṅgala*) of the Tarka-saṁgraha, as noticed by Dr. Bühler, runs as follows:—

प्रकृतीशोभयात्मादि [क्रियया] रहितं चलम् ।
कर्म्म तत्फलसम्बन्धव्यवस्थादिसमाश्रयम् ॥
गुणद्रव्यक्रियाजातिसमवायाद्युपाधिभिः ।
शून्यमारोपिताकारशब्दप्रत्ययगोचरम् ॥
स्पष्टलक्षणसंयुक्तप्रमाद्वितयनिश्चितम् ।
अणीयसापि नांशेन मिश्रीभूतापरात्मकम् ॥
असंक्रान्तिमनाद्यन्तं प्रतिबिम्बादिसंनिभम् ।
सर्व्वप्रपञ्चसन्दोहनिर्मुक्तमगतं परैः ॥
स्वतन्त्रश्रुतिनिःसङ्गो जगद्धितविधित्सया ।
अनल्पकल्पासंख्येयसात्मीभूतमहोदयः ॥
यः प्रतीत्यसमुत्पादं जगाद वदतां वरः ।
तं सर्व्वज्ञं प्रणम्यायं क्रियते तर्कसंग्रहः ॥

The introductory part in the Tattvasaṁgraha is identical with the above as is evident from the Tibetan version extracted below:—

རང་བཞིན་དབང་ལྡན་གཉིས་ཀ་དང་།།
བདག་སོགས་བྱེད་དང་བྲལ་གཡོ་བ།།
ལས་དང་དེ་འབྲས་འབྲེལ་བ་དག།
རྣམ་པར་བཞག་ལ་སོགས་པའི་རྟེན།།
ཡོན་ཏན་རྫས་དང་བྱ་བ་དང་།།
རིགས་དང་འདུ་སོགས་ཁྱད་པར་གྱིས།།
སྟོང་དང་སྒྲོ་བཏགས་རྣམ་ཅན་ནི།།
སྒྲ་དང་ཤེས་པའི་སྤྱོད་ཡུལ་ཅན།།

The work is divided into 31 chapters, *viz.*: (1) examination of nature (in Sanskrit: Svabhāva-parīkṣā, in Tibetan: Raṅ-bshin-brtag-pa); (2) examination of the sense-organs (in Sanskrit: Indriya-parīkṣā, in Tibetan: Dwaṅ-phyug-brtag-pa); (3) examination of both (in Sanskrit: Ubhaya-parīkṣā, in Tibetan: Gñis-ka-brtag-pa); (4) examination of the theory that the world is self-existent (in Sanskrit: Jagat-svabhāva-vāda-parīkṣā, in Tibetan: Hgro-wa-raṅ-bshin-du-smra-wa-brtag-pa); (5) examination of Brahma, the presiding deity of sound (in Sanskrit: S'abda-Brahma-parīkṣā, in Tibetan: Sgrahi-tshaṅs-pa-brtag-pa); (6) examination of the soul (in Sanskrit: Puruṣa-parīkṣā, in Tibetan: Skyes-bu-brtag-pa); (7) examination of the Nyāya and Vaiśeṣika doctrines of the soul (in Sanskrit: Nyāya-vaiśeṣika-parikalpita-puruṣa-parīkṣā, in Tibetan: Rigs-pa-can-daṅ-bye-brag-pas-kun-tu-brtags-pahi-skyes-bu-brtag-pa); (8) examination of the Mīmāṁsaka doctrine of the soul (in Sanskrit: Mīmāṁsaka-kalpita-ātma-parīkṣā, in Tibetan: Spyoḍ-pa-pas-rtags-pahi-bdag-brtag-pa); (9) examination of Kapila's octrine of the soul (in Sanskrit: Kapila-parikalpita-ātma-parīkṣā, in Tibetan: Ser-skya-pas-kun-tu-brtags-pahi-bdag-brtag-pa); (10) examination of the Digambara Jaina doctrine of the soul (in Sanskrit: Digambara-parikalpita-ātma-parīkṣā, in Tibetan: Nam-mkhahi-gos-can-gyis-kun-tu-brtags-pahi-bdag-brtag-pa); (11) examination of the Upaniṣad-doctrine of the soul (in Sanskrit: Upaniṣad-kalpita-ātma-parīkṣā, in Tibetan:

མཚན་ཉིད་གསལ་དང་ལྡན་པ་ཡི།།

ཚད་ལ་གཉིས་ཀྱིས་གཏན་ལ་དབབ།།

ཆ་ཤས་ཤིན་ཏུ་ཕྲ་བས་ཀྱང་།།

འདྲེས་པ་གཞན་གྱི་བདག་ཉིད་མིན།།

མི་འཕྲོ་ཐོག་མཐའ་མེད་པ་ཅན།།

གཟུགས་བརྙན་ལ་སོགས་དག་དང་འདྲ།།

སྤྲོས་པ་ཀུན་གྱི་ཚོགས་དང་བྲལ།།

གཞན་གི་རྟོགས་པ་མཛོད་བཞིན་པ།།

U-pa-ni-sa-di-kas-b̲r̲tags-pah̲i-b̲dag-b̲r̲tag-pa); (12) examination of the Vātsīputra doctrine of the soul (in Sanskrit: Vātsīputra-kalpita-ātma-parīkṣā, in Tibetan: G̲nas-mah̲i-bus-b̲dag-b̲r̲tag-pa); (13) examination of the permanence of entities (in Sanskrit: Sthira-padārtha-parīkṣā, in Tibetan: B̲r̲tan-pah̲i-d̲ṅos-po-b̲r̲tag-pa); (14) examination of the relation between *Karma* and its effect (in Sanskrit: Karma-phala-sambandha-parīkṣā, in Tibetan: Las-dań-h̲bras-buh̲i-h̲brel-pa-b̲r̲tag-pa); (15) examination of the meaning of the word 'substance' (in Sanskrit: Dravya-padārtha-parīkṣā, in Tibetan: R̲dsas-kyi-tshig gi-don-b̲r̲tag-pa); (16) examination of the meaning of the word 'quality; (in Sanskrit: Guṇa-śabdārtha-parīkṣā, in Tibetan: Yon-tan-gyi-tshig-gi-don-b̲r̲tag-pa); (17) examination of the meaning of the word *Karma* (in Sanskrit: Karma-śabdārtha-parīkṣā in Tibetan: Las-kyi-tshig gi-don-b̲r̲tag-pa); (18) examination of the meaning of the word generality or genus (in Sanskrit: Sāmānya-śabdārtha-parīkṣā, in Tibetan: S̲pyih̲i-tshig-gi-don-b̲r̲tag-pa); (19) examination of the meaning of the words 'generality,' and 'particularity' (in Sanskrit: Sāmānya-viśesa-śabdārtha-parīkṣā, in Tibetan: S̲pyi-dań-bye-brag-gi-tshig-gi-don-b̲r̲tag-pa); (20) examination of the meaning of the

---

བསྐལ་པ་གྲངས་མེད་མི་ཉུང་བས།།
ཐུགས་རྗེ་ཆེན་པོ་འདི་བདག་གྱུར་པ།།
རྟེན་ཅིང་འབྲེལ་བར་འབྱུང་བ་ནི།།
གང་གིས་གསུངས་པ་སྨྲ་བའི་མཆོག།
ཀུན་མཁྱེན་དེ་ལ་ཕྱག་འཚལ་ནས།།
དེ་ཉིད་རྣམས་ནི་བསྡུ་བར་བྱ།།

Dr. Bühler further observes that the first section of the Tarkasaṁgraha contains ईश्वर-परीक्षा (examination of God), कपिलकल्पितात्म-परीक्षा (examination of Kapila's doctrine of the soul), औपनिषदकल्पितात्म-परीक्षा (examination of the soul according to the Upaniṣads), स्थिरभाव-परीक्षा (examination of permanent entity), etc. The last colophon appears to him to be स्वतः प्रामाण्यवाद (examination of the doctrine of self-evidence). These are the very subjects treated in the Tattvasaṁgraha. So the two works are identical.

word 'co-existent cause' (in Sanskrit: Samavāya-śabdārtha-parīkṣā, in Tibetan: Hdu-wahi-tshig-don-brtag-pa); (21) examination of the meaning of the word 'sound' (in Sanskrit: Sabdārtha-parīkṣā, in Tibetan: Sgra-yi-don-brtag-pa); (22) examination of the definition of perception (in Sanskrit: Pratyakṣa-lakṣaṇa-parīkṣā, in Tibetan: Mṅon-sum-gyi-mtshan-ñid-brtag-pa); (23) examination of inference (in Sanskrit: Anumānaparīkṣā, in Tibetan: Rjes-su-dpag-pa-brtag-pa); (24) examination of other kinds of valid knowledge (in Sanskrit: Pramāṇāntara-parīkṣā, in Tibetan: Tshad-ma-shan-brtag-pa); (25) examination of the doctrine of evolution (in Sanskrit: Vivartavāda-parīkṣā, in Tibetan: Hgyur-war-smra-wa-brtag-pa); (26) examination of the three times (in Sanskrit: Kāla-traya-parīkṣā, in Tibetan: Dus-gsum-brtag-pa); (27) examination of continuity of the world (in Sanskrit: Saṃsāra-santati-parīkṣā, in Tibetan: Hjig-rten-rgyud-pahi-brtag-pa); (28) examination of external objects (in Sanskrit: Vāhyārtha-parīkṣā, in Tibetan: Phyi-rol-gyi-don-brtag-pa); (29) examination of S'ruti or Scripture (in Sanskrit: S'ruti-parīkṣā, in Tibetan: Thos-pa-brtag-pa); (30) examination of self-evidence (in Sanskrit: Svataḥ-prāmāṇya-parīkṣā, in Tibetan: Raṅ-las-tshad-ma-drtag-pa); and (31) examination of the soul which sees things beyond the range of senses (in Sanskrit: Anyendriyātītārtha-darśana-puruṣa-parīkṣā, in Tibetan: Gshan-gyi-dwaṅ-po-las-hdas-pahi-don-mthoṅ-wa-can-gyi-skyes-bu-brtag-pa).

Kamala S'īla (about 750 A.D.).

129. Kamala S'īla,[1] also called Kamala S'rīla, was a follower of S'ānta Rakṣita. He was for some time a Professor of Tantras in Nālandā whence he was (*vide* Appendix A) invited to Tibet by king Khri-sroṅ-deu-tsan (728—786 A.D.). While in Tibet he vindicated the religious views of Guru Padma-sambhava and S'ānta Rakṣita by defeating and expelling a Chinese monk named Mahāyāna Hoshang. He was of wide fame and the author of the following works:—

130. **Nyāya-bindu pūrva-pakṣe-saṁkṣipta**, called in Tibetan Rigs-pahi-thigs-pahi phyogs-sṅa-ma-mdor-bsdus-pa, a summary of criticisms on the Nyāyabindu of Dharmakīrti. The Sanskrit original of this work appears to be lost, but there exists a Tibetan translation[2] in the Tangyur, Mdo, She, Folios 106—115. The translation was prepared by the Indian sage

1 *Vide* Pag-sam-jon-zang, part i, p. 112, edited by Sarat Chandra Das, and also the Journal of the Buddhist Text Society of Calcutta, vol. i, part i, p. 10, and Waddell's Lamaism, p. 31.

2 I have consulted the copy brought down by the British Mission to Tibet in 1904.

Viśuddha Siṁha and the interpreter monk of Shu-chen named Dpal-rtsegs-rakṣita.

131. **Tattva-saṁgraha-pañjikā**, called in Tibetan De-kho-na-ñid-bsdus-pahi-dkah-hgrel, a commentary on the Tattva-saṁgraha of Śānta Rakṣita. The Sanskrit original of this work is lost, but there exists a Tibetan translation [1] of part I of this work in the Tangyur, Mdo, He, Folios 146—400, and part II of it in the Tangyur, Mdo, Ye, Folios 1—385. The translation was prepared by the Indian sage Devendra Bhadra and the interpreter monk Grags-hbyor-śes-rab.

Kalyāṇa Rakṣita (about 829 A.D.).

132. Kalyāṇa Rakṣita,[2] called in Tibetan Dge-bsruṅ, was a great dialectician and teacher of Dharmottarācārya. He flourished during the reign of Mahārāja Dharma Pāla who died in 829 A.D. (*Vide* Appendix B). He was the author of the undermentioned works [3] :—

133. **Vāhyārtha-siddhi-kārikā**, called in Tibetan phyi-rol-gyi-don-grub-pa-ces-bya-wahi-tshig-lehur, which signifies memorial verses on the reality of external things. The Sanskrit original of this work is lost, but there exists a Tibetan translation in the Tangyur, Mdo, Ze, Folios 202—210. The translation was prepared by the Vaibhāṣika teacher Jina Mitra of Kāśmīra and the Tibetan interpreter-monk Dpal-brtsegs-rakṣita.

134. **Śruti-parīkṣā**, called in Tibetan Thos-pa-brtag-pahi-tshig-lehur-byas-pa, which signifies 'memorial verses on the examination of Śruti or verbal testimony.' The Sanskrit original of this work appears to be lost, but there exists a Tibetan translation in the Tangyur, Mdo, Ze, Folios 210—211.

135. **Anyāpoha-vicāra-kārikā**, called in Tibetan Gshan-la-brtag-pahi-tshig-lehur-byas-pa, which signifies 'memorial verses on the determination of a thing by the exclusion of its opposites.' The Sanskrit original of this work is lost, but there exists a Tibetan translation in the Tangyur, Mdo, Ze, Folios 211—213.

136. **Īśvara-bhaṅga-kārikā**, called in Tibetan Dwaṅ-phyug-hjig-pahi-tshig-lehur-byas-pa, which signifies 'memorial verses

---

[1] I have consulted this work in the monastery of Labrang, Sikkim, which I visited in June 1907.

[2] *Vide* Taranatha's Geschichte des Buddhismus von Schiefner, pp. 216—219: and Pag-sam-jon-zang, p. 114. The particle 'bsruṅ' signifies "protected" and is an equivalent for Sanskrit "Rakṣita." But Schiefner has taken it as an equivalent for "Gupta." This does not seem to be correct, for the Tibetan equivalent for Gupta is "sbas."

[3] I have consulted Kalyāna Rakṣita's works in volume Ze of the Tangyur lent to me by the India Office, London.

on the refutation of God.' The Sanskrit original of this work appears to be lost, but there exists a Tibetan translation in the Tangyur, M̲do, Ze, Folios 214—215.

Dharmottarācārya (about 847 A.D.).

137. Dharmottara[1] (Ācārya Dharmottara or Dharmottarācārya) called in Tibetan Chos-m̲chog, was a pupil of Kalyāṇa Rakṣita and of Dharmākara D̄atta of Kāśmīra. He appears to have flourished in Kāśmīra while Vanapāla was reigning in Bengal about 847 A.D. (*vide* Appendix B), and is mentioned by the Jaina philosophers Mallavādin the author of Dharmottara-ṭippanaka about 962 A.D.[2] and Ratnaprabha Sūri[3] the famous author of Syādvāda-ratnāvatārikā dated 1181 A.D. Dharmottara was the author of the following works :—

138. **Nyāya-bindu-ṭīkā**, called in Tibetan Rigs-pahi-thigs-pahi-rgya-cher-hgrel-wa, a detailed commentary on the Nyāya-bindu of Dharmakīrti. The Sanskrit original of this work was preserved in the Jaina temple of Śāntinātha, Cambay, and has been published by Professor Peterson in the Bibliotheca Indica series of Calcutta. There exists a Tibetan translation[4] in the Tangyur, M̲do, She, Folios 43—106. The translation was prepared by the Indian sage Jñāna-garbha and an interpreter-monk of Shu-chen named Dharmāloka, and afterwards recast by the Indian sage Sumati-kīrti and the Tibetan interpreter-monk B̲lo-l̲dan-śes̲-rab. Nyāyabindu-ṭīkā begins thus :—" Sugata, the conqueror of lust, etc., has overcome this world, the source of series of evils beginning with birth : may his words dispelling the darkness of our mind attain glory."[5]

---

1 *Vide* Taranatha's Geschichte des Buddhismus von Schiefner, p. 225 ; and Pag-sam-jon-zang, p. 114.

2 The Jaina logician Mallavādin (q. v.) wrote a gloss called Dharmottara-ṭippanaka on Dharmottarācārya's Nyāyabinduṭīkā. The year 884 in which Mallavādin flourished corresponds to 827 A.D. or 962 A.D. according as we take it to refer to Vikrama-saṁvat or Śaka-saṁvat. On one supposition Mallavādin was a contemporary of Dharmottara and on the other he flourished a century later.

3 अत्र धर्मोत्तरानुसारी प्राह। प्रयोजनमादिवाक्येन साक्षादाख्यायते इति न क्षमे।
(Syādvāda-ratnāvatārikā, p. 10, Jaina yaśovijaya series of Benares).

4 I have consulted the copy brought down by the British Mission to Tibet during 1904. The Tibetan version has also been edited by F. J. Sherbatski and printed in Russia.

5 जयन्ति जातिव्यसनप्रबन्ध प्रसूतिहेतोर्जगतो विजेतुः।
रागाद्यरातेः सुगतस्य वाचो मनस्तमस्तानवमादधानाः॥
(Nyāyabinduṭīkā, Chap. I).

139. **Pramāṇa-parīkṣā,** called in Tibetan Tshaḏ-ma-ḇrtag-pa, signifying 'an examination of Pramāṇa or the sources of valid knowledge.' The Sanskrit original of this work appears to be lost, but there exists a Tibetan translation [1] in the Tangyur, Mdo, Ze, Folios 215—237, as well as Folios 238—253. The translation was prepared by monk Ḇlo-ḻdan-śes-rab.

140. **Apoha-nāma-prakaraṇa,** called in Tibetan Gshan-sel-wa, signifying 'a treatise on the determination of a thing by the exclusion of its opposites.' The Sanskrit original of this work appears to be lost, but there exists a Tibetan translation [2] in the Tangyur, Mdo, Ze, Folios 254—266. The translation was prepared by the Kāśmīrian Paṇḍita Bhāgyarāja and the interpreter-monk Ḇlo-ḻdan-śes-rab, in the incomparable city of Kāśmīra.

141. **Pāra-loka-siddhi,** called in Tibetan Hjig-rten-pha-rol-grub-pa, signifying 'proof of the world beyond.' The Sanskrit original of this work appears to be lost, but there exists a Tibetan translation [3] in the Tangyur, Mdo, Ze, Folios 266—270. The translation was prepared by the great Paṇḍita Bhāgyarāja and the interpreter-monk Tshab-ñi-ma-grags during the lifetime of Śrī Harṣa Deva (king of Kāśmīra, 1089—1101 A.D.) in the great incomparable city of Kāśmīra.

The work begins thus:—

"Some say that the world beyond is possessed of the characteristics of a complete separation from the link of consciousness which began from before birth and continued after death, etc"

142. **Kṣaṇa-bhaṅga-siddhi,** called in Tibetan Skaḏ-cig-ma-hjig-pa-grub-pa, signifying 'proof of the momentariness of things.' The Sanskrit original of this work appears to be lost, but there exists a Tibetan translation [4] in the Tangyur, Mdo, Ze, Folios 270—282. The translation was prepared by the Indian sage Bhāgyarāja and the interpreter-monk Ḇlo-ḻdan-śes-rab.

143. **Pramāṇa-viniścaya-ṭīkā,** called in Tibetan Tshaḏ-ma-rnam-ṅes-kyi-ṭīkā, which is a commentary on the Pramāṇa-viniścaya of Dharmakīrti. The Sanskrit original of this work appears to be lost, but there exists a Tibetan translation [5] in the Tangyur, Mdo, Dse, folio 346 f, and We, Folios 1—188. The translation was prepared by the Kāśmīrian Paṇḍita Parahita Bhadra and the Tibetan interpreter Ḇlo-ḻdan-śes-rab in the model city of Kāśmīra. In the concluding lines of the work

---

[1] I have consulted the India Office copy.
[2] I have consulted the India Office copy.
[3] I have consulted the India Office copy.
[4] I have consulted the India Office copy.
[5] I have consulted the India Office copy

Dharmottara, the author of it, is described as "the excellent subduer of bad disputants (quibblers).[1]

Muktā-kumbha (after 847 A.D.).

144. Muktā-kumbha,[2] called in Tibetan Mu-tig-bum-pa, was the author of a work called Kṣaṇa-bhaṅga-siddhi-vyākhyā, which is a commentary on Dharmottarācārya's Kṣaṇa-bhaṅga-siddhi. Muktā-kumbha must have flourished after 847 A.D., when Dharmottara lived.

145. The **Kṣaṇa-bhaṅga-siddhi-vyākhyā** is called in Tibetan S̱kad-cig-ma-ḫjig-grub-paḫi-ṟnam-ḫgrel. The Sanskrit original of the work appears to be lost, but a Tibetan translation[3] is embodied in the Tangyur, M̱do, Ze, Folios 282—301. This version was prepared by the Indian sage Vināyaka and the interpreter-monk Grags̱-ḫbyor-śes̱-rab.

Arcaṭa (after 847 A.D.).

146. Guṇa-ratna Sūri,[4] the famous Jaina author of the Ṣaḍdarśana-samuccaya-vṛtti, who lived in 1409 A.D., mentions the Tarkaṭīkā of Arcaṭa.[5] Arcaṭa is also mentioned by the Jaina philosopher Ratnaprabha Sūri,[6] the well-known author of Syādvādaratnāvatarikā, dated 1181 A.D. In the Jaina Nyāyāvatāra-vivṛti[7] it appears that Arcaṭa criticised Dharmottarācārya who lived about 847 A.D. Roughly speaking he flourished in the 9th century A.D.

Arcaṭa was the author of the following work on Logic :—

147. **Hetu-bindu-vivaraṇa**, called in Tibetan G̱tan-tshigs̱-thigs̱-paḫi-ḫgrel-wa, being a commentary on the Hetu-bindu of Dharmakīrti. The Sanskrit original of this work appears to be

---

1 སློབ་དཔོན་ཆོས་མཆོག་རྟོག་གེ་ངན་འཛོམས་མཆོག། (Tangyur, M̱do, Wo, Folios 188).

2 The name Muktākumbha is restored from Tibetan.

3 I have consulted the work belonging to the India Office, London.

4 *Vide* Satis Chandra Vidyabhusana's Jaina Logic under "Guṇaratna Sūri."

5 *Vide* Dr. Suali's edition of the Ṣaḍdarśana-samuccaya-vṛtti, chapter on Bauddha-darśana.

6 **अर्चटचर्चचतुरः पुनराह । इह प्रेक्षावतां प्रवृत्तिः प्रयोजनवत्तया व्याप्ता... ।** (Syādvāda-ratnāvatārikā. chap. i, p. 17, published in Jaina Yaśovijaya granthamālā of Benares).

7 *Vide* Satis Chandra Vidyabhusana's edition of the Nyāyāvatāra with vivṛti which is being published by the Indian Research Society of Calcutta.

lost, but there exists a Tibetan translation [1] in the Tangyur, M̱do, She, Folios 205—375. It is divided into four chapters treating respectively of (1) Identity (in Tibetan : Raṅ-ḇshin, and in Sanskrit Svabhāva) ; (2) Effect (in Tibetan : ḫbras-bu, and in Sanskrit : Kārya) ; (3) Non-perception (in Tibetan : Mi-ḏmigs-pa, and in Sanskrit : Anupalabdhi) ; and (4) Explanation of Six Characteristics (in Tibetan : M̱tshan-ñid-drug-ḇśaḏ-pa, and in Sanskrit : Ṣaḍ-lakṣaṇa-vyākhyā). In the beginning of the work it is stated that Arcáṭa was a Brāhmaṇa, and from the concluding part it appears that he lived in Kāśmīra. The Tibetan version ends thus :—

"In the city of Kāśmīra, the pith of Jambudvīpa, the commentary (on the work) of Dharmakīrti, who was the best of sages, was translated. From this translation of Pramāṇa the pith of holy doctrines, let the unlearned derive wisdom."[2]

DĀNAŚĪLA (ABOUT 899 A.D.).

148. Dānaśīla,[3] also called Dānaśrīla, was born in Kāśmīra about 899 A.D., when Mahī Pāla was reigning in Bengal. He was a contemporary of Parahita Bhadra, Jina Mitra, Sarvajña Deva and Tilopa. He visited Tibet and co-operated in the propaganda of the translations of Sanskrit books into Tibetan. He was the author of the following work on Logic :—

149. **Pustaka-pāṭhopāya,** called in Tibetan G̱legs̱-bam-ḇklag-paḫi-thabs̱, signifying the method of reading books. The Sanskrit original of this work appears to be lost, but there exists a Tibetan translation [4] in the Tangyur, M̱do, Ze, Folio 270. The translation was prepared by the author himself.

---

[1] The volume She, containing this work, was brought down by the British Mission to Tibet in 1904. I borrowed it from the Government of India.

[2] འཛམ་གླིང་སྙིང་པོ་ཁ་ཆེའི་གྲོང་ཁྱེར་དུ།།
མཁས་པའི་སྙིང་པོ་ཆོས་ཀྱི་གྲགས་པའི་འགྲེལ།།
དམ་ཆོས་སྙིང་པོ་ཚད་མ་བསྒྱུར་བ་ལས།།
སྙིང་པོ་མེད་པ་རྣམས་ཀྱི་སྙིང་པོར་ཤོག།

(Tangyur, M̱do, She, folio 375).

[3] *Vide* Taranatha's Geschichte des Buddhismus von Schiefner, pp. 225—226 ; and Pag-sam-jon-zang, p. xlvi.

[4] I have consulted the India Office copy.

JINA MITRA (ABOUT 899 A.D.).

150. Jina Mitra [1] was a native of Kāśmīra who, together with Sarvajña Deva, Dāna-śīla and others, visited Tibet and helped the Tibetans in the work of translating Sanskrit books into Tibetan. Jina Mitra lived about 899 A.D.,[2] when his contemporary kings Khri-ral (or Ral-pa-can) of Tibet and Mahī Pala of Bengal, died. He wrote the undermentioned work on Logic :—

151. **Nyāya-bindu-piṇḍārtha**, called in Tibetan Rigs-paḫi-thigs-paḫi-don-bsdus-pa, which contains the purport of Dharmakīrti's Nyāyabindu. The Sanskrit original of this work is lost, but there exists a Tibetan translation [3] in the Tangyur, Mdo, She, Folios 115—116. The translation was prepared by the Indian teacher Surendrabodhi, and the interpreter of Shuchen, named Vande-ye-śes-sde.

PRAJÑĀKARA GUPTA (ABOUT 940 A.D.).

152. Prajñākara Gupta,[4] called in Tibetan S'es-rab-ḫbyuṅ-gnas-sbas, lived at the time of Maha Pāla, who died in 940 A.D. He was a lay devotee and quite different from Prajñākara Mati, who was a monk and keeper of the southern gate of the university of Vikrama-śilā during the reign of Canaka in 983 A.D. (*Vide* Appendix C). Pranjñākara Gupta was the author of the following works :—

153. **Pramāṇa-vārtikālaṅkāra**, called in Tibetan Tshad-ma-rnam-ḫgrel-gyi-rgyan, which is a commentary on the Pramāṇa-vārtika of Dharmakīrti. The Sanskrit original of this work appears to be lost, but there exists a Tibetan translation [5] which is divided into two parts. The first part extends over Folios 1—352 of volume Te, and the second part Folios 1—328 of volume She of the Tangyur, section Mdo. The translation was prepared by the great Kāśmīrian Paṇḍita Bhāgya-rāja and the Tibetan interpreter Blo-ldan-śes-rab. Subsequently, it was looked through by Sumati and the interpreter Blo-ldan-śes-rab. The translation has the advantage of having been assisted by numerous sages of the great monastery of Vikramaśilā in Middle India,

---

1 *Vide* Taranatha's Geschichte des Buddhismus von Schiefner, p. 226; and Pag-sam-jon-zang, pp. xcvi, 115.

2 *Vide* Csoma de Koros's Tibetan Grammar, p. 183.

3 I have consulted the India Office copy.

4 *Vide* Taranatha's Geschichte des Buddhismus von Schiefner, pp. 230, 235; and Pag-sam-jon zang, p. 116.

5 I have consulted this work in the monastery of Labrang in Sikkim, which I visited in June, 1907.

under the supervision of the great wise Paṇḍita S'rī S'unayaśrī Mitra and also of the wise Paṇḍita Kumāraśrī of the model city of Kāśmīra.

154. **Sahāvalambha-niścaya,** called in Tibetan Lhan-cig-dmigs-pa-ṅes-pa, signifying "the ascertainment of objects and their knowledge arising together." The Sanskrit original of this work appears to be lost, but there exists a Tibetan translation[1] in the Tangyur, Mdo, Ze, Folios 301—308. The translation was prepared by the Nepalese Paṇḍita S'ānti Bhadra and the Tibetan interpreter-monk S'ākya-hod of the village of Seṅ-dkar in the province of Hbro (Do).

Ācārya Jetāri (940—980 A.D.).

155. Jetāri[2] or Ācārya Jetāri, called in Tibetan Dgra-las-rgyal-wa, was born of a Brāhmaṇa family. His father, Garbhapāda, lived in Vārendra at the court of Rājā Sanātana, who was a vassal to the Pala kings of Magadha. Being expelled by his kinsmen, Jetāri became a Buddhist devotee and worshipped Mañjuśrī, by whose grace he became a perfect master of sciences. He received from king Maha Pāla the royal diploma of Paṇḍita of the university of Vikramaśilā.

156. The famous Dīpaṅkara or S'rījñāna Atiśa is said, when very young, to have learnt five minor sciences from Jetāri. Maha Pāla reigned up to 940 A.D. (*vide* Appendix B), and Dīpaṅkara was born in 980 A.D.[3] Their contemporary, Jetāri, must have lived between those dates.

He was the author of the following works[4] on Logic :—

157. **Hetu-tattva-upadeśa,** called in Tibetan Gtan-tshigs-kyi-de-kho-na-ñid-bstan-pa, signifying "instruction on the real nature of the middle term in a syllogism." The Sanskrit original of this work appears to be lost, but there exists a Tibetan translation in the Tangyur, Mdo, Ze, Folios 344—354. The translation was prepared by the Indian sage Paṇḍita Kumārakalasa and the Tibetan interpreter-monk S'ākya-hod.

158. **Dharma-dharmi-viniścaya,** called in Tibetan Chos-daṅ-chos-can-gtan-la-dwab-pa, signifying "determination of the minor and major terms." The Sanskrit original of this work appears to be lost, but there exists a Tibetan translation in the Tangyur, Mdo, Ze, Folios 354—359.

---

[1] I have consulted the India Office copy.

[2] *Vide* Taranatha's Geschichte des Buddhismus von Schiefner, pp. 230—233; and Pag-sam-jon-zang, p. 116.

[3] *Vide* the "Journal" of the Buddhist Text Society of Calcutta, vol. i, part i, p. 8.

[4] The Volume Ze, of the Tangyur, Mdo, containing Jetāri's works, was lent to me by the India Office, London.

159. **Bālāvatāra-tarka**, called in Tibetan Bis-wa-hjug-pahi-rtog-ge, signifying "children's introduction to Logic." The Sanskrit original of this work appears to be lost, but there exists a Tibetan translation in the Tangyur, Mdo, Ze, Folios 359—372. The translation was prepared by the Indian sage Nāga Rakṣita and the Tibetan interpreter of the province of Sum-pa (in Amdo) named Dpal-mchog-dan-pohi-rdo-rje. The work begins thus:—

"Who by the lustre of his sermon has completely dispersed and cleared the veil of the gloom of ignorance, who is a single lamp to three worlds—may that Bhagavān long remain victorious."[1] It consists of three chapters named respectively: (1) Perception; (2) Inference for one's own self; and (3) Inference for the sake of others.

Jina (about 983 A.D.).

160. Jina, called in Tibetan Rgyal-wa-can, was the author of the following work :—

Pramāṇa-vārtikālaṅkāra-ṭīkā, called in Tibetan Tshad-ma-rnam-hgrel-gyi-rgyan-gyi-hgrel-bśad, a voluminous work, the Tibetan version of which occupies volumes De and Ne of the Tangyur, section Mdo. This version was prepared by Paṇḍita Dīpaṅkara of Vikramaśilā (who arrived in Tibet in 1040 A.D.) and the Tibetan interpreter, Byaṅ-chub-śes-rab of Shaṅ-shuṅ.

161. Jina, the author of the original work, is probably the same as Jina Bhadra of Koṅkana,[2] who was a contemporary of Vāgīśvarakīrti, about 983 A.D. (*Vide* Appendix C).

Jñāna-śrī (about 983 A.D.).

162. Jñāna-śrī, or rather Jñāna-śrī Mitra[3] (probably the same as Jñāna-śrī Bhadra, who worked in Kāśmīra), was born in Gauḍa. He was at first admitted into the Śrāvaka school of

---

[1] གང་གིས་གསུང་རབ་འོད་ཟེར་གཏི་སྨུག་གིས།།
སྨུན་པའི་རབ་རིབ་རྣམ་པར་གྲོལ་མཛད་གསལ།།
ས་གསུམ་གནས་ན་སྒྲོན་མ་གཅིག་པུ་ཡི།།
བཅོམ་ལྡན་འདས་དེ་ཡུན་རིང་རྒྱལ་གདར་ཅིག།།

(Tangyur, Mdo, Ze, folio 359).

[2] *Vide* Tāranātha's Geschichte des Buddhismus von Schiefner, p. 235.

[3] *Vide* Tāranātha's Geschichte des Buddhismus von Schiefner, pp. 235—242; and Pagsam-jon-zang, pp. 117—120.

Buddhism, but afterwards imbibed faith in the Mahāyāna. Dīpaṅkara or S'rī-jñāna Atiśa (born in 980 A.D.) is said to have been much indebted to him. Jñāna-śrī Mitra was appointed a gate-keeper of the university of Vikramaśilā by Canaka who reigned in Magadha up to 983 A.D. (*Vide* Appendices B and C). The Hindu philosopher Mādhavācārya in the 14th century quotes [1] Jñāna-śri, who is perhaps the same as Jñāna-śrī Mitra. He was the author of the following works on Logic :—

163. **Pramāṇa-viniścaya-ṭikā,**[2] called in Tibetan Tshad-ma-rnam-par-ṅes-pahi-hgrel-bśad, which is a commentary on the Pramāṇa-viniścaya of Dharmakīrti. The Sanskrit original of this work appears to be lost, but there exists a Tibetan translation in the Tangyur, Mdo, Dse, Folios 1—346, and We, Folios 188—322. The translation was prepared by the author [3] himself with the co-operation of the interpreter-monk Chos-kyi-brtson-bgrus.

164. **Kārya-kāraṇa bhāva-siddhi,**[4] called in Tibetan Rgyu-daṅ-hbras-buhi--ṅo-wo-grub-pa, signifying 'establishment of the relation of cause and effect.' The Sanskrit original of this work appears to be lost, but there exists a Tibetan translation [5] in the Tangyur, Mdo, Ze, Folios 413—418. The translation was prepared by the great Indian sage Kumāra Kalasa and the interpreter-monk S'ākya-hod. Subsequently, it was retouched and published by the Nepalese Paṇḍita Ananta-śrī and the interpreter-monk aforementioned.

165. **Tarka-bhāṣā,** called in Tibetan Rtog-gehi-skad, signifying 'technicalities of logic.' The Sanskrit original of this work appears to be lost, but there exists a Tibetan translation [6] in

---

1 *Vide* the Sarvadarśana-saṁgraha, chapter on Bauddha-darśana :—

तदुक्तं ज्ञानश्रिया

यत् सत् तत् क्षणिकं यथा जलधरः सन्तश्च भावा अमी ।
सत्ताशक्तिरिहार्थकर्म्मणि मितेः सिद्धेषु सिद्धा न सा ॥
नाप्येकैव विधान्यथा परकृतेनापि क्रियादिर्भवेत् ।
द्वेधापि क्षणभङ्गसङ्गतिरतः साध्ये च विश्राम्यति ॥

2 I have consulted the Tibetan version of this work in the monastery of Labrang in Sikkim.

3 The author of the Pramāṇa-viniścaya-ṭīkā is called Jñanaśrī Bhadra and also simply Jñāna-śrī. He is stated in the Colophon of the work to have been a native of Kāśmīra. *Vide* Satis Chandra Vidyabhusana's "Indian Logic as preserved in Tibet, No. 3" in the Journal of the Asiatic Society of Bengal, New Series, vol. iii, No. 7, 1907. Jñāna-śrī Mitra, of Gauḍa, seems to be the same as Jñāna-śrī Bhadra, of Kāśmīra, who may have left Gauḍa to live in Kāśmīra.

4 The author of this work is named Jñāna-śrī Mitra.

5 I have consulted the India Office copy.

6 I have consulted the India Office copy.

the Tangyur, Mdo, Ze, Folios 373—413. The translation was prepared by the interpreter-monk Dpal-ldan-blo-gros-brtan-pa. The work is divided into three chapters named respectively: (1) Perception; (2) Inference for one's own self: and (3) Inference for the sake of others. It begins thus:—"Bowing down to the teacher, the lord of the world, I elucidate Tarkabhāṣā (the technicalities of logic) for the sake of introducing children of small intellect to the system of Dharmakīrti."[1]

Ratna Vajra (about 983 A.D.).

166. Ratnavajra,[2] called in Tibetan Rin-chen-rdo-rje, was born in a Brāhmaṇa family in Kāśmīra. His ancestors were deeply versed in the śāstra of the Tīrthikas. His father, Hari Bhadra, was the first convert to Buddhism in his family. Ratnavajra, who was an upāsaka (lay devotee), studied by himself up to the 36th year of his life all the Buddhist sūtras, mantras, and sciences. After this he came to Magadha and Vajrāsana (Buddha-Gayā) where he beheld the face of Cakra-saṁvara, Vajravarāhī and many other deities, by whose grace he completely mastered the Buddhist śāstras. He received the royal diploma of the university of Vikramaśilā and was appointed a gate-keeper of the university (*vide* Appendix C). Afterwards he came back to Kāśmīra, whence he went through Udyāna (Kabul) to Tibet, where he was known by the name of Ācārya. He flourished during the reign of Canaka about 983 A.D. (*Vide* Appendices B and C). He was the author of the following work:—

167. Yukti-prayoga, called in Tibetan Rigs-paḥi-sbyor-wa, signifying "application of reasoning." The Sanskrit original of this work appears to be lost, but there exists a Tibetan translation[3] in the Tangyur, Mdo, Ze, Folios 372—373. The

---

1 སྨྲ་མ་འཛིག་རྟེན་དབང་བདུད་ནས།།
བྱིས་པ་ཡིད་གཞུངས་ཆུང་པ་རྣམས།།
ཆོས་ཀྱི་གྲགས་པའི་ལུགས་མཆན་ཕྱིར།།
རྟོག་གེའི་སྐད་ནི་རབ་གསལ་བྱ།།

(Tangyur, Mdo, Ze, folio 373).

2 *Vide* Taranatha's Geschichte des Buddhismus von Schiefner. p. 240.

3 I have consulted the Tibetan version in the possession of the India Office, London.

translation was prepared by the Indian sage S'rī S'ubhūti-śānta and the interpreter-monk of Shu-chen, named Tiṅ-ṅe-ḫdsin-ḇzaṅ-po.

RATNĀKARA S'ĀNTI (ABOUT 983 A.D.).

168. Ratnākara S'ānti [1] was known to the Tibetans as Ācārya S'ānti or simply S'āntipa. He was ordained in the order of the Sarvāstivāda school of Odantapura, and learnt the Sūtra and Tantra at Vikramaśilā from Jetāri, Ratna-kīrti [2] and others. Thereafter he was appointed by king Canaka (who died in 983 A.D.) to be a gate-keeper of the University of Vikramaśilā (*vide* Appendix C), where he defeated the Tīrthika disputants. At the invitation of the king of Ceylon he visited that island where he spread the Buddhist doctrine. He was the author of a work on *Chanda* (prosody) called Chando-ratnākara [3] and of the following works [4] on Logic :—

169. **Vijñapti-mātra siddhi,** called in Tibetan Ṟnam-par-rig-pa-tsam-ñid-du-grub-pa, signifying 'establishment of a mere communication of knowledge.' The Sanskrit original of this work appears to be lost, but there exists a Tibetan translation in the Tangyur, M̱do, Ze, Folios 335—338. The translation was prepared by the Nepalese Paṇḍita S'ānti Bhadra, and the Tibetan interpreter-monk S'ākya-ḫoḏ of the province of Ḫbro (Do). Subsequently, it was published by the same Paṇḍita and Ḵlog-ṣkya-śeṣ-rab-ḇrtsegṣ.

170. **Antar-vyāpti,**[5] called in Tibetan Naṅ-gi-khyab-pa,

---

[1] *Vide* Taranatha's Geschichte des Buddhismus von Schiefner, pp. 234, 235 and Pag-sam-jon-zang, pp. 117, cx. The Tibetan equivalent for the name Ratnākara Santi is རིན་ཆེན་འབྱུང་གནས་ཞི་བ།

[2] This Ratnakīrti is different from the sage of that name who was patronised by King Vimala Candra about 650 A.D. (*vide* Tārānātha's Geschichte des Buddhismus von Schiefner, pp. 172, 174, and my discussion in art. 108 under the head Vinīta Deva in the Buddhist Logic). This earlier Ratnakīrti, known through a commentary on the Madhyamakāvatāra, wrote Kalyāṇa-kāṇḍa and Dharmaviniścaya embodied in the Tangyur Mdo, Ku. The same Ratnakīrti was perhaps the author of Apohasiddhi and Kṣaṇabhaṅgasiddhi which are being published in the Bibliotheca Indica series of Calcutta under the editorship of M. M. Hara Prasād Sāstri. Two other works called Sthira-dūṣaṇa and Vicitrādvaita-siddhi are ascribed to him.

[3] For an account of the Chandoratnākara see Satischandra Vidyabhusana's "Sanskrit works on Literature, Grammar, Rhetoric and Lexicography as preserved in Tibet" in J. A. S. B., new series, vol. III, no. 2, 1907.

[4] The volume Ze of the Tangyur, section Mdo, containing Ratnākara S'ānti's works, was lent to me by the India Office, London.

[5] The Sanskrit original of 'Antarvyāpti' or more fully 'Antarvyāpti-

signifying 'internal inseparable connection.' It is embodied in the Tangyur, Mdo, Ze, Folios 338—344. The translation was prepared by the Indian sage Kumāra Kalasa and the interpreter-monk S'ākya-ḥoḍ.

Vāk-praja (about 983 A.D.).

171. In the Tangyur, Mdo, Ze, Folios 201—202 there is the Tibetan version[1] of the **Sarvajña-siddhi-kārikā**, called in Tibetan Thams-caḍ-ṃkhyen-pa-grub-paḥi-tshig-leḥur-byas-pa, signifying 'memorial verses on the attainment of omniscience.' The author of this work is named in Tibetan Ñag-ḥbaṅs which may be restored in Sanskrit as Vāk-praja. If he is the same as Vāgīś-vara-kīrti, he must have lived about 983 A.D. (*vide* Appendix C).

Yamāri (about 1050 A.D.).

172. Yamāri was specially versed in Grammar and Logic. But he was very poor. Once, being unable to support his family and children, he came to Vajrāsana (Buddha-Gayā). There he related his poverty to a Yogin, who replied: "You Paṇḍits despise Yogins and do not solicit dharma from them, hence this has come to pass." Saying this, he uttered the Vasudhara benediction in virtue of which Yamāri rose to opulence. He afterwards received the royal diploma of the university of Vik-ramaśilā.[2] He lived during the time of Naya Pāla who died in 1050 A.D. (*vide* Appendix B). He was the author of the following work:—

173. **Pramāṇa-vārtikālaṅkāra-ṭīkā**, called in Tibetan Tshaḍ-ma-rnam-ḥgrel-rgyan-gyi-ḥgrel-bśaḍ, which is an annotation on the Pramāṇa-vārtikālaṅkāra of Prajñākara Gupta. The Sanskrit original of this work appears to be lost, but there exists a very voluminous Tibetan translation which covers volumes Be, Me, and Tse of the Tangyur, Mdo. The translation was prepared by Paṇḍita Sumati and the interpreter Blo-

---

samarthana' has recently been recovered from Nepal by M. M. Hara Prasad Sastri, M.A., of Calcutta, and is deposited in the Library of the Asiatic Society of Bengal. It begins thus:—इह सत्त्वमर्थक्रियाकारित्वं तदितरलक्षणायोगात्। तच्च क्रमयौगपद्याभ्यां व्याप्तं परस्परव्यवच्छेदलक्षणत्वादनयोः। प्रकारान्तरेण करणासम्भवात्। It ends thus:— अन्तर्व्याप्तिसमर्थनं समाप्तमिति। कृतिरियं रत्नाकरशान्तिपादानाम्॥

1 I have consulted the copy belonging to the India Office, London.

2 *Vide* Taranatha's Geschichte des Buddhismus von Schiefner, pp. 247, 253.

ldan-śes-rab in the monastery of Sñe-thaṅ near Lhasa. The volume Be ends thus :—" From the immeasurable merit acquired by me by composing this regular annotation, may the world, subduing its adversary death, obtain the indestructible and perfected Nirvāṇa." [1]

Śaṅkarānanda (about (1050 A.D.).

174. Śaṅkarānanda,[2] called in Tibetan Bde-byed-dgah-wa, was born in a Brāhmaṇa family in Kāśmīra. He was learned in all sciences, and was above all an expert in Logic. He intended to write an original work on Logic refuting Dharmakīrti, but in a dream he was told by Mañjuśrī : " Since Dharmakīrti is an Ārya (a Buddhist monk), one cannot refute him, and if thou seest mistake in him, it is the mistake of thine own understanding." Thereupon Śaṅkarānanda repented and composed a commentary on Dharmakīrti's Pramāṇa-vārtika in seven chapters. He flourished[3] during the time of Naya Pāla, who reigned until 1050 A.D. He was the author of the following works on Logic :—

175. **Pramāṇa-vārtika-ṭīkā**, called in Tibetan Tshad-ma-rnam-hgrel-gyi-hgrel-bśad, being an annotation on the Pramāṇa-vārtika of Dharmakīrti. The Sanskrit original of this work appears to be lost, but there exists a Tibetan translation[4] which covers volumes Pe and Phe of the Tangyur, Mdo.

176. **Sambandha-parīkṣānusāra**, called in Tibetan Hbrel-pa-brtag-pahi-rjes-su-hbraṅ-wa, which is a commentary on the

---

1 ཚུལ་བཞིན་ཊཱི་ཀ་འདི་ནི་བྱས་པ་ལས།།
བསོད་ནམས་ཚད་མེད་བསགས་པ་གང་ཡིན་པ།།
དེས་ནི་འཇིག་རྟེན་གཤིན་རྗེའི་དགྲ་འཇོམས་ནི།།
མི་ཟད་རབ་བསྒྲུབ་གཉིས་མེད་ཐོབ་པར་ཤོག།།

(Tangyur, Mdo, Be, folio 303).

2 *Vide* Taranatha's Geschichte des Buddhismus von Schiefner, pp. 247, 349 ; and Pa-sam-jon-zang, pp. 107, 120.

3 Some maintain that Śaṅkarānanda was a personal pupil of Dharmakīrti. On this point Lama Taranatha observes :—" The Brāhmaṇa Śaṅkarānanda appeared at a much later time, and to call him a personal pupil of Dharmakīrti would be a great confusion."—Taranatha's Geschichte des Buddhismus von Schiefner, p. 188.

4 I have consulted this work in the monastery of Labrang, in Sikkim, in 1907.

Sambandha-parīkṣā of Dharmakīrti. The Sanskrit original of this work appears to be lost, but there exists a Tibetan translation[1] in the Tangyur, M̱do, Ze, Folios 24—39. The translation was prepared by the great Indian Paṇḍita Parahita, and the Tibetan interpreter-monk Ḏgaẖ-waẖi ṟdo-rje.

The work begins thus :—

"By whom connection with the world has been renounced, in whom there are no "I" and "mine," who is called free from concerns—to that Omniscient One I bow down."[2]

177. **Apohasiddhi**, called in Tibetan Sel-wa-grub-pa, signifying 'establishment of a thing by the exclusion of its opposites.' The Sanskrit original of this work appears to be lost, but there exists a Tibetan translation[3] in the Tangyur, M̱do, Ze, Folios 308—334. The translation was prepared by the Kāśmīrian Paṇḍita Manoratha and the Tibetan interpreter Ḇlo-ḻdan-śes-rab in the incomparable city of Kāśmīra.

The work opens thus :—

"The Omniscient One who is free from all mistakes and who looks to the interests of living beings in all times, saluting him and relying on his mercy, I elucidate the puzzle of 'self' and 'others' connected with the doctrine of *Apoha*."[4]

---

1 I have consulted the Tibetan version in the possession of India Office, London.

2 གང་གིས་འབྲེལ་བ་སྤངས་གྱུར་པ།།
འགྲོ་བ་བདག་དང་བདག་གི་མི།།
གཟུང་འཛིན་མེད་པ་ཅན་གསུངས་པ།།
ཀུན་མཁྱེན་དེ་ལ་ཕྱག་འཚལ་ལོ།།

(Tangyur, M̱do, Ze, folio 24).

3 I have consulted the India Office copy.

4 ཀུན་མཁྱེན་འཁྲུལ་བྲལ་དུས་གསུམ་གནས་པ་ཡི།།
དོན་རྣམས་ཇི་བཞིན་གཟིགས་པ་ལ་བཏུད་དེ།།
བརྩེ་ལ་གཞོལ་ནས་སེལ་བ་ལ་བརྟེན་པའི།།
བདག་གཞན་རབ་ཏུ་སྨྲ་བའི་འཁྲུལ་བསལ་བྱས།།

(Tangyur, M̱do, Ze, folio 30

178. **Pratibandha-siddhi,** called in Tibetan H̱brel-pa-grub-pa, signifying "establishment of the causal connection." The Sanskrit original of this work appears to be lost, but there exists a Tibetan translation [1] in the Tangyur, M̱do, Ze, Folios 334—335. The translation was prepared by Paṇḍita Bhāgya-rāja and the interpreter Ḇlo-ḻdan-śeṣ-rab.

---

[1] I have consulted the India Office copy.

APPENDIX A.

THE UNIVERSITY OF NĀLANDĀ.

(*About* 300—850 *A.D.*).

Nālandā was a village which is identified with modern Baragaon,[1] 7 miles north of Rajgir, in Behar. Though occasionally mentioned in the Pāli literature, Nālandā was not of great importance before the rise of the Mahāyāna at the beginning of the Christian era. Nāgārjuna, about 300 A.D., and Ārya Deva, about 320 A.D., were the earliest scholars to take interest in the educational institution at that village. A Brāhmaṇa named Suviṣṇu, a contemporary of Nāgārjuna, is said to have established 108 temples there in order that the Abhidharma of the Mahāyāna might not decline.[2] About 400 A.D., the Chinese pilgrim, Fahian,[3] visited this place, which he calls "the village of Nalo." He saw there a tower which had been erected on the spot where Sāriputra, the right-hand disciple of Buddha, had entered Nirvāṇa. Early in the 7th century A.D., another Chinese pilgrim, the famous Hwen-thsang, visited Nālandā and halted[4] there 15 months to study the Sanskrit language under S'īlabhadra. According to him[5] the site of Nālandā was originally a mango garden which was bought by 500 merchants at a cost of ten crores of gold pieces and given to Buddha.[6] After the Nirvāṇa of Buddha, five kings, named S'akrāditya Buddha Gupta, Ṭathāgata Gupta, Bālāditya, and Vajra, built five Saṅghārāma or monasteries at Nālandā. A king of Central India established another magnificent monastery, and began to build round these edifices a high wall with one gate. A long succession of kings continued the work of building, using all the skill of the sculptor, till at the time of Hwen-thsang in 637 A.D. the whole was "truly marvellous to behold." In the estab-

---

[1] *Vide* Cunningham's Ancient Geography of India, p. 468.

[2] *Vide* Tārānātha's Geschichte des Buddhismus von Schiefner, pp. 70—86.

[3] *Vide* Beal's Fa-hian, p. 111.

[4] *Vide* Cunningham's Ancient Geography of India, p. x.

[5] *Vide* Beal's Buddhist Records of the Western World, vol. ii, pp. 168—170.

[6] It must have been given to a Buddhist saint of a later age and not to Buddha himself.

lishment were some thousands of monks, all men of great ability and learning. They were very strict in observing the rules of Vinaya, and were looked up to as models by all India. Learning and discussing they found the day too short, day and night they admonished each other, juniors and seniors mutually helping to perfection. Learned men from different cities came to Nālandā to acquire renown, and some persons even usurped the name of Nālandā students in order that they might be received everywhere with honour. " Of those from abroad who wished to enter the schools of discussion, the majority, beaten by the difficulties of the problems, withdrew; and those who were deeply versed in old and modern learning were admitted, only two or three out of ten succeeding."[1] Hwen-thsang mentions some celebrated men of Nālandā, such as Dharmapāla and Candrapāla, Guṇamati and Sthiramati,[2] Prabhāmitra and Jinamitra, and Jñānacandra and S'īlabhadra.

Another Chinese pilgrim named I-tsing, who resided in Nālandā for ten years (probably 675—685 A.D.), says that there were eight halls and 300 apartments in the monastery of Nālandā with more than 3,000 resident monks. The lands in its possession contained more than 200 villages which had been bestowed upon the monastery by kings of different generations.[3]

Nālandā assumed the character of a university from about 450 A.D. Bālāditya, king of Magadha, who built a monastery at Nālandā, was a contemporary of the Hun king Mihirakula, who reigned first in S'ākala and afterwards in Kāśmīra. Now Mihirakula[4] began his reign in 515 A.D., and his contemporary, Bālāditya, must also have lived about that time. There were three predecessors of Bālāditya who built monasteries at Nālandā. Of them, the earliest, named S'akrāditya, must have reigned about 450 A.D. if we suppose 25 years as the average duration of the reign of each of them. The year 450 A.D. is then the earliest limit which we can roughly assign to the royal recognition of Nālandā. The latest limit which we know with certainty is 750 A.D., when Kamalaśīla (*q. v.*) was the professor of Tantras at Nālandā. But as we read in the accounts of Vikramaśilā that there was for some time an intercourse between that university

---

1 *Vide* Watters' " On Yuan Chwang," vol. ii, pp. 164—165.

2 This Sthiramati seemed to be the one mentioned by I-tsing (*vide* Takakusu, p. 181). He flourished after Asaṅga and Vasubandhu.

3 *Vide* Takakusu's I-tsing, pp. xxxiii, 65 and 154.

4 *Vide* Watters' " On Yuan Chwang," vol. i, p. 289.

Takakusu, in his " Paramārtha's Life of Vasubandhu," published in the " Journal " of the Royal Asiatic Society of Great Britain and Ireland, January 1905, maintains that Bālāditya came to the throne in 481 A.D., but this statement is by no means final. The date (452—480 A.D.) of Vikramāditya, Bālāditya's father, is also open to dispute.

and Nālandā, we may suppose that the latter continued to exist approximately until 850 A.D.

According to Tibetan accounts[1] the quarter in which the Nālandā University, with its grand library, was located, was called Dharmagañja (Piety Mart). It consisted of three grand buildings called Ratnasāgara, Ratnodadhi, and Ratnarañjaka, respectively. In Ratnodadhi, which was nine-storeyed, there were the sacred scripts called Prajñāpāramitā-sūtra, and Tāntrik works such as Samāja-guhya, etc. After the Turuṣka raiders had made incursions in Nālandā, the temples and *Caityas* there were repaired by a sage named Mudita Bhadra. Soon after this, Kukutasiddha, minister of the king of Magadha, erected a temple at Nālandā, and while a religious sermon was being delivered there, two very indigent Tīrthika mendicants appeared. Some naughty young novice-monks in disdain threw washing-water on them. This made them very angry. After propitiating the sun for 12 years, they performed a *yajña*, fire-sacrifice, and threw living embers and ashes from the sacrificial pit into the Buddhist temples, etc. This produced a great conflagration which consumed Ratnodadhi. It is, however, said that many of the Buddhist scriptures were saved by water which leaked through the sacred volumes of Prajñapāramitā-sūtra and Tantra.

---

1 *Vide* Pag-sam jon-zang, edited in the original Tibetan by Rai Sarat Chandra Das, Bahadur, C.I.E., at Calcutta, p. 92.

APPENDIX B.

A LIST OF KINGS OF THE PĀLA DYNASTY OF BENGAL AND BEHAR.

(*From Tibetan sources*).

In the Tibetan books,[1] such as Pag-sam-jon-zang, Lama Taranatha's Chos-byuṅ, etc., we find a short account of the kings of the Pāla dynasty of Bengal. Go Pāla, the founder of the dynasty, lived principally in Puṇḍra-vardhana. His successor, Deva Pāla, annexed Vārendra to his kingdom. Deva Pāla's grandson, Dharma Pāla, conquered Magadha and annexed it to Bengal. Dharma Pāla's power is said to have extended in the east to the ocean, in the west to Delhi, in the north to Jālandhara, and in the south to the Vindhya ranges. It is stated that during his reign S'ānta Rakṣita died. Now S'ānta Rakṣita visited Tibet during the reign of Thi-srong-deu-tsan in 749 A.D., and worked there for 13 years, that is, till 762 A.D. His death must therefore have taken place after 762 A.D. Dīpaṅkara S'rījñāna, *alias* Atiśa, High-priest of Vikramaśilā, who was a contemporary of king Naya Pāla of Magadha, visited Tibet in company with Nag-tsho-lotsava in 1040 A.D. during the reign of Lha-tsun-byaṅ-chub, son of Lha-lama-ye-śeṣ-ḫoḏ, who held his court at Tholing in Ñāri. These facts throw a good deal of light on the dates of the Pāla kings.[2] It is further stated that the death of Mahī Pāla is exactly synchronous with that of the Tibetan king Khri-ral. Now Khri-ral (or Ral-pa-can) died in 899 A.D.[3] This fixes the date of the death of Mahī Pāla. As the period of reign of each of the kings that preceded and succeeded Mahī Pāla is definitely stated by Lama Tārānātha, and also by the author of the Pag-sam-jon-zang, there is no difficulty in ascertaining the dates of the Pāla kings. Proceeding in this way, we can fix the dates as follows :—

1.	Go Pāla	660—705 A.D.
2.	Deva Pāla	705—753 A.D.

[1] *Vide* Tārānātha's Geschichte des Buddhismus von Schiefner, pp. 202—252; and Pag-sam-jon-zang, edited by Rai Sarat Chandra Das, Bahadur, C.I.E., pp. 112—121.

[2] *Vide* the 16th volume of Kloṅ-ṛdol-gsuṅ-ḫbum, and Sarat Chandra Das's "Indian Pandits in the Land of Snow," pp. 50—76.

[3] *Vide* the Chronological Table extracted from the Vaiduryakarpo in Csoma de Koros's Tibetan Grammar, p. 183.

3.	Rasa Pāla ..	..	753—765 A.D.
4.	Dharma Pāla ..	..	765—829 A.D.
5.	Masu Rakṣita ..	..	829—837 A.D.
6	Vana Pāla ..	..	837—847 A.D.
7.	Mahī Pāla ..	..	847—899 A.D.
8.	Mahā Pāla ..	..	899—940 A.D.
9.	S'āmu Pāla ..	..	940—952 A.D.
10.	S'reṣṭha Pāla or Praiṣṭha Pāla	..	952—955 A.D.
11.	Canaka ..	..	955—983 A.D.
12.	Bhaya Pāla .	..	983—1015 A.D.
13.	Naya Pāla ..	..	1015—1050 A.D.
14.	Āmra Pāla ..	..	1050—1063 A.D.
15.	Hasti Pāla ..	..	1063—1078 A.D.
16.	Kṣānti Pāla ..	..	1078—1092 A.D.
17.	Rāma Pāla ..	..	1092—1138 A.D.
18.	Yakṣa Pāla ..	..	1138—1139 A.D.

The researches on the Pāla kings, by the late Dr. Rājendra Lāl Mitra, arrived at a conclusion which is somewhat different from mine. Dr. Mitra's list of Pāla kings [2] is given below :—

1.	Go Pāla	..	855—875 A.D.
2.	Dharma Pāla ..	..	875—895 A.D.
3.	Deva Pāla ..	..	895—915 A.D.
4.	Vigraha Pāla I ..	..	915—935 A.D.
5.	Nārāyaṇa Pāla ..	..	935—955 A.D.
6.	Rāja Pāla ..	..	955—975 A.D.
7.	.... Pāla ..	..	975—995 A.D.
8.	Vigraha Pāla II ..	..	995—1015 A.D.
9.	Mahī Pāla ..	..	1015—1040 A.D.
10.	Naya Pāla ..	..	1040—1060 A.D.
11.	Vigraha Pāla III ..	..	1060—1080 A.D.

---

[1] Probably the same as Nārayaṇa Pāla who, in the Bhagalpur plate, is styled " the lord of Aṅga."

[2] *Vide* Dr. Rājendra Lāl Mitra's " Indo-Aryans," vol. ii, p. 232.

APPENDIX. C.

THE ROYAL UNIVERSITY OF VIKRAMASILĀ.

(*About* 800—1200 *A.D.*).

Vikramaśilā,[1] mentioned in Sanskrit Sragdharāstotra-ṭīkā,[2] Vṛhat-svayambhū-purāṇa,[3] Tibetan Tangyur,[4] etc., was a great collegiate monastery, or rather University, founded by king Dharma Pāla at the close of the 8th century A.D. It was situated on a precipitous hill[5] in Behar at the right bank of the Ganges, possibly at S'ila-saṁgama, now called Pātharghāṭā, near Colgong in the Bhagalpur district. Dharmapāla endowed

---

[1] *Vide* Tārānātha's Geschichte des Buddhismus von Schiefner, pp. 234-242, 259-261; Pag-sam-jon-zang, pp. 113, 117, 118; and Sarat Chandra Das's article in the "Journal" of the Buddhist Text Society of Calcutta, vol. i, part i, pp. 10—12; and his "Indian Pandits in the Land of Snow," pp. 50—76.

[2] The colophon of the Sragdharā-stotra-ṭīkā runs as follows:—

श्रीमद्विक्रमशीलदेवमहाविहारीय राजगुरुपण्डितभिक्षु श्रीजिनरक्षितकृता बालार्क-वृत्तिटीका परिसमाप्ता (Sragdharā-stotra, edited in the Bibliotheca Indica series by Satis Chandra Vidyabhusana, p. 50).

[3] वाराणस्यां नगर्यां च विहारे यत्र धार्मिके ।
तदा विक्रमशीलस्थि विहारे वसदुत्तमः ॥
धर्मश्रीमित्रो नामोऽयं भिक्षुः पण्डितकञ्चुकः ।
धर्म्मं दिदेशयामास नामसङ्गीति च कथाम् ॥ (Vṛhat-svayambhū-purāṇa, edited by M. M. Hara Prasad Sastri, chap. vi, pp. 320—321).

[4] Numerous Sanskrit works such as तारैकविंशतिकास्तवचे संक्षेप, तारा-चिरम-बोधम् etc., were translated into Tibetan in the monastery of Vikramaśilā, as is evident from the Tangyur, Ṛgyud, La, Folios 11—26, 54, etc.

[5] At the distance of a day's sail below Sultanganj there is a steep hill called Pātharghāṭā overhanging the Ganges, which here is *uttaravāhini* (or flows towards the north). This corresponds exactly with the account of Vikramaśilā given in Tibetan books. There are also ruins of Buddhistic images at Pātharghāṭā. For its old name S'ilasaṁgama *vide* Francklin's "Site of Ancient Palibothra," pp. 54—55, Appendix p. xiii. General Cunningham identifies Vikramaśilā with modern Silao, which is a small village three miles to the south of Bargaon (ancient Nālandā) and six miles to the north of Rajgir in the subdivision of Behar (*vide* Report of the Archæological Survey, vol. viii, p. 83). But this identification does not tally with the description found in Tibetan books, for the Ganges never passed by Silao, nor is there any hill near to it.

the university with rich grants sufficing for the maintenance of 108 resident monks besides numerous non-resident monks and pilgrims. At the head of the university was always a most learned and pious sage. Thus at the time of Dharma Pāla, Ācārya Buddha-jñāna-pāda directed the affairs of the university, and during 1034—1038 A.D. Dīpaṅkara or S'rījñāna Atiśa was at its head, and Sthavira Ratnākara was the superior of the monastery. The famous Tibetan scholar Nag-tshul-khrims-rgyal-wa, better known as Nag-tsho Lotsava, who came to take Dīpaṅkara Srījñāna *alias* Atiśa to Tibet, resided in the monastery of Vikramaśilā for three years, 1035—1038 A.D.[1] Kamalakuliśa, Narendra-śrī-jñāna, Dāna Rakṣita, Abhayakara Gupta, S'ubhakara Gupta, Sunāyakaśrī, Dharmākara S'ānti and S'ākya-śrī Paṇḍita also belonged to the university of Vikramaśilā. Provision was made specially for the study of grammar, metaphysics (including logic) and ritualistic books. On the walls of the university were painted images of paṇḍitas eminent for their learning and character. The distinguished scholars of the university received a diploma of "Paṇḍita" from the kings themselves. For instance, the distinguished logicians, Ācārya Jetāri of Vārendra and Ratnavajra of Kāśmīra, were granted such a diploma. The most erudite sages were appointed to guard the gates of the university. These were six in number, each of which had to be guarded by scholars designated "Gate-keepers" (called in Tibetan Go-sruṅ, corresponding, perhaps, to our Dvāra-paṇḍita). During the reign of Canaka (955—983 A.D.) the undermentioned eminent logicians acted as gate-keepers :—

(i)—At the eastern gate .. Ācārya Ratnākara S'ānti.
(ii)—At the western gate .. Vāgīśvarakīrti, of Benares.
(iii)—At the northern gate .. The famous Naropa.
(iv)—At the southern gate .. Prajñākaramati.
(v)—At the first central gate .. Ratnavajra of Kāśmīra.
(vi)—At the second central gate Jñāna-śrī-mitra of Gauḍa.

The university of Vikramaśilā is said to have been destroyed by the Mahomedan invader Bakhtiar Khiliji[2] about 1203 A.D. when S'ākya-śrī-paṇḍita, of Kāśmīra, was at its head.

---

1 *Vide* Kloṅ-rdol-gsuṅ-hbum, vol. xvi.

2 *Vide* the Tibetan-English Dictionary compiled by Rai Sarat Chandra Das, p. 869; Waddell's "Lamaism," p. 16.

The Turuṣkas or Mahomedans attacked Magadha several times. Thus Tārānātha, speaking of Ācārya Kamala Rakṣita who was at the head of the Vikramaśilā university at the end of the 10th century A.D., observes :—"A minister of the Turuṣka king, out of the Karṇa land in the west, together with 500 Turuṣkas, drew to Magadha to plunder. They plundered the sacrificial materials, but when they began to walk all in a body to the Ācārya (Kamala Rakṣita) the Ācārya got into a rage and walked up along, throwing a jug, filled with water, over which he had spoken the mantras. On the spot a great and indomitable storm collected, out of the wind came forth many black men armed with swords who fell upon the Turuṣkas; the minister himself perished spitting blood, and various contagious illnesses repulsed the others in such a way that none of them could reach their native country, and a great terror came over the Tīrthas and Turuṣkas—Tārānātha's Geschichte des Buddhismus von Schiefner, pp. 266, 261.

GENERAL INDEX.

D

F

Q

R